American Nature Writing 2000

American Nature Writing 2000

selected by John Murray

Oregon State University Press
Corvallis

The paper in this book meets the guidelines for permanence and durability of the Committee on Production Guidelines for Book Longevity of the Council on Library Resources and the minimum requirements of the American National Standard for Permanence of Paper for Printed Library Materials Z39.48-1984.

ISBN 0-87071-551-8
© 2000 John Murray
All rights reserved. First edition 2000
Printed in the United States of America

Oregon State University Press
101 Waldo Hall
Corvallis OR 97331-6407
541-737-3166 • fax 541-737-3170
http://osu.orst.edu/dept/press

For Christine

Restoring our right relationship [with nature] requires learning, or remembering, a way to be in the natural world that doesn't desecrate or overrun, but that maintains and respects. This comes through attentive love: through action based on the love that comes from being aware, listening, noticing what the place and its inhabitants need and desire. Attentive love requires an ethic of humility, the opposite of arrogance. It sees excessive control as a liability; it respects and reveres the process of life ... it requires faith in ourselves and in the other.

—Marybeth Holleman, "In the Name of Restoration"

☙

Contents

Preface

That it will never come again
Is what makes life so sweet.

—Emily Dickinson

This year's annual, the seventh in the series, is devoted to the writings of women for three reasons: First, to honor the memory of Patricia Hall Murray, who passed away on Earth Day, 1998. Women such as my mother, with their ardent dedication to the family, quietly but powerfully help to make the world a better place. My essay pays final tribute to the woman who first introduced me to nature, as she read the stories of Ernest Thompson Seton beside my bed when I was a child. Second, it seemed to me such a special collection was the best way to mark the beginning of a new century and new millennium and hopefully a new era in human affairs, a time in which civilization becomes more fully integrated with nature. Third, I hoped that such a unique celebration would further encourage women writers—particularly younger women writers—to write about nature. In the next century mother nature is going to need all the help she can get.

Next year's volume is already being planned. If you have a selection or know of a selection that you believe would contribute to that anthology (which will have no restrictions by gender), by all means send it to me at P.O. Box 102345, Denver, Colorado 80250. I am particularly interested in nature writing (i.e., writings of any genre with a strong natural content) from the following groups: (1) writers known only locally or regionally but with national potential, (2) writers from the Midwest, Northeast and South, (3) writers with experiences in nature abroad, (4) writers concerned with nature in an urban or suburban context, and (5) writers from ethnic groups offering alternative perspectives on nature (such as African American, Asian American and Native American). Working together—readers and editor—we can continue to build anthologies that, like this one, hold both literary excellence and thematic and stylistic diversity as the standard.

The *American Nature Writing* series is designed not only for the general reader interested in enjoying some of the finest current writing in the genre, but also for teachers, students and practioners of the nature essay. For teachers in particular, the anthology can be helpful in writing workshops, contemporary literature courses, composition and exposition classes, literature seminars, interdisciplinary environmental studies courses, and field study courses. Although several fine anthologies representing the better-known nature writers are available, this is the only series consistently to feature the work of the younger, emerging nature writers. In that sense, it holds a particular appeal to those just learning about the genre, or about prose writing in general, as well as to those who delight in discovering fresh new talents.

I would like to thank Warren Slesinger of Oregon State University for his enthusiastic support of the series, and all those readers who generously sent me their writings over this past year. I look forward to hearing from more of you in the next twelve months.

—*John Murray*

Introduction

❧

I have seen the extreme vanity of this world.
—Mary Rowlandson,
A Narrative of the Captivity of Mary Rowlandson (1676)

i.

The story is told in our family of Celinda Fuller White, my great-great-great grandmother. After an ordinary and uneventful childhood on the Midwestern frontier, Celinda was abducted by Indians one day while picking berries. She was fourteen years old. For the next four years she lived among the Shawnee, finally escaping at the age of eighteeen. For the rest of her life she remained close to the tribe, for she had been married to the son of a chief, and her log-cabin home became one of their last meeting places. In a corner of the basement in my father's home there is a heavy wooden box filled with artifacts— peace pipes, stone axeheads, projectile points, bear claws, a fox skin— that have come down to us from that distant time. I have often thought what a story she could tell. A brief biographical sketch of her life survives only because her son, Charles White Evers, my great-great grandfather, wrote an eight hundred-page local history (published in a ten pound leather-bound edition by J.H. Beers & Company of Chicago).

Of his mother he wrote:

> *In her flight she came to a river beyond which she saw some*
> *men, at work, to whom she called, at the same time leaping into*
> *the water. She was none too soon, for her pursuers were on the*
> *bank before she could swim to the far side, which she did with*
> *great difficulty, in her exhausted condition. The men's rifles*
> *shielded her from further danger and she was restored to her*
> *surviving kindred. With all the hardships she endured in*

common with the Indians while in captivity, they treated her
kindly and she always had a sympathetic word for them. Our
house was a great resort for them, because she fed them, and
could talk with them, both in word and sign language."

Some of the earliest writings by women about nature in North America are captivity narratives, most notably the account written by Mary Rowlandson, who was abducted during the Wampanoag uprising of 1676 in colonial Massachusetts. When I reflect upon the last three hundred years of nature writing by women in America I think first of this signal body of writing, for it is in these simple but powerful journals that we first see European-American women separated from their native culture and put in close and continual proximity with wild nature. These first-person chronicles form the experiential and literary foundation for the immense body of nature writing by women that has followed. From these hardy pioneers and their personal records of capture and liberation, of courage and compassion, have come the many women authors who now loom large in our national literature.

One thinks first of such figures as the essayist Margaret Fuller, who was so admired by Henry David Thoreau and Ralph Waldo Emerson, and the poet Emily Dickinson, for whom nature was a central theme. By the late nineteenth century women writers such as Harriet Beecher Stowe (*Palmetto Leaves*) and Isabella Byrd (*A Lady's Life in the Rocky Mountains*) had begun to write popular nonfiction books about nature (central Florida and northern Colorado, respectively). Their works moved the process of literary empowerment one step further—from factually-based adventure narratives to unified personal essay collections. At the turn of the century writers such as Ella Higginson (*Alaska, The Great Country*), Mary Kingsley (*Travels in West Africa*), and Mary Austin (*The Land of Little Rain*) continued to advance the cause of women in this regard, as all three became nationally recognized as professional writers. Overseas, the historic process was at work, as well, in the celebrated African writings of Beryl Markham (*West with the Night*) and Isak Dinesen (*Out of Africa*) during the 1930s and 1940s.

The life and career of Rachel Carson (1907-1964) represents both the culmination of a long struggle for opportunity and achievement and the beginning of a new period of increasing involvement for women writing about nature. The title of Carson's graduate thesis—"The Development of the Pronephros During the Embryonic and Early Larval Life of the Catfish"—gave little hint of the stellar works of literature that were to come. Later, in best-selling books such as *The Edge of the Sea* and *The Sea Around Us,* Professor Carson (for she taught marine biology at both Johns Hopkins University and the University of Maryland) proved herself every bit the equal, if not the better, of any man (Edwin Way Teale, Aldo Leopold, Joseph Wood Krutch) then writing about nature. Her masterpiece *Silent Spring*, which detailed the deadly genetic effects of DDT, inspired President Kennedy to form a commission that led to the banning of the pesticide in the United States. Carson remains the standard against which the careers of all other women nature writers are judged.

Since then, many gifted women writers have followed in Carson's footsteps. One thinks of Annie Dillard, whose nature book *Pilgrim at Tinker Creek* was awarded the Pulitzer Prize for general nonfiction in 1975. Now a professor of English at Wesleyan College in Middletown, Connecticut, Dillard is especially committed to fostering the work of younger women writers. Another noted natural history writer who came of age in the seventies was Dian Fossey, an associate of anthropologist Louis Leakey (best known for his work among the hominid fossils of Olduvai Gorge in Tanzania). Her work *Gorillas in the Mist* focused on the plight of the upland gorilla in the volcano mountains of Rwanda. Following Fossey's tragic death, a major studio film was made by Universal Pictures about her ground-breaking work in Africa, with actress Sigourney Weaver in the role of the naturalist. More recently, in the 1980s and 1990s, acclaimed works by such writers as Terry Tempest Williams (*Refuge*), Linda Hasselstrom (*Land Circle*), and Gretel Ehrlich (*The Solace of Open Spaces*) have continued to demonstrate the ability of women to move and change the world through the force of their words and the clarity of their vision.

ii.

What struck me the most as an editor in compiling this unique collection was the rich diversity of the writings, whether in terms of geographic location, theme, style or authorship. Three generations of contemporary women nature writers are represented here. The youngest writer was twenty when she wrote her essay (Emma Brown). The oldest writer is fifty-nine (Pattiann Rogers). Most of the contributors fall somewhere between these outer boundaries—of the elder practioner and the emerging author—and are established, middle-aged members of the guild, with at least one book or significant periodical publications. Geographically, the selections range across the continent, from rural Georgia (Janisse Ray) to wild Alaska (Marybeth Holleman), from the rolling countryside near the nation's capitol (Lisa Couturier) to the rugged western mountains (Trudy Dittmar), from the Louisiana backcountry (Alianor True) to the deserts of southern Utah (Kate Boyes). Some writers speak of the gentleness of nature (Adrienne Ross) and others bear witness to its mercilessness (Susan Marsh). The selections also vary considerably in length, ranging from essays that can be read and appreciated in a few minutes to those that require the better part of an hour to read and ponder. Taken together, they provide a continent-wide view of a literary landscape every bit as diverse as the geographic territory that is America.

Although a common myth with respect to the eastern United States is that the region has been extensively humanized over the centuries and is lacking in wild areas, the women writers in this volume demonstrate that the east offers natural wonders every bit as lovely and striking as the west. Two pay tribute to the eastern sea coasts. For Jan DeBlieu, the mid-Atlantic beach is quite literally her home, as she, her husband and young son maintain permanent residence on the Outer Banks of North Carolina. The dunes and lagoons, oak woods and salt marshes are her natural habitat: "Every day I set aside time to explore unfamiliar terrain and wonder at the great schools of fish, the falcons and sea birds that [migrate] past the islands with the tug of seasonal currents." Further north, Dartmouth English professor Cynthia Huntington writes of her summer cottage on Henry Beston's Cape

Cod. The coastal sanctuary is a place of peace and calm, storms and tempests, sea gulls and blackbirds, a "landscape of memory" with unusual power to uplift the spirit and enrich the journey of life. Elsewhere in the east, Janisse Ray and Alianor True write of the naturalist's life in the Old South, of wild deer and leopard frogs and forests where honeysuckle fills the air with sweet fragrance. For Lisa Couturier and Julie Dunlap, as for the majority of Americans, nature is synonymous with the parks and forests of urban and suburban areas. Both women, who live in the greater Washington area, have found that nature is a powerful sustaining force, regardless of her size or scope.

The women writers of the west inhabit a landscape defined mostly by its open spaces—large expanses of public domain in which the human spirit finds a natural residence. The nature writers of the region are shaped by this abundance of wildness in a variety of ways. Susan Marsh is intimately familiar with the Yellowstone region and relates some of her backcountry experiences with grizzly bears. As a Forest Service ranger in the Tetons, she has seen the aftermath of grizzly attacks, and knows all too well the ferocity of the species. Similarly, her Wyoming neighbor Trudy Dittmar, living in a remote cabin, is often face to face with the local moose, a species every bit as dangerous as bears in certain situations: "Moose don't threaten, but neither do they make haste to yield." Geneen Marie Haugen, like Janisse Ray, looks at the effects of hunting on the land and on herself. Her essay probes the ambiguous and often contradictory depths of the subject. Further south, Susan Zwinger describes a harrowing hike in the depths of the Grand Canyon, a trip on which she learns as much about herself, and about conquering the landscape of fear, as she does about the great barranca and its layered geology. Finally, Alaskan writer Marybeth Holleman offers an extended meditation on the complex, interdependent relationship of human culture and nature in the wake of the 1989 *Exxon Valdez* disaster, a shipping accident in which a grounded supertanker disgorged eleven million gallons of crude oil into the pristine ocean waters of southern Alaska. In its lingering aftermath, she asks for "small acts" of "attentive love" that can, over time, "grow into long deep ocean swells" of positive change for nature.

Regardless of whether the writers are inspired by the countryside of the east or the old frontier of the west they are equally committed to nature, and to using language in its behalf. They know that words have power and books can change the world, if only one reader at a time. Their writings collectively attest to the fact that the genre is alive and well, even as the new century and the new millennium, those rarest of historical twins, emerge from the birth-canal.

iii.

It is an axiom of intellectual history that political and social forces drive all great periods of artistic creation. This was as true during the Golden Age of Greece as it was during the Italian Renaissance or the French Revolution. We now find ourselves in a similar period, as all around the globe people restlessly seek a future in which culture and nature are more fairly balanced, and the ancient dream of universal human freedom is more fully realized. One has the sense, in the writings gathered here, that nature writing is poised at the beginning of a period of wonderful exuberance. All of the excitement that attends the beginning of a new century, and the start of a new millennium, is actively stimulating this historic genre. I believe that as nature writing attracts more and more gifted young talents, and addresses increasingly the political and social issues of our time, it will gain in stature and maturity, offering what Barry Lopez has called "a literature of hope." Nature teaches humility, generosity and balance, and nature writers share these values with a world often lost in hubris, greed and disorder. The best works of nature writing are yet to come, and they will most certainly be concerned with these and other eternal verities.

Moose

Trudy Dittmar

It was early May and the woman was out saying a final goodbye to winter. She'd gone up into the high country where the snow was still firm, snowshoeing one last time. She crossed a little meadow and was tromping along not too far from the edge of the forest. It was very bright and hot in this meadow high up in the sun, and she'd just stopped to take off her jacket and tie it around her waist, when suddenly she noticed a cow moose about fifty feet ahead, at the edge of the trees.

The woman saw no sign of a calf, but it's likely that somewhere nearby there was one, because the cow was coming at her. Though she saw this, such details as the flailing forelegs, the boot-sized hoofs flashing down through the air at her, did not really register—it all happened too fast—and when the moose suddenly jerked to a halt and swerved away, she had no idea why. All the woman knew was that at that moment her feet were swept out from under her. She was plowing through open snow for some seconds and then she was plowing along through the trees. Fortunately the blanket of snow was still fairly thick, because by the time the moose got its leg free of the webbing of her snowshoe, the woman had been dragged a good distance. She was scraped and lacerated on all her exposed parts, and she had two broken bones.

You hear stories like these in every barroom in moose country. You hear them told in the morning gatherings of cronies in the local cafes. There are stories of bull moose in rutting season charging head-on into cars, trains, and bulldozers. There are stories of moose in no particular season at all turning on a dime and driving someone up a tree. Sometimes there's a warning: the ears flatten, the mane goes up, the moose does a thing that looks like he's sticking his tongue out at you. Other times there's nothing; the moose just comes. Anyone who spends much time in moose country hears lots of these stories. Though there's often a comical edge to them, they always involve a good bit of damage, and anyone who hears enough of them learns to be circumspect.

One crisp morning in rutting season I see a bull moose in the willows with a rack as wide as a redtail's wingspread. In an instant he's pricked his ears up, and with that giant rack bouncing in the air above him he's taking one of those big one-two-three kind of trots toward me. One-two-three, he stops, looks, and I'm off into the trees, scanning hard for one I can climb. Late one afternoon in the forest in summer, I'm lost and retracing my steps to a fork in the trail where I suspect I went wrong, when I see a big cow and her calf up ahead just where the crucial fork ought to be, and she's watching me. When the calf tries to nurse, she jerks from him, head tossing, and backstepping respectfully, I show her emphatically that I'm off. The light's lowering, I'm not sure where I am, and to figure that out I need to check the very spot she stands on, but instead I migrate right off the trail and go floundering off through the trees.

Another time, emerging spider-fashion from a steep climb through deadfall, I come face to face with a moose on a mountain top, his rump two feet from my destination, the door of my jeep. And still another time, a moose blocks my way on a granite trail, wide enough at his end for him to turn comfortably, but at my end a tad too narrow for me to turn with my pack on—a cliff wall jutting up inches away on one side of me, on the other a precipitous drop. These moose don't threaten, but neither do they make haste to yield. In both cases all I can do is wait for them to get bored and vacate the only path I can take, but I'm spared the boredom that usually accompanies idle waiting by one hearty spritz after another of anxiety.

Moose can be difficult. You try to give them a wide berth. But at the same time they're unpredictable—there's no standard MO with a moose. Despite all the bar and cafe stories, and despite those few times when I felt I was about to be grist for one for one of those stories myself, in the gamut of moose ways the moments of bluster are far more rule than exception, and almost all my encounters with moose have been very different from what the stories depict. They'll surprise you by what they will do, but what they *won't* do can surprise you more. A moose is enigmatic. A moose is, at times, a bottomless thing.

Of course on many counts a moose is a perfectly fathomable thing, no enigma, but quite explicable in terms of its adaptations to its environment. Many of these adaptations are apt and resourceful, prime emblems of how cunning nature's workings can be. And they're all the more prime perhaps, and all the more cunning, because they're frequently effected through features that seem so awkward and nonsensical, even comical sometimes.

No need to go further than the moose's physique, for an example. People who live in moose country have a particularly keen sense of the animal's drollness, and to borrow one local depiction, a moose looks like it got caught in a crusher and smooshed end to end. Its head and neck escaped the crusher, but the big compression pads of the crusher caught it right at the chest and right smack on the rear and squeezed hard, and when the moose came out he had a short little body humped up at the shoulders, his head much too big for it, his legs way too long. In contrast to his black chocolate trunk, these legs are grizzled like an old dog's muzzle, and his neck has a thing called a "bell" hanging from it, a clapper-like furry flap dangling down. The nose end of his face looks too big for the rest of it—his face is nose-heavy, wide and huge-nostrilled, finished off below with a pendulous upper lip—and against the bigness of the nose end of the face, the smallness of his eyes way up back of the muzzle is unsettling. He looks disproportioned and ungainly, a ragtag mix of a lot of things, none of them fully realized—the head an early attempt at something equine, the slope of the back from butt up to shoulder hump suggesting a start on a giraffe, abandoned early, before the designer had the courage to take the design all the way.

But a moose body is far from the work of a crusher, and there's method in the madness of these oddities. The modified giraffe aspect angles the neck well for eating from trees. The rangy legs help here too, for rising on its hind legs a moose can reach branches twelve feet up, and it can straddle saplings, riding them down between its long forelegs to get at the top shoots and leaves. And these four-and-a-half foot high moose legs maneuver easily in all sorts of elements and conditions. Moose can run soundlessly over a littered forest floor at thirty-five miles an hour; they can move with little effort in snow nearly two feet deep; they can plod over quaking muskegs where other large animals would flounder, swim sixteen-mile stretches of Great Lakes at a clip, and they've been seen crossing mud holes, buried to the withers in soupy mire. As for the big head, long faces are a standard adaptation of large herbivores, providing space for large grinding teeth to deal with the silica and cellulose of plants and the moose's extra-long jaws enable him to include in his diet not just the tender herbaceous forbs and grasses and aquatics, but the tough woody plants as well. Then too, the pendulous muzzle, being nearly all muscle, enables him casually to strip shoots of their leaves, and the long snout contains phenomenal numbers of nerve endings, enabling him to detect the faintest smells. And though a moose isn't averse to sticking his head under water (they've reportedly uprooted aquatic plants from eighteen feet deep) the long face lets him browse much underwater vegetation while keeping his eyes on what's going on around him, if he likes. Although his vision isn't reputed to be the best at midday, it's good in dim light, and he can rotate his eyes independently to front and rear, so he can even watch behind him without turning his head. Even the strange "bell" or dewlap has a beneficial function, for in addition to being a visual status symbol for males (the bigger the better), it's also thought to be a retainer for a special saliva containing sex pheromones.

It's always a little startling, the moose's oddness, the silliness of his disproportions, as if nature had played a joke on him, but all these idiosyncrasies give the moose flexibility, they expand his ecological niche, so as curious as they are, you can get to the bottom of them. But though these oddities, once deciphered as deft adaptations, explain the moose rather nicely, they don't cover all the ground for me. You can see a moose every day and not fail to be struck by these oddnesses, these sillinesses, even once they've been explained; but eternally striking or not, they're not enough to account for the discomposure I feel whenever I notice a moose watching me.

Whenever during my rambles, a dark place in the landscape materializes into a moose, what really startles me is the way he just stands there, looking. There's a thicket of willows up ahead, or a little pool choked with water plants, or a shadowy jumble of evergreen trunks, and suddenly the image of a moose coalesces within it, and I'm unnerved by the exotic stillness of him. Some would attribute his composure at these moments to bad eye sight. He's not just standing looking at you, they'd say; he doesn't see you at all. But in all these cases, whether he's seen me or not, he's heard me, he's smelled—whatever. For who knows how long, he's known I was there. In all these cases, a deer would have frozen, then bolted. Ears sharp, an elk would have focused intently for an instant, and then he'd have been only a rusty flash among the trees. Other members of the family Cervidae are always nervously vigilant, but the moose just stands, looking. He's focused enough, sometimes quite alert, even stirred up. But most often he is merely casual, not frozen as if hoping for camouflage, but fidgeting nonchalantly, nipping buds or munching aquatics as he watches, chewing cud, flicking his ears at flies. His stillness is not lack of motion so much as cool silence and calm—and it unsettles me.

It's as if moose have a big still place in them, like a deep lake whose surface is never ruffled, its waters dark, cold, shining, and smooth. They are like the rocks in a landscape, the cliffs, the outcroppings. It sets a jolt in my blood, this quality, so alien in a wild animal. It triggers an eerie thrill.

Of course, you might chalk this quality up to a position of sureness. Only wolves and bears are their enemies—bears only when they've been wounded, and in this country there are no more wolves. But in the fall I see the trucks go through town with moose dead in the back, long grizzled legs jutting up out from under the tarps, big palmate antlers jutting out just beside them, their heads now where their butts should be. And so the position-of-sureness theory doesn't quite work for me.

A moose can be dangerous, I know that, but when all is said and done he rarely threatens, rarely uses his formidable store of fierceness on anyone; and as if this were some kind of Eden—as if god were in his heaven and all was right with the world—when faced with a gun a moose many times just stands there, looking on. It is as if moose were informed with a simplicity so pristine that they don't grasp life's dark complexities. It is as if they are victims of a kind of innocence, cruelly exploited. How do you *really* explain such behavior?

On the coldest of days in a very cold time, a moose came to my doorstep. He came in a dream. It was not a sleeping dream, and not a daydream either, but a waking dream that was focused, although I, the dreamer, had no idea on what. But there was a focusing, a searching on the part of' the dreamer, a stretching of all the invisible insides of the dreamer toward something. It was a focusing not *on* a thing, but *of* a thing; the dreamer's heart.

I was in my cabin, a dark speck on a bare knoll over eight thousand feet up the leeward slope of the Wind River Mountains, just a few miles from the pass that traverses the western end of the range. Through the fine snow sifting down outside the windows you could see no farther than a few feet. Without sensory clue, I knew there was a visitor. I opened the door. He stood close by the doorstep, a huge dark form suspended in an ether of snow.

He didn't speak, but I heard him. He said to follow him and I did. Down the knoll and over the bench to the river bottom. Across the river and up through the trees. Over the ribbon of snow that in summer is the road to the pass, and into the trees beyond it, climbing through them up sharp-planed slopes and down their nether sides, then up and down again, over wave upon wave of trees. Climbing and impossibly climbing, effortlessly, the moose form just ahead of me slow and indifferent and steady, like the constant procession of the planets traveling their ellipses, the perpetual spinning of the atoms in their orbitals.

Then we were at the top of Union Peak, on the crest of the highest slab of all the raw jagged slabs of granite that protrude from that mountain's top like massive knife blades standing on edge. And suddenly, as if I were two people, observer and observed, I saw myself from a long distance, as if through a telescope back in the cabin I'd left behind. I saw myself there on the slab at the moose's side, the two of us distant and tiny yet oversized in proportion to our surroundings, and despite all the snow sifting down through the miles between observed and observer, silhouetted against the sky.

Standing beside him, I touched the moose's neck. I didn't stroke it, but simply laid my hand upon the side of it, flat. He stood motionless, made no reaction, but his lack of reaction itself was a kind of response. He was a moose and he let me touch him, and I felt the life of him.

He never betrayed the faintest awareness of me. You would have thought he was alone. It didn't matter; alone or not, he guided me. He stood at the top of an undistinguished peak in the storm of winter and looked out from it, and I followed his gaze and saw what he saw.

For a few moments the land was rushing before us, like a fast-forward of terrain photographed from an airplane, and us flying in it, our eyes the camera's eye. We stood stationary on our mountain top and the land rushed south to north at us as we scanned down the southwestern slope of the Wind River Mountains, into the plains below, on down over their vast sweeps to Rock Springs and past, toward the southern border of the state. We scanned south or it rushed north, one or the other, all of it snow, all of it empty landscape, bleak and cold and lifeless with snow.

And then the rushing had stopped and there was the huge white curve of the top of the world, not south any longer, but the cold arc of ice which held the North Pole. Then that curve of ice lengthened, we saw a vast arc of the globe, many degrees, and then we had a still more distant view. We saw down past the vast cap of ice to where the landforms started, the Scandinavian peninsula, its great lobes flat and edged with intricate indentations, sharp-edged as a sawblade and totally white. Beyond, a vast expanse of Eurasia, cold and still and white. A third of the globe white and inert and silent encompassed in our view, even as we stood on the rock blades of the mountain looking out over ridges of forest behind vast veils of falling snow.

White and white, nearly the whole eastern part of the Northern Hemisphere, every peninsula of it, its coastlines hard-edged and sharp white against gray sea. I kept looking, expecting something, a bit of motion, a spot of color, something to hook onto but all the way, down, as the curve lengthened, as the expanse grew, revealing more and more of the world, there was nothing but snow-covered continent and grey water all the way down.

It lulled me, that dream. There was a peace in it. All still, all white. Beautiful. But cold. So cold and still it frightened me that this should be my vision, that when I called out for a truth, this was what the moose showed me.

There's a theory that evolution is based on a struggle among genes, not bodies. It represents a twist on the traditional Darwinian view. In the competition for fitness (i.e., to leave more offspring), natural selection rewards individual bodies with variations best adapted to the environment, with the result that as their descendants increase in numbers, their species evolves into one which embodies universally these particular adaptations. Individuals are the basic unit of selection, say traditional Darwinians, while genes, which furnish the ingredients of variation, are just outfitters, as it were. But biologist Richard Dawkins' theory of genes as the agent of Darwinian processes would have us recognize that the gene is the true replicator on this planet, not the moose, not the fruit fly, not us. After all, in sexual reproduction an organism doesn't make a precise copy of itself, a gene does. And whereas the particular organism is relatively short-lived, the tiny bit of hereditary material Dawkins defines as a gene is long-lived, as it (or the information encoded within it) passes intact not only through generations of a species, but often beyond species, sometimes even throughout all the five kingdoms of life, informing everything from humans to willows to morels to kelp to streptococci. The bodies genes pass through are just vehicles, says this theory, each a unique and temporary combination of genes; but the genes (unless zapped by mutation) are constant, reproduced unaltered again and again. And since the true replicator is the gene, not the organism, says the theory, it's not the organism, but the gene that's the contender in the struggle for fitness, while bodies like us, moose and humans, are secondary.

Ultimately the gene works not for individuals or species or any other taxonomic division, but for itself. "Natural selection favors those genes that manipulate their own propagation," says Dawkins, and so the gene programs us organisms, its vehicles, to do whatever is necessary to increase its numbers in the gene pool. And if we humans have deceived ourselves in this matter, thinking that we bodies are the ones with the stake in the struggle, it's because in organisms as complex as we are, the most effective programming plan hit upon by genes so far in the course of their evolution is to help us cope with limitless unpredictable environments by setting us up with an enormous plasticity of mind. Subject as our intelligence makes us to vast combinations of circumstances, it behooves our gene passengers, in short, to provide us with a consciousness so sophisticated that as decision-makers—at many levels of action, at least—we're emancipated from our master genes. That we're deluded in this matter is to be expected. It's hard to detect that we're mastered, when we are also master. Hard to detect that we're vehicles when we also have a big share of free will.

I hadn't yet heard this theory the day I had my moose dream, but many of its implications go hand in hand with intimations that raked my soul that day, and it may well have been the tip of some such iceberg that I was intuiting when the moose showed me the picture of a winterbound globe. The theory has its critics, and being no more than a casual student of such things, I can make no claims for its validity other than to note that some fine scientific minds (among them Francis Crick, of the double helix) have received it enthusiastically enough to build upon it. All I can say is that here and now, many moons past the day of the moose dream, I find the paradoxical logic of it all quite compelling, even rather lovely. But if it's true, the world is a colder place.

And we are cold in it, if it's true; and not just in what openly passes as our darker side. We've been inexorably forced to acknowledge the predatory protoreptilian parts of ourselves—their work is everywhere and hard to escape—but even by virtue of what we call our goodness, we are cold. For "natural selection favors those genes that manipulate the world to ensure their own propagation" and if a "superficially selfless" gene (as another writer has called it) will do better at getting its information passed on, then even altruism rears a selfish head.

There are all sorts of animal behaviors that involve altruism. Mice, for example, engage in grooming each other, and it seems a benevolent thing for them to do. But mice separated from other mice develop nasty sores on parts of their heads they can't reach, and so when one grooms another it's likely not out of good will alone. Support is offered in exchange for support. Altruism is reciprocal. Myriad examples of such behavior have been the focus of extensive, distinguished research. A lot of this behavior occurs among kin (ground squirrels screaming to warn relatives of danger); but a lot of it extends beyond kin, occurring among kind, as in the case of the mice mentioned above; and some extends beyond kind, across species (one ant species protects aphids in exchange for sugar they harvest), and even across kingdoms sometimes (another ant species living in the bull's horn acacia attacks all that tree's enemies in exchange for nutrients it produces, and even clips surrounding vegetation competing with the acacia for growing space and light). Throughout the web of living creatures, one after the other is doing something for another in expectation that the favor will be paid back.

I think of an acquaintance who was always flattering others—very effectively generally, but if you took close note, suspiciously much. "She's a compliment junky," a friend said, explaining her. "She puts out as much of it as she can in an effort to get as much as possible of the same thing back." Richard Dawkins wouldn't extrapolate from the evidence of reciprocal altruism in animals to human beings, but some of the biologists whose work he draws on would, and so would a number of evolutionary psychologists. According to them we've evolved a stake in good reputations on this sort of basis: if you do good to others, they'll do you good back. At some point in the labyrinthine course of human evolution, they say, via some subtle turn it became important not just to be good, but to appear to be good; just leaving the impression of goodness could gain the desired "reciprocation" for us. And the subtle adaptive adjustments didn't stop there. For as humans developed in astuteness, it came about that if we tried knowingly to deceive others we showed our hand in small ways—the others just might see through us—and so it became adaptive behavior to mime our concept of goodness to our own selves, deceiving ourselves about our goodness in order to do a better job of deceiving others about it. Ground-breaking researcher R.L. Trivers has related his genetic model of reciprocal altruism (the term is his coinage) to many of our overtly fine moral sentiments, suggesting that sympathy, gratitude, generosity, guilt, righteousness, and others are not as purely virtuous as we've thought all these centuries, but instead have been targeted by natural selection for improving our ability to deceive, to discern deceivers, and to escape having our own deceptions discerned. And all of this is related to getting our genes to the next generation—or, as Dawkins would have it, to the genes getting themselves there.

In spite of myself (and the anguish that invoked the dream moose), when I read of this research and the hypotheses it generates, my intellectual excitement is exquisite. My mind takes in these theories with bated breath. It's all so amazing, this business of the gene that shapes us to shape ourselves for the good of its survival—if valid, it's another gigantic strike for the elegance of the workings of nature—but it's a cold world. With the immense flexibility of our natures we're given the choice of goodness, unselfishness. And yet even our unselfishness is selfish. And even our choice isn't a choice.

You can flip that back on itself, of course. If the choice isn't our choice, you can say, the selfishness isn't our selfishness. It's the gene that's selfish, not the carrier of the gene. If I'm deviously supportive, only superficially altruistic—if I'm too hotly engaged in this struggle for fitness to achieve the disinterest necessary to qualify even my highest feelings as true love, it's not me but the genes in me that are behind it, and I'm off the hook. . . .

The Arctic tern, though indigenous to the coldest latitudes, flies ten thousand miles to avoid the hibernal extremes of its native habitat. Some bats drop their body temperatures to as low as twenty-nine degrees Fahrenheit, and hang themselves up for the winter just about dead. Other mammals increase their body heat. Some tiny ones raise it considerably, insulating themselves underground or undersnow right at the onset of cold weather, but the arctic fox needn't do so until the outside temperature drops below minus forty Fahrenheit, and even then, with only a minimal increase in body temperature he can sleep safely on open snow at minus eighty Fahrenheit for up to an hour, so well insulated is he, fur covering even the pads of his feet. Some amphibians burrow down into the mud all winter so as not to freeze, managing minimal respiration through their cloacas, even through their skin, while the wood frog buries itself in shallow soil of the forest and, by a miracle of biochemistry, freezes till spring. Although as the water in the spaces between his cells freezes he gets hard as a board, as long as the glucose his cells are packed with keeps the living matter of those cells free of ice, when he thaws out in spring he will start jumping again. As the days grow shorter many plants begin to dehydrate their cells. Consequently, although water by necessity freezes inside the plant, as in the wood frog it does so only in the spaces between the living cells, and so the plant, like the frog, goes on living in the frozen state. In some cases even the nature of the freezing within plants is different from usual; in a process called vitrification, the ice forms without crystallizing, so there are no sharp edges to puncture and destroy the cells. And some plants, like spring beauties and snowbank buttercups, even manage to develop while deep within snowdrifts, utilizing the meager light that penetrates snowpack to do some minimal photosynthesis.

Dealing with cold isn't easy. It requires ingenious biological plans. But even the cleverest accommodations to winter fail to exempt the plant or animal from the rigors of cold. There's always a sacrifice; winter exacts a harsh toll. It inflicts brutal physical hardship. Sometimes it dictates total suspension of activity, even of consciousness; the very life of some organisms is in abeyance for months at a time. Even then, winter kill is a fact of the season; whatever plan a species follows, there is always a percentage of the population that doesn't make it through. But tough on the world as it is, winter is not evil. It has nothing to do with morality. It's just a neutral coldness, part of the cycle of things. While one pole of the earth has its turn tilting toward the sun, the other tilts away from it, that's all.

The moose pays his winter dues like everyone. He makes a modest migration, not far south generally, mostly just down from the mountain tops, though because of his long flexibly-jointed legs he needn't even make the trip too early, deferring departure from subalpine bogs and creek bottoms, if he wishes, till the snowpack is close to two feet. He makes a dietary adjustment, switching from nutritious pond weeds, sedges, and tender leafy shrubs to woody shrubs and trees, and this requires increased fermentation time in his rumen to deal with the heavy cellulose load. As his dry weight consumption reduces by half, he metabolizes body fat stored during the summer, losing weight slowly but steadily till spring. To compensate for lowered nutrition, he sheds the weighty antlers that would drain his energy (seventy to eighty-five pounds of calcium grown in one four-month season, exceeding all other antler growth), and without going into torpor, he lowers his body temperature, reducing his basal metabolism and thus the energy demand on his food. He starves in bad seasons, if snow is too high; if he's weakened by too poor nutrition, he's susceptible to pneumonia, parasites, other disease, wolves.

Most of his adaptations aren't spectacular, but more often than not they cut the mustard. He has ten-inch guard hairs and a dense woolly underfur—in the wintertime an inch or more thickness of it on the inch-thick hide of his back—insulation to suit him for life in some of the coldest places, the high places in altitude and latitude, boreal forests of circumpolar lands. When the grasses and ferns and low shrubs of summer are two feet under in winter, he rips the bark off aspens with his lower incisors (like all cervids, he has no front teeth in his upper jaw), and straddling aspens weighed down by ice, he bends them down farther, to get at the finer twigs at the top of the tree. With his long, loose-hinged legs he moves fast even through deep snow, and when the snow surpasses the comfortable limit, moose, like deer, do a thing called *yarding*, several of them staying in a small area, or yard, and continually packing the snow down in a number of criss-crossing trails. Snow, in fact, is his winter comforter; when things are at their roughest he burrows down and insulates himself with a covering of it.

It's said that in the Middle Ages European moose were sometimes used as draft animals in Scandinavia, drawing sleds long distances through deep snow much faster than relays of horses could. It's even been reported that American moose were occasionally broken to harness. I don't have too much trouble believing it. Until not long ago some miles west of me there was a couple who hosted gatherings of moose every winter for years. All they did was put out plenty of hay and the moose came back and stayed every winter, munching, around in their yard from November to April, clomping around on the hay-bestrewn wooden deck that belted their house, and if the couple had wished it, I bet at least some of their moose guests would have stood for being harnessed up.

The moose is as winter a creature as almost any. His adaptations aren't as dramatic as those of some organisms, but in their understated way they're about as effective—in fact, in allowing him to go about the business of living almost as freely and fully in winter as in summer, they're more effective than most. When winter comes, the moose doesn't go around it or away from it, he doesn't switch to a whole new game plan, he doesn't shut down; he just lives in it, taking it as it comes as straightforwardly as he takes summer. He does more than survive the cold world; he makes it his home. Like my dream moose, he moves through it with something like the sangfroid and disinterest that characterize nature itself.

Last spring I stood on a rise at the border of forest. The pink petals of least lewisias hid beneath the new blades of grass at my feet. At the bottom of the long, steep slope below me there was a trickle of a stream and a deep streambank, eroded—an expanse of watery mud, black and textured with pocks. I saw something moving, and then he materialized, as usual. It was a bull moose in velvet, in mud above his knees. He was stuck, and even those long loose-hinged legs wouldn't get him out of it. He plunged and plunged, and it was to no avail. His feet were tangled in submerged roots perhaps, or perhaps due to illness or age he was simply too weak to defeat the suction's drag. But the moose showed no signs of panic. He worked for a while and then rested with complete unconcern. I'd once read an account of something similar, but hadn't quite believed it. The writer was a high level national parks official who'd watched a moose plunging in a quicksand of volcanic ash, and that's how he'd put it: between times he "rested with complete unconcern."

I stayed for a long time and watched him. But I was far from camp, and finally I had to leave. Still, I stayed for close to two hours and watched him, as he plunged and rested and plunged and rested, and when I left he didn't look any closer to getting out. Perhaps when the temperature dropped that night the mud would firm up and, the suction reduced, he'd get a foothold. If a grizzly didn't happen upon him first. I left reassuring myself with that rather strained notion. Perhaps the coldness he knew so well how to live with would save him here.

I philosophize on the neutrality of winter. On the beauty of the cold world the moose showed me. But when a bear surges over the top of the hill before me and, in his rolling gait, pours down its side toward the trees where I stand, it's all I can do to keep my wits about me. My heart can soar at the notion of the vast indifferent plan of nature, I can theorize what I theorize, I can know what I know, but when even just the metaphor for death comes, my heart freezes in me. I'm as far from the peace of that dispassionate power as I can be in those moments. Is the rest all delusion, hypocrisy?

The image of the moose in the mud says it isn't. Even the bones on the porch of my cabin this bitter fall say no. I went up to look before the snow should be final and found a profusion of them helter skelter in the willows around that stream, some flecked with matter, dried gut like scraps of rawhide. A long jawbone, a large femur, but I couldn't find a skull. I'd left the jeep on the log road and hiked in on impulse, no pack on, no water. While I was searching, I got more and more nervous as a strange leaden sky filled the east. By the time I got back to the jeep my whole body was shaking. A fall blizzard on the mountain is beautiful as long as you're not caught in it. I'd gathered the large ones, the whitest. Back home the books seemed to confirm that some were moose bones. I've spread them in a line under the porch rail. That way most of the day they catch the sun.

from *The North American Review*

Mapping the Sacred Places

Jan DeBlieu

I once drew a map to my home on the North Carolina Outer Banks for a friend who wanted to visit. I was new then on Hatteras Island, new to the salt-scorched landscape and interlocking planes of earth, sea, and sky. I felt newly awakened as well, as if I had spent the previous years with my eyes and my thoughts half-lidded. Every day I set aside time to explore unfamiliar terrain and wonder at the great schools of fish, the falcons and sea birds that migrated past the islands with the tug of seasonal currents.

Since there was not much to show on my map—just a single road beelining down a skinny arm of sand—I decorated it with my own favorite landmarks. On the north end I put three arches covered with a mane of vertical lines; these were the grassy, camel-hump dunes that fronted the ocean. Halfway to my house I drew a tuxedoed heron with hot-pink legs; this marked the marshy flats where I had stumbled on a group of black-necked stilts and the messy stacks of twigs they used as nests. Last I drew a stick-figure crustacean waving a flag on a nearby beach. I went to that beach often to watch ghost crabs skirmishing, shoving each other with round, pearly claws as if locked in mortal combat. Next to the figure I penciled in the words, "Ghost Crab Acres."

I meant the map to be comical, but also to honor places on Hatteras where I had witnessed something important or particularly beautiful. I am not much of an illustrator, and at completion the map looked like something a first-grader might have drawn. My friend called a few days after she received it. "Are these amusement parks or something?" she asked. I realized sheepishly that the connection I felt to each landmark was too personal, too powerful, to be explained by a simple drawing.

Now I wish I had kept that map for myself, or made another. I wish I had drawn a new map with equally foolish figures for each of my nine years on these islands. Put together they would compose a running chronicle of the places I have held dear here, a mental history of my courtship with the land.

I am more insular these days, and too caught up in the eddies of family life to do much. While still curious about the natural forces that play across the islands, I no longer have the same white-hot drive to observe and learn. I live on a pinesheltered ridge on Roanoke Island, out of sight of the ever-shifting horizons. The latest atlas of my world would mark hideaways in the dunes and marshes, but also the houses of close friends, the bookstore in nearby Manteo, and the grassy field where I take my young son to romp.

We map, each of us, mentally and physically, every day of our lives. We map to keep ourselves oriented, and to keep ourselves sane. "The very word 'lost' in our language means much more than simple geographical uncertainty;" the urban planner Kevin Lynch once wrote.....it carries overtones of utter disaster.... Let the mishap of disorientation occur, and the sense of anxiety and even terror that accompanies it reveals to us how closely it is linked to our sense of balance and well-being." And we map the places we love in much more detail than the places we dislike. "The sweet sense of home is strongest," Lynch wrote, "when home is not only familiar but distinctive as well."

Recently a friend pointed out to me that these sandy reefs where I find my own sweet sense of home have been mapped (in the standard, two-dimensional sense of the term) longer than any site in North America. In 1585 an unknown British draftsman, sailing to the Outer Banks with a military expedition, drew a sketch of the land's lay believed to be the first European depiction of the New World.

The drawing scratched out on parchment shows six rectangular islands positioned like beads on a string. Behind them, to the west, lies a massive mainland with squarish inlets and coves. The draftsman must have been either seasick, homesick, or inept as a cartographer, for he rendered a clunky, unimaginative chart of a coastline that to my eye has as much grace and nuance as anywhere on earth.

A scant two years later the Outer Banks were set down on paper with more precision by the English artist John White, who voyaged to Roanoke Island with a group of men and women hoping to establish the first British colony in the New World. (Cut off from all contact with England during the war with Spain, the colony mysteriously disappeared.) White himself returned safely to England in the autumn of 1587 and completed a series of drawings of the land then called Virginia. His three maps of the Outer Banks, engraved and published in 1590, must have been compiled using compass readings and astronomical observations, the only techniques of survey known in his time. They are astoundingly accurate. One, titled "The Arrival of the Englishmen in Virginia," shows British barks in a serpent-plagued Atlantic just offshore from a row of pleasant-looking, forested islands. The second and third maps depict the Outer Banks virtually as we know them today: as arching dribbles of sand reaching far to sea; as less like *terra firma* and more like the delicate stroke of a calligrapher's pen. A wide sound separates the banks from a mainland fringed by rivers and creeks. White believed the islands to be slightly wider and more eastward reaching than they later proved to be. But all reefs change shape with the tides and seasons. Who can say that the banks of four hundred years ago were not a bit plumper and more deeply arced than the banks of today?

It is fun to compare those early visions of the islands to later images produced by technology White and his contemporaries scarcely could have imagined. On March 12, 1969, the Apollo 9 space capsule orbited 120 miles over North Carolina. Although most of the continent was obscured by clouds that day, the skies above the eastern seaboard cleared long enough for an astronaut to snap a photograph that has become a signature image of the Outer Banks. To the east sparkles the black surface of the Atlantic, falling away with earth's curve; to the west lies the torn, lake-dappled membrane of the mainland. The Outer Banks sweep down the center in a plume of sediment-laden water, a single dry, sandy wisp.

Maps can never capture the essence of the land, any more than a photograph can depict a person's soul. Yet they so fascinate us that we draw them, etch them, paint them in a profusion of forms. One chart of the banks shows the location of four hundred-odd shipwrecks that have occurred off this "Graveyard of the Atlantic" since 1585. The map on the wall of my study is engraved in the style of scrimshaw, with hachures marking the scooped edges of land, the intestinal courses of salty creeks. Five tiny lighthouses dot the ocean shore, showing the location of the banks' famous beacons.

A controversial rendering of the North Carolina coast was published in 1978 by four geologists who wanted to warn potential buyers of the toll that erosion can exact on island property. The Hatteras Island village of Rodanthe, where I first lived on the Outer Banks, was rated as extremely prone to flooding; it now has the highest rate of erosion along the North Carolina coast. Although we loved the town, my husband and I were chastened by the geologists' advice. When time came for us to buy a house, we settled on higher, drier land.

In the early 1980s oceanographers began using infrared cameras mounted on satellites to measure the surface temperature and chlorophyll content of ocean currents. For the first time scientists could watch the raucous mixing of water masses off the coast. East of the Outer Banks, where the warm Gulf Stream runs headlong into cold plumes from the Labrador Current, the satellite sensors produce charts that are vivid and jarring. Where the naked eye would see only indigo water, the sensors paint a cauldron of hot fuchsias and golds colliding with icy knots of cobalt and jade.

To me these high-tech snapshots stir images of far more complex and enticing maps than I have ever seen set down on paper. What fluid, invisible highways are buried in the shifting currents, out of range of human sight and understanding? What wavering routes carry copepods, crustaceans, tunas, triggerfish, rays, and red drum to their far-flung summer and winter waters?

It is in the imagination, I think, that the art of mapping reaches its apex.

In 1960 Kevin Lynch published a book entitled *The Image of the City*. It describes a study by Lynch and several colleagues on the perceptions of people living in Boston, Los Angeles, and Jersey City. Lynch found that residents of each city drew maps with common features, such as main highways and government buildings, and that they would go out of their way to pass parks and green areas. Beyond that, the maps were highly idiosyncratic. From the mapping exercise and a series of interviews, Lynch concluded that even lifelong urban residents are not able to absorb all the images with which cities are so thickly piled. To give order to such a chaotic world, they choose a few important sights and use them as navigational posts.

If Lynch had taken time to look beyond the visual dissonance of city centers, I am convinced he would have found a similar filtering reflex among rural people. The capacity of the human mind is too limited to take in every detail of the landscape, be it town or country. We simply can't process the images with which we are besieged. And so we map, making note of what sights we deem, in a glance, to be vital.

"Visitor and native focus on very different aspects of the environment," writes the geographer Yi-Fu Tuan. The visitor's on-the-spot mapmaking "is often a matter of using his eyes to compose pictures." In contrast, Tuan writes, the lifelong resident moves through her environs with a shrewd and prejudiced eye. She knows which routes will clog with afternoon traffic, and which neighborhoods harbor muggers or snarling, unchained dogs.

Shortly after I moved to Hatteras I got a taste of how limited was my own vision of the island compared to that of a native. One day I took a walk to the shore of Pamlico Sound by way of a road through a small neighborhood. On my way home a fisherman stopped me to chat. "You interested in that land down there?" he asked, nodding toward the sound where a vacant lot was posted with a "For Sale" sign.

I shook my head. We hadn't yet saved the money for property.

"It's a nice, high piece," the fisherman said. "Not too many left like that. You might ought to take a close look."

As he drove off I stared toward the lot in question. It had struck me as no different from the surrounding properties, many of which were too wet for septic tanks. Momentary paranoia set in: Was the fisherman making fun of me? Trying to sell me a bill of goods? I walked back to the lot and noticed for the first time the gradual rise in the road, the dome in the land, the absence of the marsh plants that dotted adjacent sites. By island standards it was a veritable bluff, if not quite a mountain. How long would I have to live on Hatteras, I wondered, before I could discern all the subtleties of its spread?

I know now that my mental map of Hatteras will always be less richly detailed than that of a true islander, because I lack the islander's cultural ties to the land. Certain places there became sacred to me because of a few elucidating, extraordinary brushes I had with the natural world. But if I had grown up on Hatteras, my list of sacred places might include the Rodanthe Community Center, or a historic lifesaving station where my grandfather served, or a beach where the annual town picnic is held. In strong, stable communities, residents develop traditions that consecrate certain sites, not just grand public parks or monuments, but meeting places that tend to be, in the words of the landscape architect Randolph Hester, "dilapidated, familiar, homey, and homely."

Fourteen years ago Hester conducted a study on the precious communal places—what he called the sacred structure—of Manteo, a town on Roanoke Island near my home. Until the 1960s Manteo was the most important town on the Outer Banks. As the county seat, it held administrative offices and a large courthouse; as the primary trade center, it held grocery, and variety stores, family restaurants, and a commercial wharf on Roanoke Sound. All that changed, however, as the banks evolved from an enclave of fishing villages into a seaside resort. By 1980 several of the most important businesses had moved to the growing oceanfront town of Nags Head, and the Manteo waterfront was lined with vacant buildings.

Hester was then a professor at North Carolina State University in Raleigh. He had long been interested in the subconscious attachments people form to places. A few years before, while redesigning a day care center in Cambridge, Massachusetts, he had used an unconventional tactic to probe his clients' feelings. "The center was in a beautiful old Victorian building, nice but really funky," he said. "Everyone liked it. Before I drew up a design I did a standard survey with parents and teachers to find out what their values were and what kinds of activities they'd like to see in the center."

The survey indicated that the clients wanted a bright, state-of-the-art facility, "the kind of place you'd find in the suburbs," he said. "To achieve that, we would have had to raze the building. I was shocked."

Acting on a hunch, he approached a few parents and teachers and asked if they would repeat the survey under hypnosis. They agreed—

and gave entirely different answers. "The single most important thing was, they wanted to plant a tree outside that would be big enough for kids to climb," Hester said. "And they wanted some sort of natural area, like a creek, where kids could explore and chase butterflies." He drew up two designs, one based on each survey. The parents and teachers voted overwhelmingly to accept the plan that left the building little changed and created natural play areas outside.

I don't pretend to know what that means," Hester said. "But a psychologist friend of mine believes that people have all kinds of subconscious desires that they can't articulate. When they're presented with an option that honors those desires, that's the option they choose."

ₑ

With Manteo's unemployment rate running higher than any in the state, the mayor and town commissioners desperately wanted to build a new economic base. The obvious solution was for the village to capitalize on its quaint layout on Roanoke Sound, in hopes of attracting tourists. Roanoke Island was already known as the site of Sir Walter Raleigh's Lost Colony. The National Park Service had established a Fort Raleigh Visitor Center on the undeveloped north end, and each summer a local theater company presented an outdoor musical about the colony's mysterious demise.

Hester's assignment was to design a layout of the waterfront that would entice developers to open inns and shops downtown. Everyone talked as if a tourist-based economy would eliminate all woes. But turning a workaday downtown into an upscale tourist district is no simple feat. And as Hester soon learned, residents were close-knit and proud, both of the island's history and of their blue-collar heritage.

"The reality of daily life just seemed blurred with the mythology of the place," he said. It was an Andy Griffith Mayberry community, except that people would talk about Sir Walter Raleigh as if they had just seen him sailing in the sound. After a month we began to get a sense that people weren't willing to sell the soul of the community, even for economic development."

He arranged for a class of design students to make activity maps by studying the way residents used various parts of town. And he noticed that the same residents passed his office several times a day. Many of them routinely met friends at a local cafe or drugstore fountain. "People would go to the post office and take an hour and a half to get their mail. They'd park at a gravel lot on the waterfront, then go check the water, then run into a friend and end up going for coffee. They weren't downtown to get their mail; they were there for news."

It occurred to Hester that the townspeople might be underestimating their emotional ties to the plainer features of town, much as the Cambridge parents and teachers had underestimated their fondness for the old building that housed the day care center. "There are all sorts of social pressures to abandon the old in favor of new, shiny development," he said. "And we buy into them, whether we want to or not."

He began trawling for information about the most popular meeting spots and landmarks. He talked again and again with longtime residents, pushing them to describe their feelings about their favorite places. "Each of them would articulate little pieces of the sacred structure," he said. "I'd probe, and they'd send me in the right direction. It was difficult because they didn't know themselves that the town had a sacred structure."

One frequently mentioned site was a waterfront park where, years before, commercial boats had tied up to refuel. A local man had erected a jagged cement cross there, culled from the rubble of a demolished elementary school. According to local legend, the cross miraculously appeared in the cement as a wall of the school was being pummeled by wrecking balls. Another site was the gravel parking lot on the old wharf, where each Christmas townspeople festooned a cedar tree with lights. Locals considered their hangouts at the cafe and the soda fountain to be precious, along with the public docks on the waterfront. Unadorned and run-down, these gathering points were exactly the places that would be destroyed by a wholescale redevelopment. Hester arranged for a community newspaper to run a survey about residents' attitudes toward specific town features, "and then things really started to gel."

Despite their deep desire for a stable economy, townspeople decided they did not want Manteo to be completely gentrified. Hester made a map of the downtown's most sacred places, then drafted a land-use plan restricting development at these sites. "I knew it would scare off most developers," he said. "And it did. In accepting those limits, the residents gave up millions of dollars in potential income. But they managed to preserve the community's character and flavor."

When Hester mapped the sacred structure of Manteo, he marked places of particular significance with a heart. He hoped, everyone hoped, that would be the end of it. When we draw maps to fix our position in the world—whether mentally, emotionally, or physically—we do so prayerful that the lines we set down will still be true next week, next year. We are often disappointed.

On a mild winter day the Manteo waterfront is deserted except for a pair of fiftyish women in docksiders and jogging suits eating ice cream on a bench. Sailboats and cabin cruisers ride a calm gray tide in the slips of a new marina. A boardwalk constructed twelve years ago, largely by local volunteers, leads past a new inn, the old gravel parking lot (now paved), a sandwich shop, a condominium complex with an interior courtyard and shops, and—hidden from the street by the hulking condominium building—the park with the partly crumbled cement cross. Across a creek rocks a handsome replica of the three-masted bark that brought the first colonists from England. I go to the waterfront occasionally to eat lunch. Each time I find it pleasant, but not holy. It does not speak to me or anyone I know in any meaningful way.

Sadly, there is question whether the sacred structure of Manteo has proved strong enough over the past decade to withstand the forces of change. Locals still stroll the downtown streets, meeting neighbors on their way to the post office. But the docks where they gossiped are gone, replaced by the marina and a cramped public boat ramp on the out-of-the-way north end of downtown. The drugstore soda fountain burned some years back. Patrons have not taken to the fashionable ice cream parlor that replaced it. In a few years the post office may be forced by space limitations to move to the outskirts of town.

Few people remember Hester's map of sacred places.

Hester is now a professor at the University of California at Berkeley. He was clearly distressed when I told him of the changes along the Manteo waterfront. "The community worked so hard to prevent a tourist takeover," he sighed, "but the sense I'm getting is that the takeover happened anyway once they let down their guard." When I mentioned the post office's possible relocation, he curtly added, "That's what happens in most towns—they dismantle those centers of activity and then lament that the downtown is empty."

Yet even with its slicker countenance Manteo is beloved by my neighbors, who have lived here all their lives, and who will never live anywhere else. They hold in their minds a nostalgic map of past experience overlaid by the pragmatic map of the present. One shades the other. Neither dominates.

"Making an actual, physical map of something you feel in your heart can be quite a powerful experience," Randolph Hester told me, rather wistfully. And so I draw maps when I should be working, seeking to tap that power. Seeking to keep my bearings in a shifting world. I watch a flock of grackles invade the pines in my yard, and dream of Hatteras Island. As soon as I moved from there the sharp images I held of that landscape began to fade. Through the years many of the places I loved have been taken from me. The beach I called Ghost Crab Acres was sandbagged to slow erosion. The salt flats I nicknamed Stilt Field were flooded to attract ducks. An overgrown road where I went to spy on night-herons was sternly marked with NO TRESPASSING signs. Yet I map with those spots still prominent in my mind.

I map in concentric circles, my Roanoke Island home at the center. I place the barrier islands, eight miles to the east, an inch from my own bedroom, closer than the grocery store and jail that are just down the road. When I visit Hatteras, I tip my heart to the camel-hump dunes, the flooded marsh, the sandy ruts that lead to Pamlico Sound. Driving by, you would not know they held anything special at all.

—from *Orion*

Tempest and Staying In

Cynthia Huntington

⮑

Tempest

All day it was so hot the world burned. The water slid back and forth along shore, uncoiling like a muscle. Sand sizzled as the waves broke and drew back, dragging pebbles into the cool depths where they bounced and simmered in the froth.

Tern chicks crouch on hot sand under this breathless sun. They hide in jeep tracks or in footprints for shade, while their parents fly back and forth, making sharp cries and diving over the water. The birds' voices are shrill, hysterical in the heat. Back and forth they fly, searching, crying, then they stop against the air, fold their wings and plunge straight down, twisting slightly with wings back and head tucked for a deadfall dive, shearing off just at the surface. They rise and dive again and again for the small fish, flying endlessly back and forth from their hot nests to the glaring surface of the water. They are so pure a white, so definite and sleek and gleaming a white and their cries are like the sound of wires dragged across metal, high and cutting, yet distant as a signal from space.

⮑

I stood chest-deep in the current, feeling the salt sting my insect-bitten skin. I squinted up at the sky where blue and silver lights bounced into my eyes. The sun had weight, leaning on my bare shoulders, leaving a hot scar on the flesh it pressed. The pigment in my cells rushed forward to darken, little dye pots breaking open and spilling to dim the gleam of pale skin. Drying myself, I brushed glowing crystals of quartz from my arms and legs, each grain separate and precise and final as my flesh is not: one atom of silicon nested between four atoms of oxygen in exquisite, repetitive symmetry. Time made these crystals, uncounted, undisturbed quantities of time, balancing molecule on molecule. Cell by cell, over millions of years, my body is preserved in stone: patterns of tissue and muscle fiber replaced as semiprecious stones, the spirit light of bone growing ever more stable. Agate, jasper, amethyst, lapis…a sea change, pearls that were my eyes, this corpse of light.

Back in the shack, a glass of water overturned on the floor spread out and evaporated before we could move to wipe the spot, leaving a dark stain on the boards. Not enough for a fly to drink.

The flies wanted something else: they hung in mid-air or dropped suddenly on to an arm or leg, insensible of danger, ignoring the hand raised against them. It's our sticky selves they desire, taste of sweat and salt, the rich bitter blood. I slapped a fat one that grazed along my shoulder. He fell out of the air stupefied, half dead already, slowly turning wing over wing in hallucinatory mirage currents of heat. I wandered from bunk to windowframe, lay down and stared up at the ceiling, scratched at a great bite on my thigh until it opened; a splash of alcohol there, and I winced and swore as it seethed through my cells. Time simply passed; the earth turned slowly, and we rode it around with the patience born of having no choice. You couldn't call it waiting exactly—the way waiting points forward, directed outside the moment—rather we remained, hot, heavy, and yes, patient, riding inside time. Bert squatted on the porch in a slab of shadow, scratched a reed pen over worked and reworked lines of a drawing, connecting certain marks and pressing others back into oblivion. Crouched there on his haunches, he looked for all the world like some old savage, drawing the four directions with a stick in the dirt. I stared at my hands, turning them over and back, tracking alluvial cracks the sun made translucent, feeling the blood swell in my fingertips, stalled, lingering, before it was pushed back through the blue wrist vein. I stared at the white chips of my nails as if the faintest coolness was coming off their hard surfaces; I stared, allowing my eyes to rest on the nearest thing and slowly divine its contours. The thing might have been a tabletop or the view from a window, but because I was lying down it was not, it was only my hand against the red bedcover and I stared at it as if it were not mine, as if I could be far away or someone else and when that did not work I got up and drank a cup of cold, iron-flavored water and heard again the terns crying below on the beach, a sound which had continued to rise and fall even though for a while I had stopped hearing it.

&

Now toward evening a red-wing shrills from the weathervane. A sparrow chirps busily in the tangled bay and poison ivy outside the window, rattling the branches to stir up a small breeze. Within the shadow of deep grass a toad pants. Light clouds pushed out of the east give the sky new depth, breaking up that unrelieved glare of midday, and the waves turn over with a gratified sigh. I go out on the deck and look out. Far out a boathorn speaks deeply; now grass moves, and unmoving branches, dead sticks with no green, darken slightly, pulling a new dampness from the air. They may not be quite dead; they may be wanting to put out leaves, or to hold on until the world moves again under them.

The horses come down the beach, mounted by unschooled riders, following single file behind the leader. From far off only their movement stands out, that up and down canter as they cross below, while the bumpy shape of a large boat offshore seems not to be moving at all until I turn back and the horizon is empty.

It is evening coming, and rain coming on. Behind these first puffy clouds a phalanx of low dark ones frowns on the horizon, gathering force, and the northeast breeze blown ahead of them feels wet and cool. This wind carries water and oxygen to quicken the world, freshening cells of leaf and hill. A breeze blows across the chipped waves. Each wave that breaks sprays particles of seawater up into the air; as the wind carries them inland we taste salt.

&

Blackbirds are massing on the next hill, making chittery, tossing flights, settling down and rising up again in annoyance. Down on the beach the gulls circle and float in broad ellipses. There is a general rising and falling: leaves flip on the branches, grasstops shake, and towels fly up on the line. My hair whips into my face; the wind pulls it straight back, then everything sags and settles.

The air smells of wind and pepper; the birds' voices are shrill as they swoop back and forth, and light flutters on the grass, showing silver, then deep green. All along the foredune the grass is bent before the wind's motion. The shack stands to take the measure and shape of the wind pushing at it. One has to give, and for now the wind divides. Sand dances in short leaps inches off the ground, each grain landing to dislodge the next, making dust clouds along the tops of the dunes. Skeins of sand whirl down the slope of the nearest big dune, twisting and twirling. The beach roses in front of the shack look surprised, their branches flailing the air, as the wind pushes the ground away beneath them, grain by grain, persuading the multitudes singly, a force no force can halt.

ॐ

But now it seems to stop. Grass luffs in the dying breeze and a cool dampness settles over the valley. In the quiet a bobwhite repeats his urgent greeting, saying hopefully it is not too late.

I walk across the ridge and down into the valley by the pump. The sky turns light grey, seeming to absorb the cloud shapes that dashed across it, and the horizon darkens as wind flails the grass and disappears. I can't tell if the wetness beading my arms is sweat or mist, if this air grows heavy with rain or fire.

The blackbirds have left the bayberry. Beside the pump the huge bush is dark and silent; no alarm sounds at my approach. For weeks they danced and called and flew in circles over our heads when we appeared at the top of the path. The male whistled and flew around us while she fled to a nearby bush crying help. He fluttered, she moaned, all the while we pumped the buckets full and tugged them uphill, feeling guilty and harassed.

But yesterday all that was over. The pair flew past us unconcerned, as if nothing marked that spot, once so hotly defended.

Perhaps the nestlings have fledged and flown, but I suspect disaster: the marsh hawk. She has been around all week, raising panic in the valley every evening as she hunts along the ground and beats the grass for signs of life. I approach the bayberry cautiously, but nothing happens. I circle the bush, twelve feet across, looking for the well-hidden nest, but I see only tangles, thorns, and a deepening dark within. It is so quiet down here. Up above me, over the hill, the whole gang of blackbirds flies about full of weather news and excitement, swooping and calling back and forth.

&

The first drops make small depressions in the sand, and the sand begins to give up the heat borne down on it all day. A reversal is beginning: the earth's warmth will go back up into the sky and the sky will let go cool drops into the sun-warmed earth. This afternoon animals hid in the shade; now they will come out. Rain cools the hissing fringes of the waves. Darkness begins to contract horizons; I stare hard at what is near, shifting into shadow: twigs and branches, the scuffed depressions in the sand where we have walked back and forth, a darkening stalk of high grass. Branches and leaves become one mass as the ground rises into them; back-lighting gives shape to taller grasses, detail lost, the ground all one color. The rain still holds back, letting go in fat drops, a few here and there; you can walk between them.

As simply as that, the rain hitting my face, standing below the hill in the open, the change happened. I felt it like a gear slipping into place. A muscle relaxing across my shoulder, the board sliding into the notch, giving room to move without constraint. As the rain fell into the earth which pulls everything to itself, it seemed all space fell into order, pulling me with it. Clouds gathered weight and broke, falling into the earth, to lie upon the leaves and strike the bare hills, to break over our heads. And I stand here among birds and blowing grasses, adding my mass to that summoning, part of the storm falling towards me, falling as the earth falls, forward, circling back.

☕

I stood there below the hill, feeling the beating of my chest against the air. Then I looked up and got my breath pulled out of my throat. A crowd of gulls was passing overhead, flying back into the dunes as they do every evening. White and dark, they take the wind under them, moaning as they leave the beach, flocking up to the slopes where they sit in disgruntled company on the sand, all facing one direction. Tonight though, with the light on their backs, against the darkening east, they seem strange, more than themselves.

Tonight they touch the outlines of the timeless. Black against a pale, curdling sky, they cross the sky in whirling spirals. In their passing are one thousand thousand summer evenings. They fly into the gathering storm, light glancing on their wings, the black, winged ones, shapes that cross the earth at night. Touched by those shadows I turn invisible. They have always been here and my life is so brief. I stand in the open and watch them come, flexed, wing against wing, above the wind-furrowed grass, as they fly back into the dunes, swirling down to disappear behind the hill where storm clouds are massing.

☕

For an instant I seemed to remember something I'd been trying to say for a long time, something I knew, but did not fully understand until that moment—then that low, mumbling chorus overtook me. And then there was nothing left in me to think it. I was flown through, emptied and taken back. When I came back to myself I knew that I had been lifted, not in joy but in dread, and I knew that it did not matter. Raised up by the black wings or the white, you're equally gone, emptied. And then there is no remembering and no question.

I'm left here. Shake it off and turn back. Climb the hill and look out over the horizon. Now the rain breaks in ribbons driven sideways into my face, and a storm wind keens across the emptied landscape. I turn toward the shack, walk a few steps, then begin to run.

☕

An eerie darkness is gathering over Euphoria. Thunder rumbles across the waves and the sky turns weirdly stark and violent; the walls shake in sympathy. I close the door with difficulty, leaning on the wind to ease the wood over the swollen sill. The big board falls tight into its latch across the doorframe. Then the room is small and filled with us.

Cold now in my summer dress, my skin wet, goose bumps rising along my arms, I go to stand next to Bert. He takes me under his arm, inside the thick shadow of his shoulder, his body's heat. We watch together from our window as the combers fume and churn and plow up on shore.

We light the stove and set out lamps, confident in our small shelter, as the storm sweeps down on the land. Fill the lamps and check the water supply, eight buckets full, count our store of batteries for flashlight and radio, put out candles. Make everything tight and ready. We'll keep an ear on the weather station just to be safe—though it's not yet hurricane season. Hazel has left us a red flag to fly from the roof as a distress signal—but who would see it here? If a hurricane were forecast, we'd shutter the windows, unhook the propane tanks, and try to get out. Euphoria would likely stand as she has before, but the wind could shatter glass; a fuel tank toppled over could ignite.

Dark closes fast now, rain pelting the windows. For dinner we choose something from our store of cans and it is wonderful, miraculous that someone put this food into a can—beef stew, as it happens—that someone prepared it for us. Clear water in the pan, rice measured out; we'll ladle the stew over it as night comes down and the tide leaps up the beach. Wind luffs the sides of the shack, bursts of rain, and then the warm stillness flowing back. Rice grains rattle in the tin; they scratch as I stir them into the water. Whoosh of the can opener biting into the lip, grinding metal teeth around the sealed diameter. We are rich and wise, in possession of metal tools, fire, shelter and light. Cooked food, and blankets folded across the beds. For thousands of years we have sought this shelter. In tents or houses, in walled fortresses or circles of wooden huts where the fire crouched, smoke seeping into the breath and bones of the people. For thousands of years we have spoken to each other in the hush of coming storms, passing pots back and forth, drawing near the fire. I slice crusty bread as Bert pours water into the basin; the lampglow shines in his eyes. Beyond his watching face, his spirit watches.

We wash the dishes by lamplight, using as little water as we can manage. I sweep the floor and tidy up in the first burst of energy in days, folding and stacking towels rescued from the line, clearing tables of books and papers. We lean together beside a lamp to take up the endless game of gin rummy, slap the cards down, add up the points in the summer's tally. Wind tests the cracks, bursts of rain rocking us, and then stillness—it's still coming.

☘

The storm picks up again with a gash of light and a sickening thud as thunder hits the hill behind us. The shack shakes from roof to floorboards, down through the underpinnings, then rain gushes down with a sudden release and blows in sheets against the windows. It is a rolling, summer storm, a real Cape Cod tempest. The air crackles with static. Nothing comes through on the radio. Then a giant spark rips down the sky, white light slashes across the room followed by a violet strobe.

We stand stock-still in the middle of the room, pulled to our feet as lightning rips open a landscape rendered bright and flat as nightmare. A flash, a print on the retina, and in the swift dark the dying rumble of thunder subsiding, rolling over, like furniture dragged across a floor. The vision given by lightning is too quick; it reaches the brain just as darkness closes back in. We see a landscape of memory, lingering for moments on the back of the brain. The shack jerks and rocks as lightning shoots down; the world disappears and reappears, time seems to stop: the water is lit up bright and flat as an electric sheet and the dunes rise up in their Egyptian stillness.

We stand, surrounded by wind, inside the shack that trembles with its fury. The stove pipe beats back and forth, shaking down a black rain of fat sooty drops, and rain is driven down inexhaustibly, running over the sides of the shack. We hold on to one another, transfixed, as Euphoria sails into the storm.

Staying In

Morning. The storm has passed and left behind a steady rain that promises to pour down on us for days. The wind bangs the shack like a wooden gong and glass rattles in the window frames. There is no going out: it's given that we will stay inside, listening to the rain beat the walls, occasional thunder growling up. The temperature has fallen thirty degrees and streams of water shove under the door; we put down newspapers, then towels, until everything is soaked and the smell of wet newsprint clings in our nostrils. We wear all our clothes, sweatshirts and jeans and sweaters, in layers mismatched and lumpy. There's no dry firewood; the gas stove boils water for tea. No fire, tea and crackers, and wearing all our clothes.

℞

Afternoon. We rested and read all morning, tired after a sleepless night. I tried to get out a little bit during a seeming lull, but the rain soaked me through, and when I came back it was hard to get warm again, with tea and blankets and my last dry socks. The windows press fog and mist and we are cut off, asail and adrift in the grey, beating rain.

We take up a lot of room, suddenly large as we move around the shack. I feel dangerously shut in, blinded by the closed door and rain-soaked windows. To go from the table to the cupboard I must displace Bert, who is sitting on a camp chair beside the cold stove. To make a third cup of tea, Bert has to get past me at the table; if he wants to sit there too I have to get up and pull out the bench, and move books and papers, cups and spoons out of his way. We maintain an elaborate courtesy. I think of old hut dwellers who would live like this whole winters. The smell of smoke and stale bodies, wet socks, and the fear of going mad. I fall asleep in self-defense, a stale, unrestful sleep, visited by dreams of giants.

For lunch I make a pot of soup, using the last of the potatoes and onions, some sausage and dry milk. When the wind turns we get an occasional patch of radio. A station somewhere in Maine is playing all the songs of 1958 from two o'clock to three-thirty. "Davy Crockett,

King of the Wild Frontier," leads off. I count the hours until supper. If we were in town today, we would go to the movies or sit in a bar with friends....

🐌

Second morning. Last night it was hard to sleep because we hadn't moved all day. I lay in my bunk and heard the rain beat only inches over my head, its mental chatter like the details of many lives dropping singly and together. Outside, each creature crouched in its shelter: the owl, the hawk, the tidy, plush bodies of mouse and mole. Nothing was hunting or hunted; every beast and fowl and creeping thing was gathered into its place. What were the terns doing? The adults leave the nest to ride out the storm on the waves, but how were the chicks surviving? Could they last a second night in this heavy rain, with nothing to protect them—or had the storm tide already washed them out? Lying there I imagined scenes of desolation. Shipwrecked sailors wandering the dark, how long a man might search for shelter here. Bert began snoring then in fitful bursts, as irritating a sound as you could possibly imagine, and louder than the rain.

We woke to find the door still leaking. This was not amusing. The boards are soaked through now, and along the back wall a thin stream of water courses downward, winding past the windowframe and across the floor where it drips out through cracks in the boards. The wind shudders and pushes, body of wind, big shoulder heaved at the walls. We can see nothing from the windows; the shack is cold as a tomb, wreathed in cloud. Shut inside, we glare at each other over tea. I sit in bed with my journal and find I have no thoughts. Words advance across the page in merciless progression; sentence follows sentence, idea flows out of observation, words putting out more words and none of it means anything to me today. The pages feel thick and soft in my hands. We lie on the beds and read, or dial the radio across the numbers of distant cities. Voices scratch out of the metal box like a needle pulled across grooves.

🙠

Afternoon. My book this week is peopled with characters suffering from bad marriages and too much gin—it seemed witty enough on a bright, noisy day when I borrowed it from a friend in town. We eat an endless bowl of soup, dipping out of the pot that never diminishes. We start to hate the soup. I make another pot of tea; the crackers are stale and damp. This matters more than either of us could have imagined. The rain persists. Bert says he'll take a walk anyway; I say he might as well swim in a whirlpool. He comes back quickly and spreads wet sheets of clothing over chairs and I only just mention having told him so. We play Scrabble. We play gin rummy, peeling the cards up from the soft, fibrous wood. Bert's raincoat hangs on a chair like a dejected visitor, melting into a pool on the floor. We move our chairs to the furthest corners and plan separate vacations. The wind makes the most godawful noises. Arias and death-cries, keening and barking, terrible scrapings and thunder of something falling over. It shakes the walls to get our attention but when I listen it still doesn't make sense.

"Do you realize that when Picasso was my age he had already invented and discarded Cubism?" Bert says, looking up from his sketchbook.

"Picasso was a shit," I tell him.

"Maybe you *have* to be a shit to get anywhere. Be selfish, just live in the work. Let somebody else clean up." He pauses. "I don't know if it's healthy for an artist to be in a relationship."

I ignore this last. "Well, when Keats was my age he was already dead."

"Why do you always have to make it be about you?"

🙠

Time grinds to a stunning halt after this exchange; we're quiet and glum, padding about in our socks and long underwear, feeling snappish. Why do I live with this hulking, hairy, stale-smelling, large and surly creature? We turn on the news and get a weak signal, then static: the batteries are failing. We're cut off from the world: does no one think of us, or care to ask how we survive? Boredom relives boredom, running mental films of random action, exhausting with its "she said," and "then that happened," how it all comes to nothing. Stand in the middle of the room and listen: the afternoon seems tranquilized, spent of passion, gently breathing. Then a quick blast throws a truckload of sand at the walls and the shack staggers, sways, and rights itself.

ॐ

Night. This night comes early, black night in which everything disappears. Then wind, thunder again—it's hard to believe no one's angry. What does the air hit to make it stop so suddenly? A light sways violently offshore, then light opens into light; the waters sheen electric pale. The shack trembles like an animal that smells fire. Tucked up in blankets, not really warm, I fall asleep feeling sorry for all of us.

Shadows pile up at the door. Ghosts of lost creatures, sailors, ancestors, all I have tried to put away from me here, cry out, demanding comfort. Go away. Get on, you storm voices, you mysteries, leave me alone, you damned lost endless multitudes, and the hell with you. Where you come from there are more of you, endless yous, the centrifugal force of your woes pulling me toward you, and I will not go. I do not want to go with you because I know you are dead. A shadow stands on the doorstep, rain pasting his clothes to his body, his hair slapped to his forehead, a streaming wraith wrung out in the sea's agitation, with the deadlight shining in his eyes. His silence is a demand; he says nothing. If I bring you into my bed to warm you you still are dead and I am cold from holding you. No—you nothings, you dead voices, you windborne sorrows, no to you.

ॐ

In my dream a lamb roast is turning on a spit; tents billow in gaudy colors across a desert camp. I dream the elders are gathering, caravans arriving by day and night, and the lamb turns on the spit, its skin splitting, black char of fat and the head revolves over and around, righted and spun downward, staring from burnt eye-sockets. Meat, hot and running with fat, savory with herbs, the smell of the animal growing stronger in the fire.

In the dark a skunk comes knocking, treading up the path, wet fur effusing skunk stink. I wake and taste it in the back of my throat, through my sinuses, inside my lungs. He bangs once at the trash can and pads off. I wait, listening. The rain has stopped. I listen some more, then get up and open the door.

The quietest night, weighted with damp, lies on the world. A faint glow of moonlight burnishes the clouds, and night sleeps. It is right to say the storm has lifted; I can feel the air spring back under it, the grasses uncoiling. There is the blink off and on, around and back, of Highland Light, not visible for days.

The stairs hang down like a bridge between lives; a soft radiance is on the sand. Grasses bend seed plumes toward the flowing dunes, their lapped curves standing still a moment in their constant retreat. Offshore, boats circle their anchors, afloat on the consciousness of water, and the moonlight wakes a struggle of roses gripped down in sand. Their blossoms clenched tight, roots pulling hard to earth, they bury themselves holding on. Behind me, the shack is dark as a shell; the whisper of surf breaking on the beach below is like the jet stream around a disappearing space craft. The shack rises up behind me. Sheer and hollow, wingless, it rises as the ground flows out beneath it. I am standing here on the night earth on my two white legs, on moving ground, out here awake in the moonlight, not dreaming, alive in the dark before naming.

—from *The Salt House: A Summer on the Dunes of Cape Cod,*
a work-in-progress

High Country

Emma Brown

Mike Turner was not supposed to pass by this place, but we look for him anyway. You never know what a person might do when he ducks out from under his roof and arrives under this big Wyoming sky: itineraries are disregarded and whims grip the heart. The meticulous, well-researched plan for the perfect trip, dubbed 'Wander into Wonder' by this minister who was taking a sabbatical from his church because he felt he needed time and solitude to decide what came next, and the book-lined idea-thick office in which the plan was made, the desk on which the topos lay, at which he sat, concentrating and dreaming, piecing together an adventure from guidebooks and memories of this place he'd visited twenty-five years ago—I imagine all of these seemed far away and irrelevant when his feet were finally upon the earth and he smelled sage.

And so we look despite the improbability of finding him. The gurgling purr of a grouse in the dense growth of the lower elevations just before a thunderstorm, when things feel ominous, becomes a cry for help. A pair of cheap black plastic sunglasses, modelled after a more expensive brand, found on the east side of Texas Pass, a pair of men's underpants left on a rock above Billy's Lake, a howl at Shadow Lake, reports of a black dog that looked like his along the road in Big Sandy Opening, at the Big Sandy trailhead, at the Elkhart trailhead, on the Scab Creek trail, at Green River Lakes, all within hours of one another— all of this information offered by people who don't want to know that this experienced backpacker, father, husband, and minister has disappeared. They are grasping, and we with them, at nothing, but the planes have stopped circling and the Sublette County Sheriff's Department has called its people off the search. The people who are supposed to find him are giving up, and the small, unlikely things are something, at least.

ℛ

I am a ranger in the Bridger Wilderness, in the Wind River Range, in northwest Wyoming, and my brother Sam is by some coincidence my trail partner. Our job is to backpack. There are other things, too—removing aluminum foil from fire rings, picking up trash, smiling and answering strangers' questions. There is frustration because visitors seem determined to love this wild place to death. There is boredom, sometimes, and exhaustion, often. But these things are forgettable. What I will remember best is walking among granite and sky, and the green smell of lakewater in my hair; I will remember too that someone else's tragedy worked its way into me and became part of my story.

Sam and I hear Aaron's voice crackle from our radios somewhere near Island Lake. Radio conversation at times resembles the backcountry equivalent to soap operas; we try to piece together the development of real-life dramas from the snippets of transmissions we can hear. It is our entertainment. Aaron is reporting that he has met a family whose father has not shown up for a planned rendezvous at a spot called, ironically, Dad's Lake. The man is two days late. I am occupied with sore feet and a candy bar.

That afternoon we walk and listen to the chattering radio. The man is six foot six with a fu manchu moustache and glasses. He has a black dog, Andy, who carries a red pack. We find the term fu manchu hilarious. We cannot resist gossip about those whose voices float from the radios at our hips, and we do not think too much about the man who hasn't shown up to meet his family.

It is not uncommon for people to be reported missing in the Winds, and then show up hours later. Sometimes the late arrivers have stopped at a lake to savor the silence, sometimes they have been delayed by illness or weather. This summer, one party was three days late after being chased off the trail by a moose; another man, legally blind, lost his way after breaking his eyeglasses while fishing. A helicopter found him waving a sock to attract attention. The newspaper said the man was wearing shorts and a tee shirt and suffered from 'severe bug bites.' I suppose we think that Mike Turner, the man with the fu manchu, is no different, and that is why we can consider all of this just entertainment, a distraction from the usual routine of our jobs.

Days pass and Mike Turner does not stumble out of the woods. Helicopters and fixed-wing airplanes buzz low over the middle part of the range, where I am hiking on my days off. I notice in the distance, among the gray of rocks, bright spots—backpackers' tents, packs, jackets—that appear and then are hidden as the land shifts with my perspective. Somewhere in this range he is a bright spot among gray, I think. They cannot help but find him. It occurs to me that this man simply cannot be lost up here. The peaks of the Continental Divide cast shadows during the morning hours from the east, and the flatness of roads and homes and telephones spreads to the west—anyone would know where to find refuge. Something else must be wrong.

More days pass. He was supposed to be at Dad's Lake two weeks ago; his name and photograph have made the national news. Everyone has an opinion about Mike Turner's whereabouts. Janet from the fish biology department is hopeful; she thinks he's curled up sick on the side of the trail somewhere. If I were a betting man, says one fisherman as he casts into the blue of Rainbow Lake, I'd bet he's dead. Most everyone agrees in a somber tone and with a slow shake of the head.

He was planning on covering so much ground, and so much of it off of trails, that it is hard to know where to concentrate the search. He left three alternate itineraries with his family, each for a different combination of weather and snow conditions, and the people who know him say that Mike is the kind of guy who will happily follow whim to peaks and ridges that capture his fancy. He could be anywhere, people are saying, within the folds of these mountains.

It is because of a mistake of mine that Mike Turner becomes to me more than another missing person. At the Big Sandy trailhead, on my way into the wilderness for nine days of work, I meet three men. Their eyes are red; they drove all night last night from Caldwell, Idaho to ask backpackers to watch for signs of Mike. The two younger men introduce themselves as members of Turner's congregation; the older looks me in the eye and says, I'm his father. He is referring to one of the younger men I have just met, but misunderstanding, I believe I am shaking hands with the father of a man who is most certainly dead. This man is quiet and composed but urgent; he presses me for every bit of information I have learned in the past several days—about the multiple reports of black dogs with red packs, about howling at Shadow Lake, about a stray black lab along the road near here. I tell him what I know without listening to my words; I am trying to imagine what this man is feeling, trying to understand how it is to be spending these valuable days waiting at a trailhead, entrusting his son to other people, to strangers whose bodies allow them into the mountains. I cannot fathom his patience. I say goodbye to them and walk upstream along Big Sandy Creek, envisioning this man, his body stiff with age and worry, lying awake at night, taking inventory of the possible horrors his son has lived. Through small lush meadows and still tracing the stream, I imagine this man's eyes shining, reflecting the stray light from the moon in the dark of an unfamiliar room at the Big Sandy Lodge, and I understand that Mike Turner is real.

Cindy tells me quietly that I need not look too hard for Turner. The Sheriff's office has pulled most of its people; the search has lost its urgency, but I don't want to give up on Turner. I ask those I meet on the trail whether they have seen a man with a fu manchu moustache, or a dog. They all know about the missing backpacker; Turner's friends have alerted everyone in the backcountry. No one has seen anything. One man, whom I meet on a little-used trail through an area that narrowly missed the heat of the Boulder Creek burn of several years ago, says, you know, he was asking for it, coming out here alone, traveling cross country over dangerous terrain. There is no sympathy in his voice. Others echo his sentiment: Turner was silly, naive, foolhardy to undertake such a journey.

It is my habit to nod politely when I am in uniform, even to the most outrageous of comments. But I cannot bring myself to be diplomatic with these people, who are attacking what I believe is Turner's desire to take risks, to seek solitude in an increasingly crowded place. Don't you see? I want to say. He was not after just pretty scenery— trees silhouetted against brilliant sunsets, mountains drawn into rippled granite and draped with snow—and he was not after simple escape from traffic jams and email. The Mike Turner I imagine was in search of wildness, joy and perhaps freedom, and that journey required an embrace of danger. Have you progressed so far, I want to ask, that you cease to be wild and consider the pursuit of wildness foolish? I have never met Mike Turner but I admire the vitality I imagine to be his, and I am grateful that there are people like him who recall how to live fully while acknowledging the risk of death.

Cindy drives to Lander to tell Turner's family that there is almost no chance we will find him alive. She returns shaken—she coordinated the search effort that failed to find a missing life. There is a memorial service for Turner at a hidden place called sacred by those who know it, where you feel you are in the middle of things; there, you close your eyes and feel the stretch of Fremont Peak, flanked by Jackson and Sacagawea, soaring against the horizon while the world immediately before you slips and dives into Long Lake Gorge. In the parking lot afterwards, a man on his way home spots a black dog that looks like Andy. People who are struggling to say goodbye to Mike Turner spend fruitless hours searching for his dog, for a clue, and there are tears bidden by a new hope that precludes healing.

After nine days in the wilderness I am met by a ranger at the trailhead. After small talk, I ask, any word on Turner? And he says yeah, they found him. Is he dead? I ask. Yeah, he says. A hiker from Colorado found him. He was under a rock, near Alpine Lakes. 'Parently he's been dead for a while now, and he doesn't look too much like himself. Oh, god, I say. How about his dog? They found the dog a few days ago, he says. Poor bastard was starving. They say he's been over Indian Pass three or four times, looking for help and then going back to check on Turner. At least, I say, his family doesn't have to wonder.

Back in town I stop by the general store to pick up the local paper, The Pinedale Roundup, which says that a rock shifted as Turner was crossing a boulder field on August 2. He was not hurt, just caught in a landscape of rock. I wonder about those first moments. He took one of thousands of steps that morning, a rock that looked stable moved, and there was the sudden tingle of adrenaline that accompanies the unexpected. The shifting stopped, and he discovered with relief he was intact, uninjured. His blood flowed again. He probably didn't recognize immediately that he was stuck in such a final way, but realization along with disbelief must have risen in a nauseating wave as he struggled to free himself and could not. I wonder how long he struggled, how much sweat he gave, before he let go of disbelief. He took his pack off, says the paper, and arranged food in a circle around him. I imagine Andy stood above him, first cocking his head quizzically, then whining insistently. Mike was stuck only twenty five feet from a lake— maddeningly close. When his water was gone, he attempted to throw the water bottle into the lake and then pull it back via an attached cord. But he failed, and there was nothing to drink, and he became drier. He could reach his journal, and a pen. He wrote that he was afraid no one would find him because he was a mile west of his planned route, and only his head and shoulders were visible from the air. He wrote letters to each person in his family, took care to seal them in plastic and put them in an obvious place. He was planning on death.

The paper says he died on August 11 of either dehydration or hypothermia.

Mike Turner lived for nine days with the knowledge of his death. Nine eternities, Hank says. I remember the unseasonable storms of the first week of August, imagine him drenched and wedged with night falling. I imagine shivering. I think of the sun at midday, how hot and bright things are among rocks in that summer sun. There is thirst, and his tongue growing thicker in his mouth as his body becomes dry. I, the atheist, clutch my arms to my chest and hope that Mike Turner, the minister, found peace in the company of his god. The eleventh of August was the day after Aaron's report, the day the search helicopters first flew, the day two of our rangers stood atop Indian Pass not five miles away, the day we laughed lightly about things I don't remember anymore. I hope he did not hear the helicopters fly over him without pausing; he had torture enough without the pain of the almost-but-not-quite.

I have left the mountains, now, gone back to the city for the winter. I think of Mike Turner often. Images of a man I have never met ambush me during inconvenient moments, and I am grateful. To live fully, accepting the risk of imperfection and mistake and even death as a result of living with energy and simple joy, is to be wild. It is almost easy to become wild when I am living in the mountains, when the rivers are running through me and the sky lifts my eyes; and then it is easy again to believe that wildness is not possible in a world grown cramped and tight with humans and human things. These visions of a man who, in my imagination at least, embraced life, and the accompanying memories of hikers who shared a physical wilderness with Mike Turner but who scorned him for his risks from the perfect safety of their own well-worn trails, remind me that wildness is not exclusively of the external, experienced world. It is a quality developed and carried internally. There are places in which wildness is easier to learn, but I can carry my wildness anywhere.

—first publication

Coming of Age in the Grand Canyon

Susan Zwinger

&

Morning, 9:20, already a late start in Grand Canyon National Park. I sit in the dirt drawing *Oenothera caespitosa marginata,* an immense primrose that flings open gleaming petals shamelessly, gloriously. Drawing, my form of meditation, precludes worry. I've come here to study natural history pensively, slowly. Above me, the trail zigzags 450 feet straight up the sandstone cliff like a high-top bootlace. Soon I am climbing straight up it, out of breath, slowing people down. At the top, Michael, the trip's photographer, strides jauntily to the edge. I gaze at him in horror.

Last night, as cracked, brown fingers traced the route on a topography map, I realized that this hike would demand I do what every cell in my body told me not to do many times over. The longest hike of our nineteen days on the Colorado River, it would loop up one wild canyon, through Surprise Valley and down another, no turning back. I had serious doubts. Our trip had begun ten days earlier at Glen Canyon Dam with forty people, including much media, for the purpose of celebrating both the eightieth birthday of professional river runner and lifetime environmentalist Martin Litton, and his umpteenth time rowing the Colorado River through the Grand Canyon by oar and small wooden boat. Fortunately, a number of people had left us along the way, driving off at Lee's Ferry or hiking out of the canyon at various locations. The hard-core group remaining wanted not only to honor our elder, the Grand Old Man of the River, but also to explore, to research the return of the beaches after the spring 1996 deliberate flood to restore the river's wild condition, and simply to have a fantastic time. Along with David Brower, Martin Litton was responsible for saving the Grand Canyon from becoming just one more trash-covered, heavy-metal-deposited, slimy lake bottom. How great a world treasure we would have lost without Litton. This particular hike could include neither Litton nor most of the group. Barton, a computer specialist from California, had regaled us with tales of the grandest topography of the entire Colorado River journey. "There's a scary part where you squeeze along a narrow ledge forty feet above Deer Creek in a fantastic narrows," he had said, "but you can always turn back." My hands had curled shut like claws. After eight miles and 2,500 feet altitude gain and loss, I'm going to turn back? Factor, our half mountain goat, half encyclopedic trip leader, then told us that we must complete this nine-mile loop in five hours in order to be back in the dories in time to row to our next camp.

Now the trail turns sharply up a narrowing canyon sixty feet above thundering Tapeats Creek. I concentrate on the river's roar below: golden and turquoise, brown and white water. Silk and foam; silk and foam and danger. The trail drops down and crosses the river. Forming a human chain, we each step three feet down into waist-deep current. My sandals disappear from sight; my feet creep by Braille over stones slippery with algae. In the deepest water, I pull Barton back, forgetting he is barefoot. The water roars higher and higher on my chest (his waist). A slip, a break in the human chain could mean being swept downstream and pummeled on large boulders.

As Barton climbs out, his foot is spurting blood. The snow-cold water from the 8,000-foot Arizona mountains has spared him pain until now. This country, which unfolds the most spectacular exposure of geologic beauty anywhere on the planet, is unforgiving.

While they patch up Barton, I travel on ahead after Lili, the videographer. I hand her the heavy video camera and tripod up a small cliff. She technical climbs and mountain bikes most weekends. I used to technical climb in my twenties and feel ashamed of my loss of skill and courage. Still, my body remembers the moves and delights in translating a cliff face into stair steps and handholds.

Climbing is all about changing perception, which, come to think of it, is this entire canyon, this entire journey. The rock walls, the immense mesas, the roaring creeks are changing my perception of myself every moment. They are resculpting me relentlessly, cutting down a mile into my bedrock beliefs.

❧

We travel a leisurely, flat two miles up canyon. Barton tells stories of other rivers he plans to run all over the world. He has ceased thinking about his toe, a discipline I know from backpacking. Just can't be an issue. We have seven more miles, 2,000 more feet to climb and another major crossing.

Our conversation bubbles along like a mountain brook, while the Tapeats turns ominous. Only April 12, and heavy May-like volumes unleash from the mountains. The winter of 1997 has seen record levels of snowfall all over the West. The snowpack is at record highs; flooding is prevalent all over California, Oregon and Washington. Here, the snowpack in the Arizona and Utah mountains translates into amazing hydrology: streams gushing under pressure from holes in the rock, creeks swollen above their normal obstacles and banks, and magnificent botany. The entire desert canyon shimmers with vivid greens; cactus flowers explode in saturated color.

Upstream, Thunder River roars in from the northwest. The Tapeats accrues depth; rounded river cobble expands to hip-wide boulders. Plunging over table-size stones, snowmelt transforms its glassy-rilled surface into roaring tumults around white air sockets—a raw-thunder sound. I am watching it out of the corner of my eye with trepidation. I cannot believe that water four feet deep is good for a 5-foot, 4-inch woman.

We sail right past the crossing cairn in disbelief, and add another half-mile onto our trip by backtracking. Clasping hands, we again form the human chain; this time Barton wears his mountain boots. The first step down takes me up to my midriff with foam bulldozing my chest. Fear, which I usually put off until midstream, begins at once. This time, a fall would mean being swept downstream and possible broken bones or death. Barton yells at the top of his lungs at me to move ahead. I am pulling him back. It requires all my will to step one foot forward. At this speed, water multiplies its weight by thirty times against any obstacle.

A brilliant orange Indian paintbrush bobs on shore. It burns into my brain with a hot blade of irony. This is the last flower I will ever see.

The icy river numbs everything below midthigh, so I cannot feel where my feet should go; my body disappears in the water's rapidly sliding layers. Barton grabs ahold of Factor, who stands like a pillar near the other bank. For several moments—an eternity—I am alone in the roaring river. It takes all of my courage to work over to Factor.

Thus far, I have kept up just fine, but stopping to put my socks back on, I fall to last place. Slowly, Factor talks me up the next 900-foot elevation gain, up a canyon wall near the vertical drop of Thunder River from Thunder Spring. Factor, ever wise and encouraging, plucks a geological detail from his voluminous knowledge and points out a hill of Shinumo sandstone protruding 300 feet up into the overlying shale. The Shinumo was an ancient island in a 1.2 billion-year-old sea—the time it required to lay down enough fine-grained shale to cover an island. In my mind, I bury my island home in Puget Sound with seventy-five million years of sediment, then wonder if I should send my backup disks to the mainland.

At each switchback, my body aches with the lack of oxygen and refuses to go on. At each switchback, I force against my anaerobic cells. Solo, I would have stopped to conquer my blood-sugar problem by now, but here I ignore the dizziness and nausea, gulping a granola bar on the way up.

Lili drops behind for a long video shoot across a quarter-mile of empty space to the brightly clad human specks stuck to the vertical, red limestone wall. I am no longer last-that horrific moral pressure is off. Two more switchbacks and I am on that red wall, its shelf trail hanging me in space. This time I revel.

I am right on the edge. I gaze straight down, then straight across space, the plummeting side gorge we will cross, to the spot where volumes of white water, Thunder River, shoot out of a solid wall of stone. From high above, the water bores down through limestone, through anastomotic tubes until it hits an impervious layer of Bright Angel shale and exits dramatically. When the Colorado River carved straight down through the bedrock, it exposed two round holes anywhere from six to fifty feet wide. To see an "unexplained" and perfectly round exit high on the canyon wall with a waterfall pouring out of it is uncanny.

What joy! My spirit shoots through that giant canyon wall of resistance and flies with the white water out into open space. It flies across chasms toward the hanging rock garden and lush cottonwoods nourished by the falls—our haven for lunch. At each switchback I pause now, not from exertion, but from ecstasy.

There is such raw power in being balanced on this narrow trail. The minuteness of my fellow humans crossing the deep canyon on a red limestone wall hundreds of feet thick, the multiplicity of flower and mesa and stone and tree, the surreal image of a river shooting straight out from a wall of stone and falling a thousand feet-and the knowledge that with one leap I would fall 700 feet, to blend with the Indian paintbrush quivering in an up-canyon wind.

&

It begins raining again. The other eight hikers tuck back into deep red monkey flowers, ferns, lichens, mosses, and lush cottonwood trees, gathering around Factor for his stories. He once climbed down and through these labyrinthine tunnels carved by the water. He crawled and slithered until he could peer out from within the limestone cliff face just as the water does before it plunges.

I long to hear these stories; the stories Factor carries from twenty years of breakneck explorations reverberate in my own abbreviated experience like harmonics on adjacent strings.

Yet, I also want to perch out here alone on this windswept switchback to watch the virga and snow stream diagonally from their laden clouds—clouds that tear like scrims across the mesas layered in the distance, a preternatural distance broken by mile-high earth tables that are striated Prussian blue, maroon, cobalt, deep eggplant. I want not only to watch these storms, but also to smell and embrace them. To be swept along by the ever-spinning music of Grand Canyon thermal systems.

Another 300 feet straight up red limestone and we climb out on the cusp of Surprise Valley, a wide, gently sloping piece of the Tonto Platform, a classic hanging valley. In a hotter month, this long, waterless traverse is potentially dangerous. Today, a vigorous stroll takes us through tall spikes of century plants and yuccas, through deep-purple larkspur, past trombone-shaped purple blooms of Colorado four o'clock, *Mirabilis multiflora,* odorous mint sage, and thorny-fingered mesquites. The Tonto Platform seems impenetrable until a rift suddenly opens up—as if the Earth had ripped. We drop into Deer Creek drainage.

And drop and drop and drop and drop. Stepping down three-foot rock shelves, scrambling down ten-foot chutes, or picking through talus the size of pickups loses its charm. I feel wretchedly guilty because I am slowing my companions way down. I find myself down-climbing first, in front of the last few people. Suddenly, I gaze out into empty space. The trail disappears.

I stop dead in my tracks. A good route finder from years of hiking cross country, I see no trail up. No trail down. Just a bone-gray talus cliff face with 570 feet of exposure. Below spreads a luxurious valley where Deer Creek sparkles like a strip of tinsel.

A slim pale-gray line—only ten to twelve inches wide in spots—dots the face of the cliff for 300 feet. Could this be a track on the otherwise near vertical face where I am supposed to stick like a fly? Once again, every cell in my body cries, "Absolutely not." I think of backtracking, of crossing Tapeats Creek twice by myself-in the dark.

I put Jen, the twenty-three-year-old cook who does not yet know she is mortal, in front of me. Head down, I stare at her heels. Never did two heels look so fascinating. My feet step out into space, following Jen like two dumbstruck puppies.

Two thirds of the way over, I gaze straight down. My spirit seizes like an unoiled engine. There, 570 feet below, some ridiculously cheerful grasses blow in the wind. No respect for my terror. Yet, something strange shifts within. The wind whirs past, whipping up the vast empty space into something tangible, terrible and delicious. Something immense is born from utter nothingness. My skin springs wide open and swallows the air, my hair whips around like schools of silver jacks flashing in the ocean; my feet sprout roots that pull up from the talus like Velcro, then reattach with every step.

I gape at space, I court space, I leap through space.

Hahhhhh, I *am* space!

We drop off the slippery gray talus into the red limestone, rest below a waterfall jettisoned through anastomotic tubes straight out from the cliff. I pray that all wild such rivers—within me and without—remain free flowing.

In another half-mile, I am leaping with Jen across Deer Creek. To pass the time as we trudge out the hot, red-dust valley, we fall into a deep discussion about our mothers. She wants to know why many women her mother's age won't take physical risks. Why won't they come out here into paradise? Why does their sense of adventure end when children leave, when a husband leaves? All very painful questions, incomprehensible to someone as dynamic as Jen.

As we brainstorm ways to inspire women to run their own wild rivers, I envision her mother white-haired, parchment-skinned, puttering about her garden, snipping away at the wilds that make it through the chain-link fence.

"How old's your mom?" I ask.

"Forty-five," says Jen quickly, embarrassed for me.

Forty-five! Chronology clubs me over the head again, as it so often does in this canyon, this time with a stinging pleasure. Like I've just dropped a twenty-year-old mind into a fifty-year-old body and gotten away with it.

The wide, dry valley suddenly pinches into a narrow slot canyon where Deer Creek bores through solid stone. Its hue turns from the terra cotta of the dust to the aquamarine of the Pacific in strong sunlight.

The stream drops forty feet below the ledge where we walk. Our path curls back and forth along the constricted parallel walls of bulging stone. At two points it is so narrow that we must squeeze by an overhang that pushes our bodies out over the chasm. My change in perception jars me: *This* is the "scary" part Barton described? After the gray talus exposure, this narrow ledge embraces me.

To keep from staring down in terror, I gaze straight across forty feet to the other side of the slot canyon. There! A dozen red oxide hand prints left by the Ancient Ones who once farmed down on the Colorado. I shudder at the vertiginous climb that was required for them to press their hands to the stone. A twelve-hundred-year-old prayer to this slot canyon. Hands seamless against the wall. Palms flush to stone.

—from *American West*

Chorus

Alianor True

There is a certain comfort in waking to the same sounds every morning. When dawn stirs beyond my window and the sky lifts with the light that will become day, trilled mating calls surface from the woods around the house. Single amphibians, crying out to each other, and up, into the still winter air. By eight o'clock, sunlight soaks my wood-planked room, and frog calls are complemented by pips, flutes, and harsh caws. Musical noises, invitations to rise and meet the day, and whatever it may hold. This early air is ripe with the unrehearsed rhythm of tweets and chirps, chatter and screeches. The swish of distant traffic slides in every few minutes. Yet nothing permeates the air so much as the constant sound of frogs. Their rhythmic, repeated calls float about the forest, surfacing in hoarse harmony. They drip through the trees and vines like water, like sunlight, pervasive and insistent. A collective gathering at waters' edge, drifting up through these big woods and capturing the silence, fast and tight.

These habits and noises of frogs are new to me, like most of what I have seen in the past few weeks. I was raised in Georgia, where the soft pulse of cricket chirps lulled me to sleep from the azeala hedges lining the house. Here, in North-central Louisiana, on a plot of land settled deep in the mixed pine and hardwood forest, tiny frogs compose the background music, filling the air with the hope of spring and distant summer. Their songs diffuse and coat the forest with a steady resonance, embracing the trees and the clearcuts, the honeysuckle and the holly. They punctuate the day, rising and failing with dusk and dawn, and filling the space in between.

This old land is vaguely familiar to me, combining harbored memories with images of the environment I grew up in. Any walk around the property is almost dreamlike; I am unable to recall the exact state of this forest the last time I saw it, over fifteen years ago. I can recognize bits common to Southern ecosystems: the poison ivy snaking up bared tree trunks, spiny sweet gum balls collecting in the gutter, crackled brown oak leaves the size of my father's hand lying along the path to the shed. There are lichen-patched trunks of trees I can not name in their barren winter state, combined with the recent network of saplings and vines that fill in the forest floor and past that, the clearcut, and wide sky-baring soil. This visit has been an exercise in learning and understanding the new of now and the old of my childhood. Listening to the calls of frogs and birds, feeling the tender buds of pine saplings bend in my fingers, gathering the stories of my ancestors who lived here, and composing my own story to tell.

I walk our dirt road, the private path that serves more as a rutted driveway to the house than any sort of thoroughfare. A glance to the north opens into the clearcuts just beyond the property line. Not more than four years ago, that land belonged to my great aunt and her brother. A mature collection of Southern hardwoods, trees that saw my grandmother as a child, and her father before her. A vast tract bordered by relatives' land brought our extended family's holdings into the thousands of acres. Now that clearcut land belongs to absentee owners who live in Dallas, and to a local timber company who manages it. Owners who opted to slash it bare, and replant it with Loblolly pine, Pinus *taeda,* the tree that has managed to turn the Southeast into America's timber basket. Supplying mills around the South with pulpwood and lumber, and supplying us with paper napkins and bags, two-by-fours and particle board. That land, what used to be our land, will never again be worth what it was.

Scraggly yellow-green saplings stretch up from the red clay soil to my waist, a few ambitious ones reach my shoulders. Puddles dot the clearcuts on both sides of our road, water filling in vacated stump holes and lingering hollows left by heavy equipment. These cuts have attracted game, creating more than four miles of additional edge habitat. Tracks and droppings from deer and rabbits abound, far outnumbering my footprints. The grasses and shrubs have shot up, a thick tangle of dried browns, thistles and thorns. Hawks and eagles skim the cuts, swooping low over the land, where once they were unable to penetrate the canopy of hickory and oak, sweetgum and black walnut.

This narrow road was once the Ruston-Columbia Highway, wagon teams straddling the ruts on one of the few alternatives to waterway traffic in pre-railroad days. I imagine my great great great grandfather, Lewis, came upon patches of the expansive old growth hardwood forest I read about in history books. Millions of acres of unbroken woodlands stretching in every direction, a seemingly endless ocean of forests breaking away from the Mississippi as his raft floated downstream. Lewis Dickerson settled in the woodlands of Louisiana before they were accessible by railroad and interstate. Before logging dominated the landscape, when cotton bolls littered the hardwood forests between pastures, and the changes wrought by the Civil War were not seeds of thought in any one's imagination. I arrived here as a distant bud on the family tree, great granddaughter of Ricardo Lafayette Dickerson, a grandson of Lewis. Four generations of Dickersons have left a series of impressions on this area, a circle expanding out and out as each child claims his or her own land and passes it along to their children and they to theirs. Imagine dropping a pebble into still water, and watching the concentric ripples that expand outward to shore. That is my family, ripples and waves on this Louisiana landscape.

My grandmother was the last of my direct relatives to be raised here. Even as a child, she witnessed pastureland and timber sales from nearby forests, hardwoods harvested in a season, and replaced with pine. These days the highways rumble under the weight of heavy logging trucks, chainsaw repair is a viable job, and their distant hum is always heard in one direction or another. When the wind is just right, blowing south from Hodge, or northeast from Monroe, the stench of the distant paper mills infiltrates our remaining stand. A premonition of what is coming, and a reminder of what has come.

♋

Continuing along our road, I hear brief trills from the most populous frog, *Pseudoacris triseriata,* the striped chorus frog, calling from every corner of the clearcut and the remaining woods. Ascending in pitch just more than half an octave, each utterance in the call is a distinct note. It is similar to running a mallet over five wooden xylophone pegs, or a fingernail along the edge of a comb where the tines change from thick to thin. It is without tone in some respect, there is no resonance, no fluted melody as in a bird song. This chorus is raspy and hoarse. Quick, each note is staccato, each complete trill lasts just more than a second. These frogs do not call out in the silence alone, like a bird, penetrating the still air with one single voice. It is a voice of unison, tens of dozens repeating the sound in turn, layers of voice from every direction.

It is mating season for the striped chorus frog, these few weeks in late January that run into March. It is time to gather at the edge of the puddle, the pond, the waterfilled ruts along the road, and sing. While the females sit by idly, barely able to utter a raspy syllable or an ill-defined peep, male frogs croak with all their might, voices amplified by the vocal sacs beneath their throats. Gathering at breeding sites, flaunting his vocal powers in the hope of attracting a female, a male frog will attempt to prove to any present female that he is worthy. The one worthy of mating, worthy of her heavy labor of eggs and the tadpoles they will become.

This marshy woodland is ripe with frogs, breeding in shallow depressions following temperate winter rains. I have heard the voice of the green frog, *Rana clamitans,* whose call is similar to a plucked cello string. The call of the spotted chorus frog, *Pseudoacris clarki, is* not musical, more like a saw, and strictly nocturnal. I suspect *Pseudoacris crucifer,* the northern spring peeper, and *Acris crepitans,* the northern cricket frog, but have yet to single out their cries among the clutter of calls rising from the forest floor. It is a wonder any female can single out the voice of a suitable mate, one of her species, among the clatter. Yet the sheer number of frogs in these woods illustrates the art of their successful propagation. It is evident that the female frog has developed a discerning ear, discriminating from many voices the one she is seeking. With each species harboring its own distinct expression, mixups are rare, even when many species are gathered at the same site, each staking its claim among the watery edges and still air.

Procreation is a clumsy affair for members of the order *Anura*. External in nature, it is unadorned and immodest, a case of the simplest auditory attraction. When the female is sufficiently attracted to her mate, she approaches him, and he grasps her from behind between the fore and hind limbs, in a process called amplexus. The male hangs on clumsily as he is dragged along in her wake, releasing his sperm as the eggs emerge from the female. It is a simple act, no penetration, no sharing of fluids, no lengthy ritual preceding the drag-walk. A male frog will seize any female that approaches him, as many as he can. A female might share her purse of eggs with a number of suitors. Each batch is guaranteed a different chance of survival over the coming weeks. This mating is opportunistic, and brief, a short lived justification for the weeks of singing. A watery copulation, small wet bodies sliding abreast one another, webbed feet slipping in mud.

A slow scrutiny of nearly every puddle and stream of water along our road finds shadowed clumps of frog eggs near the center. Finding them is not like spotting a bird's nest, and knowing that inside may rest a set of dappled blue eggs. Before I arrived, I carried no intuitive notions of frog eggs, their shape or location. I've never thought of what form may precede a tadpole as a bud births a leaf, a cocoon a butterfly. Before long I am noticing rounded, lumpy, mushroom-type balls near the center of many puddles. Pale brown, and still, the same shade as the clay sediment in the water. I am curious, what is that form, not unlike a brain or cauliflower, encased in bumpy soft folds? I break a branch from a beech sapling, and commence to poke. With the disturbance, the brown sediment rinses away, and I behold a mass of clear jellylike balls, each about the size of a marble, clustered together to form a grapefruit-sized clump. And near the center of each small sphere, a thin, bright green line, with the approximate, but shrunken, shape of a tadpole.

As I break apart the mass to take a closer look, it is slippery, and cool, and no smell lingers on my fingers or in the air. It feels like gelatin, smooth and firm, and breaks away in clean curved planes. It is hard to get a grip on, and slips out of my fingers again and again before I can gain a closer look. The egg jelly is completely clear, without any tint or coloration. Inside each marble of jelly rests a light grass-green sphere, in which the embryo lies. A deep green slit with a rounded hump that will transform into a fin, a small pointed tail with a pale brown, almost translucent, tip emerging from the inner sphere. These pre-tadpoles are at most a half inch long, encased in their jellied womb. At once, as I realize what I am examining, my curiosity rises. How long before they hatch, how will they look, what will happen to the abandoned jelly casings? Will I be able to see the tadpoles? How long before I see miniature froglets hopping around this puddle?

I have noticed several more clumps of eggs these past few weeks. More lumpy masses, lightly coated with a micro-thin layer of sediment. I recently spotted a ragged and torn-looking ball of eggs. Coaxing it towards me with a knobby pine twig, I saw the outer layers had been ripped apart, and shredded strands of dirty embryonic jelly waved back and forth like hair under water. There were no eggs in this section, but a collection of intact eggs remained further inside the cluster. Was this ball of eggs predated? A raccoon? Possum? Bird or snake? Or had those eggs near the outer layer of the mass simply hatched? I saw no signs of life, no tiny tadpoles lurking about or hiding under the debris in the puddle. I have no way of knowing if that messy mass is simply the way hatched frog eggs look, or if they were snatched up by a hungry creature in the night. I resign myself to waiting for other tadpoles, other egg clusters to give me clues as the weeks edge past.

The state and condition of hatching frog eggs is only one question I have about these noisy creatures. I have yet to spot with my own eyes an adult frog lurking near any of the puddles or streams around the land. They escape me without fail. I hear them singing constantly, but never in the same area in which I stand. If I am walking on the road as it runs along the clearcuts, I hear them set deep in the woods, or in the wide puddles within the cuts. If I step into the woods and creep towards that direction, they will gradually cease until I no longer know what direction I am supposed to be heading in, and I hear them further away, or behind me, where it was quiet as I was walking through. But I always hear them. Always, from ahead and behind, at my distant sides. In the woods, along the road, from the house and the porch. But they never chirp within a thirty-foot radius of where I stand, no matter how that location changes. So I'm not betting that I will ever see them, resigning myself to the elusive presence of phantom frogs. I have chosen the striped chorus frog from a chart on the basis of its breeding time, its voice, the characteristics of its eggs. What it may be, rather than any definite form I have witnessed leaping around these woods. So, that is my best educated guess. *Pseudoacris triseriata,* is that you?

There is an idea that comes to mind when I ponder what I have witnessed and learned in my brief time here. I think of the frogs, their pervasive presence, and the promise of next spring's population. I think of what Aldo Leopold called the "*numenon,*" the imponderable essence that makes a place unique, that lends it a distinct flavor in character. Take that aspect away, and it is a different place. He was referring to the sand hills of Wisconsin, writing that "everybody knows ... that the autumn landscape in the north woods is the land, plus a red maple, plus a ruffed grouse. In terms of conventional physics, the grouse represents only a millionth of either the mass or the energy of an acre. Yet subtract the grouse and the whole thing is dead... A philosopher has called this imponderable essence the *numenon* of material things." The constant chorus of frog songs, the eggs and the tadpoles I see flitting about cloudy puddles, these compose the *numenon* of these woods, on this stranded plot of family land. There is no other sound so constant and identifying as the call of the striped chorus frog among and beyond the oaks and hickories, the beeches and pines. Without that clamor, without their presence, these woods take on a different tone. Not only is it an audible difference, but a loss. Frogs have been singing throughout these woods as long as there have been puddles and rains and seasons telling them when to sing, and what song to listen for. The past 150 years of my family's presence is a blink in their ecological history; people who built a road for them to cross, cut the trees of their shade, built obstacles in houses, sheds, and driveways. Ripples and waves.

It is hard for me to imagine the land Lewis Dickerson saw when I stand in the clearcut, my five foot seven inch frame standing taller than anything else, and to think of the trees that once dwarfed him and several generations of my family. It is hard to find a peace with the family members that sold this plot, this history. It is even hard for me to understand the craze of tree cutting that has befallen the region. Yet

I can be calmed with the knowledge that this land will persist, and the frogs' presence here is proof of that. While I may have chosen a different past for this land, one has been chosen for me, and regardless of my preferences, it will always have a history of its own. I'd like to believe that just because the future of this land will be starkly different than its past, that its story, and my family's and my own, is not lost inside those differences. We will remain what we define ourselves to be, and we can shape the histories we want to leave behind us. Our heritage rests in our own hands.

&8

It is March now, and slight shadows dart around the puddles, those few that are still holding water after nine dry days, and ragged abandoned egg casings litter the cracked edges. After a week's vacation, I notice the stillness in the woods upon my return, the absence of the chorus I have become so accustomed to. There is still plenty of noise in bird calls and squirrel chatter, the wind in the swaying loblollies, the water dripping outside my window. Sweet-gum balls dot the roof in an unpredictable rhythm, dogs bark. But mating season for *Pseudoacris triseriata* has ceased, thus too have the trilled calls filling these big woods. I miss that sound, the comfort of rising to their song each morning. That sense of continuity and regularity, knowing what to expect in the coming day and the next.

I feel my sense of place, and belonging, in witnessing their song, and the songs of others. The regular pace of nature in bird calls, in cricket chirps, in the chorus of mating frogs. They are connections to this land my family came from and the one remnant that remains among the encroaching pine plantations. Connections to the land that will outlive all of us, my father and me, my children and theirs. Perhaps these descendants will return to this land one February or early March, and witness the simple pleasure of mating frogs and their tadpoles. Or perhaps they will form different perceptions of this land and their history, noting instead some other imponderable essence, some other creature or feature that designs a distinct mold in their mind of what this land is, and will be. This plot of land has much to offer and discover, many secrets and stories between the roots and the canopy, the clearcuts and the clearings.

I invite all my descendants to help shape its future, to discover their own *numenon*, their own chorus, here on this land they too will call their own.

—first publication

The Queen and I

Adrienne Ross

Fragile wings beat into a black-veined blur as the bees tried to fly through my bedroom window and back outside to the garden. The bees craved light. Once inside my room, the bees forgot how they had entered. Their evolution had left them unprepared for following summer light falling through glass windows. When a bee finally calmed down, I'd catch her in a glass teacup and release her outside, watching her fly to the orange nasturtiums like an infant kept too long from the breast. There was a certain *noblesse oblige* in my actions. If the bees were grateful they gave no sign. Off they went, without even the proverbial backward glance, to where the hot July days were sending sunlight falling in sharp, shining sheets over our tattered rose bushes and scraggly lawn.

I didn't release the bees out of a fondness for insects. I tolerated the spiders spreading their delicate webs in my bathroom corners. They were my allies, eating the flies and whatever else was wandering through my basement rooms. And how could anyone hate butterflies or ladybugs? For all the others it takes an act of sheer intellectual will to remember I share the same protein and DNA biochemistry as the creeping, crawling creatures I collectively ignore, dismissing them as bugs. If any insect could inspire some dim interest, it was bees.

A lay naturalist, I'm always eager for a good natural history book. Years ago, I picked up William Longgood's *The Queen Must Die*, an excellent introduction to the eccentricities of bees and beekeeping. Longgood's bees were honeybees. The bees exploring my scented candles, their fuzzy black bodies crowned with a yellow cap and tipped with a gold ring around their tails, were bumblebees. Pulling Longgood down from my library shelves, I read that:

Bumblebees are . . . socially inclined but considered to be more primitive in development than honeybees. The female is impregnated in the fall and she alone survives the winter, snuggled into a hole in the earth . . . . Come spring . . . her offspring forms a working colony . . . they gather nectar while their mother devotes herself full time to laying eggs . . . .

All too often, books serve as my guide into nature. Now I had creatures available for personal study. Was it pollinating behavior when a bumblebee arched her fuzzy body and rubbed her thin legs over the powdery remains of my Aurobindo Quiet Mind incense sticks? What was the function of the translucent droppings the bees left on the red and yellow wax hanging from my brass Hanukah menorahs? Not territory marking, that much I knew, for bumblebees use visual landmarks to find preferred foraging sites and once there don't monopolize feeding territories. The longer I watched the bumblebees, the more enchanted I became with their short, intricate lives. Without sugar to maintain energy, adult bees can die within a few hours, and in my rooms, they were dropping like flies. Losing even part of a day trapped in my bedroom was too long in a life that lasted two or so weeks.

Soon there were too many of them. Every morning, I'd pull out the teacup and get as many bees outside as I could. I'd cook breakfast, call clients and by mid-morning four, five, sometimes six or more bees would be buzzing, huzzing, *hizzing* above my shoulders.

Except they weren't only flying. Honeybees fly. Bumblebees fly and crawl: across the beige carpet in my home office, across the white linoleum in my bathroom (making it impossible for me to step out of the shower without first being sure nothing was moving between the bath mat and my slippers) and to my horror, across my bed.

Noblesse oblige collapsed before raw survival instinct. The spiders and I could share the same habitat thanks to mutually exclusive niches. The bumblebees were invading my space. I wanted them gone from my life. I just didn't want them killed.

All the environmentally responsible exterminators I called said the same thing. Honeybees could be removed by a beekeeper needing a new hive. Bumblebees were commercially worthless. They produced no honey or anything else that could be sold. Or at least nothing that could be *immediately* sold. Bumblebees are worth billions of dollars to North American farmers if only for their role in clover pollination. Here in Seattle, all the bees could pollinate were the ruby roses outside my bedroom window, the purple phlox and columbine draped in long wandering tendrils across our trellis. There was only one thing to do with bumblebees.

"We use a spray," the exterminators explained.

"What does it do?" I asked, as if I didn't know.

"It's made of chrysanthemums. It won't hurt you at all. Don't worry."

"What does it do to the bees?"

"Kills 'em. Kills 'em dead. But don't worry. It won't hurt you at all."

The exterminators insisted the bees were coming into the house from a hole in the outside walls. Inside the wall would be their nest. The only holes I found were where my window didn't quite meet the frame. Could the bees be nesting outside, I asked the exterminators , wriggling into my bedroom and then forgetting how to wriggle out? Highly unlikely, I was told, so I kept searching for the entry hole. While I didn't find any bees, I did discover a hornet's nest hanging from our garage roof. If bees inspired mixed feelings, hornets were nothing but gleaming, ebony messengers of dread.

On a butterfly field trip the summer before, I'd made the mistake of wandering off into waist-high grasses. Suddenly, I had been surrounded by large, dark insects. As I tried to spot their field marks I felt a deep, searing sting followed by several more on my legs, and another on my arm. I stood frozen in an awful, primal fear before I threw my butterfly net into the air and raced from the hornets' nest hidden in the grass.

Standing in my driveway, I squinted into the bright sun to watch the hornets. How many times had I or my housemates opened the garage doors, not knowing they were there? If the nest continued to grow, we would no longer be able to open the doors without bringing down an insect battle squadron.

🐝

Discouraged, I returned to my bedroom where the bees were buzzing with unfailing persistence against my window panes. The summer was razor hot and as short-lived as the bees. Outside my windows were marigolds with their ruffled petals, pink daisies, blood-crimson roses and ghostly white morning glories encircling the Douglas fir towering over our backyard. So many flowers waiting for bees. So many bees wanting nothing more than to wriggle their plump bodies into a flower's embrace, and then dart to the next encounter, the legs of these infertile female workers sticky with pollen that brought cross-fertilization to the flowers and food to their hive's young. It was a relationship as old as the flowers themselves extending back some 100 million years ago into the Cretaceous period.

It was then that bees and flowering plants developed their mutualistic relationship. Bees and other insects provided pollination, while plants reciprocated with nectar and other desired services. Bees are believed to have played a major role in the Cretaceous' explosive diversification of plant species. Regardless of which came first—the flowers or the bees—this long-standing relationship became so successful that now a majority of the world's flowering plants require insect pollination to reproduce. Watching the bees flit from our zucchini plants to the orange nasturtiums, I couldn't help but respect the erotic certainties of their lives.

Stepping carefully around the bees crawling across my rug, I glanced out the window to watch the hornets making their black darting flights. Knowledge is power, and power cuts both ways. Watching the ebony hornets gleaming in the sunlight, I wondered if knowledge wasn't power as much as it is intimacy. The more I learned about the bees, the closer I came to sharing their lives. No longer just some kind of a bug, the bees had become as real as I or my housemates and with as much right to go about their lives.

If I knew anything about the hornets shielded behind the fragile gray walls of their hive, I wouldn't be able to call in the exterminators. I'd have to surrender the garage, and then the driveway, the back yard and sooner or later my private basement entrance. I uneasily decided not to learn anything about hornets.

One of my housemates called suddenly from the backyard. He pointed towards our compost bin, his brown skin shining in the sunlight, excitedly crying: "Wasps! Wasps!"

Great, I thought as I walked outside. *Bees in the bedroom. Hornets in the garage. Wasps in the compost bin. What's next? Hordes of locusts? Plagues of grasshoppers?*

My housemate pointed to beneath a western red cedar's sheltering limbs. No one in the house knew how to care for compost . For years lawn clippings and weeds had been thrown in the plastic bin and forgotten. I frowned as I noticed the neat rows of diamond-shaped holes lining the bin's emerald green walls. There were no wasps in sight, but soon enough a bumblebee alighted on an opening, quickly disappearing inside. Another bee emerged from the same hole and took off for the daises, followed by another bee. Hovering in the air was a bee eager to get into the bin.

Foraging, I thought, with quiet satisfaction. The bees were returning to the nest, their legs thick with pollen, while others were flying out to find food for the colony. More than finding the nest, I was seeing something completely new. I felt familiar gratitude for a world so worthy of curiosity.

Against all the exterminators' predictions, the bees were nesting outside, slipping through the cracks in my window frame. Every time I turned on my full-spectrum office lights the bees would circle my shoulders as I wrote grants for environmental education programs. As beleaguered as I felt, I still couldn't call in the exterminators with their green-trimmed jumpsuits and deadly chrysanthemum sprays.

℮

A week later, a chance conversation at a folk dance introduced me to a local beekeeper.

"Removing the bees won't be a problem," she said with an easy smile and a shining confidence at the first mention of the word *bees*. "I'll get the nest and set them up in my garden. It's filled with flowers. They'll do fine."

"These aren't honeybees," I warned. "They're bumblebees. They're worthless to you."

My companion waved her hand nonchalantly. I glanced down at the dark yellow business card she gave me. Embossed in black ink was an illustration of an ebony-haired woman wearing a long Victorian gown not so very different from her own floral print dress. The woman gazed in seeming contentment at a hive encircled by bees. *Beauty and the Bees Honey* , read the card, *Sally Harris, Beekeeper*.

Bees are bees to this woman, I thought, *and she's one of them*.

"How much will it cost?"

"Nothing. But I'll need help," cautioned Sally as she sipped her ice water. She tugged her hand through thick black curls. "Someone will have to suit up to help capture them."

"Sure," I said, hoping the speed of my reply covered my inner cringing. Trapped in the sticky web of my own good intentions, I smiled weakly and said: "I can do that."

ꝏ

Sally came by late the next afternoon with an empty gallon yogurt container, trowels, hand hoes and two white beekeeper suits she placed on our weathered worm bin. I picked up the thin suit with dismay.

"I thought these were made out of canvas."

"Oh, no," Sally said with a smile as she slipped off her sandals. "Just cotton. That's usually thick enough."

"What do we wear under it?" I asked hopefully.

"This is fine," shrugged Sally, indicating our pastel tank tops and shorts. "But you'll need boots past your ankles to stuff the pants into."

I ran into my bedroom and pulled my hiking boots from my closet. I also pulled out my long-sleeved teal polypro shirt, making sure to zip up the neck after I yanked it on over my tank top. I tugged the matching pants on over my hiking shorts. At Sally's amazed stare when I returned, I said only: "If the bees don't get me, the heat will."

I stepped into the one-piece bee suit, flipped the black mesh hood over my head, and secured it with an intricate array of zippers and velcro. Completely impervious to the bees (or so I hoped), we advanced on the compost bin. The bin tipped over easily. A black, *buzzing* cloud of bees flew up, so many darting and circling that I couldn't count them. Sally pulled a three-pronged hand hoe through the bramble and brown leaves. She scooped bees and egg clusters into the yogurt container, closing it tightly as she said: "I'm not seeing a queen."

My heart sank. The colony wouldn't survive without the queen. All their collective lives were dedicated to keeping her alive and feeding the endless clutches of young she spewed out. If the queen was still in the compost it would only be a matter of time before the bees returned to my bedroom.

"Sally, we've got to find the queen," I insisted urgently. Sally calmly pulled back clumps of scratchy twigs and moldy brown leaves. The buzzing grew to a dull roar. Bees swooped, encircled our heads, darted between our arms and legs. Unlike honeybees, bumblebees don't die when they sting. I could be stung over and over again, enclosed by a thick ebony cloud of enraged bees. One bee droned louder than the others. I wanted to run but primal instinct rooted me in place. I swirled my eyes sideways. A bumblebee was perched on my hood not two inches from my left eye.

"I need to get away from the bees," I croaked, my voice leaden with fear.

Sally nodded unperturbed as she searched for the queen. I stepped from the cedar tree's shadows and back into the afternoon sunlight. It was only three feet but that was far enough for the bees. I was out of the orbit of their tattered hive and lost queen. I was beyond the range of their interest. I stood breathing hard, sweat clinging to my warm clothes, as drawn to the sunlight as the bees. Our worlds were so different. What the bees sensed so alien to what I saw and knew. The light we could share: that same distant warmth keeping us alive.

I let myself feel my terror as I stood still in the sunlight's brilliance. I could hide nothing in the light's illuminating safety. I walked back to Sally strangely unconcerned by the whirling bees.

Sally handed me the scratched yogurt container.

"I've looked everywhere," she said, "and still can't find any queens."

"Queens?" I stammered out. I stared at Sally in confused frustration. Successions in honeybee hives are fights to the death. Wild bee queens will kill in competitions over nest sites. "Queens? There's only one to a nest."

"That's honeybees. Bumblebee nests will sometimes have an old fertile queen and several virgin queens that haven't left to find their wintering sites."

"I don't want to hear this," I moaned.

"Look, there may be several queens in this nest, there may be just one. Either way, I haven't found any. She may be flying. We'll never catch her then."

"I thought queens only flew on their mating flights or when they swarmed," I said frowning, knowing that singular mating flight was a queen bee's initiation from virginity to lifelong motherhood. "Let me guess. That's honeybees, right?"

Sally nodded. "Want me to check the container in case I got a queen without realizing it?"

We put the yogurt container on the rickety picnic table. Carefully, Sally opened the lid.

"There she is!" Sally cried. She slammed the lid shut, giving me only a brief glimpse of a bee larger and more elongated than the plump fuzzy workers.

Sally left with the queen and what we hoped were enough workers to start the hive anew. A dozen or more bees circled their destroyed hive or dropped down to explore the moist brown darkness that had sheltered their queen. Within a few hours most had disappeared into the sunlight and the sweet embrace of irises and snapdragons. Some bees would be assimilated into a new hive, genetic outcasts working for the survival of another queen's line. Others would die soon, their legs sticky with pollen they no longer needed.

The hornets were soon gone, too. The next day, I came back from grocery shopping just as the exterminator was pulling out of our driveway. A single hornet circled where the nest used to be. Scraps of papery gray walls skittered in the late afternoon breeze. No sense of obligation could make me miss them.

I called Sally. She had placed the bees (". . . along with some leaf mulch so they'd feel at home. . .") under the rhododendron bushes in her front year. Now bumblebees were buzzing and nuzzling flowers wherever she looked.

I walked out to the compost bin. There was no *buzzing* in my ears. Nothing small and black darted past me or glinted in the sunset glow. Relief mingled with sadness. Somewhere the bees from my garden were sinking into a gladiola or pink dahlia before daylight ebbed away. Now that I was no longer living with the bees I could appreciate their simple, unfailing perseverance. Life is short. And full of flowers.

—first publication

The Faith of Deer

Janisse Ray

It was stormy—tornado watch—but drizzling more than raining, and the men stood tiredly in little groups waiting for rain, and for the prizes to be distributed. It was after dark and Claire and I had walked up among them. A few poles hung with floodlights, but the lights were painfully bright—they would erase your vision—and made pools that the men stayed out of. They would stand in the dimness with the light striking half their faces, watching us.

The men were all in camouflage, every one of them, army-green and gray-green, a mockery of leaves and woods so they were a wilderness unto themselves. They had been out early in their stands this first day of hunting season and many of them had hauled heavy deer to trucks through underbrush, and even hunted again in the evening if they had not taken a buck in the morning. Their shoulders slumped and their faces were expressionless. Many of them did not have much life in their eyes, like overturned bottles. Or maybe it was the light that drank.

They were grim and they looked hungry, despite lines of food—Brunswick stew and chicken-and-rice and sausage. Some of them would talk among themselves, and we would hear shreds of it as we passed, and they would use names with each other and expressions that we did not know, but mostly they stared straight ahead, or at us, or toward the shelter, where a man with a microphone had begun to pull names from a box. As if this weren't a party but a holiday to be endured.

I say men although there were women. Maybe fifteen hundred hunters milled around, packing themselves into the long shelter that used to be a hog barn before the Sheriff cleaned it out. A beaded curtain of raindrops separated the men in the shelter, who were tight against each other, and tired and warm, from those who were outside, in the drizzle. Here and there a woman, pale-faced and thin-haired, stood with her man, also watching us.

One young buck, passing, openly eyed my pelvis and laughed, a hungry laugh, then glanced up at my face and down again, so there was no mistaking. Not long after that Claire recognized someone she knew, and we stood with him for a long time. He was married and had two teenage girls safe at home.

"Any luck today?"

"I got a buck but not a big one," Groover said.

"Will it win anything?"

"Not by a long shot," he replied. "But with so many door prizes I'll take something home. They've started calling names."

That's why the ticket cost $15, he explained, because of all the giveaway—stands and orange vests and guns and camouflage coveralls and hats with labels like Lewis Battery & Electric and Carter Farm Supply.

He said the man who'd won, they thought, was the Sheriff himself's brother, who'd got an eight-point, and that was the biggest so far, but it hadn't been dark long and more were coming in.

"I want to see the deer hanging," I said.

"I can't," Claire said.

"I'll be right back."

I threaded my way through the dim outskirts of the light, stepping carefully. Pines buckle up around their trunks, and the dirt won't stay flat there, so you have to be particular when you're walking in the dark around pine trees.

Underneath a couple of droplights, two deer carcasses hung from an A-frame rack. At each a man worked intently yet carelessly with a knife, which made small noises. The man's hands seemed frustrated as they moved around the strung carcass. Flesh tore audibly.

To the side, the remains of butchered deer were piled, head after head with the bodies removed, the skin hanging unfilled and wadded on the bloody ground, and torsos as well, having been separated from the heads, with some of the meat gone. Entrails were slung together with the heads, some of which had been engraven with two deep notches where racks had risen. Ribs that had so shortly before held beating hearts lay in the sparse pine needles, and in the dirt.

The butchering men were packing ice-laced coolers with their meat. A deer could fill a cooler, the man closest told me.

"You're throwing all that meat away?" I asked him, the one who'd spoken.

"There's nothing left on it," he said. But I could see the bright, pretty flesh hanging from the deer carcass, with its two planks of fleshy ribs. The pockets of meat made me hungry, and made me think of my dogs.

"All it's good for is the dogs," he said.

It wouldn't do for Claire to see this, she loved animals so, and the deer eyes stared crazily off in every direction, as if confused or, too, blinded by the bleak lights. And the way the bucks on the crossbeam were slung up by their hind legs was obscene.

It was a continuous butchering. The men would take the front shoulders, the hams and the sweet strip of tenderloin along the back, the backstrap, and discard the rest.

When I got back to Claire we decided to move into the shelter, and not right away but not long either we ran into Jackie, who we know from school and who, like Claire, loves horses. Her husband had taken a deer early in the morning; this was the first year of hunting for her son, eleven, who'd gotten off a shot but missed.

When I was growing up, Jackie and her sister had been the only hippies in our little town. I worked at the library in high school—they were out of college and moved back to their father's land, and I would see Jackie occasionally coming for books. Her legs would be unshaven, and I could not understand what ran her life.

That was then. Now we stop and talk when we meet in front of the school, picking up our children, or when we're setting up the haunted house at the carnival, and she just gave me periwinkle seeds from her yard.

"We eat every bit of the deer," she said. "Even the spare ribs."

When Claire and I moved on again, leaving the lee of Jackie's family, we waded into the throng, nodding and speaking, waiting until men moved aside, squeezing themselves into masses of green, to make a path for us through the forest of their bodies. We were being heavily watched. Neither of us had been back long, and so we were new and unfamiliar, and we looked out of place.

When rut comes on the bucks, October, their necks begin to swell and they go mad with desire. They fight among themselves to prove their worthiness as mates, rushing together with ears laid back, antlers clashing, lunging sleek, summer-fattened bodies against each other. They breathe through their mouths and their entire bodies quiver. The drive to breed is so strong they attack saplings and rub them raw with their antlers; they tear up the earth in wide circles with their scrapes. In frenzied pawing they rear up and hook low-hanging branches above them. Wildly amorous, they begin to run the does, attempting to sniff their vulvas and their urine.

Then while we moved through the dark mob of men in the shelter, a man stepped to block our way, asking me if I remembered him and I didn't, although he looked kind enough, with warm eyes, behind glasses. The ones without glasses, who can see without aid, like hawks—they are like wild birds, waiting to be released.

Another friend of mine says she knows I'm lost when I start talking about eyes being warm. Or kind. She can forget trying to talk any kind of sense into me.

This man wore camouflage too, and a ball cap. He brought his face close to talk, closer than any man or woman there would have done, and his eyes kept flickering over my face.

He told me his name and I remembered him. Three or four years before, on a visit home, I ran into him at the library. It was a weekday and he was in overalls, reading a book. He was out of work, he said, farming part-time with his cousin for the time being. I went home and inquired of Mama; he'd been married a time or two, had a couple of children, been arrested for growing pot.

Now, in the shelter, he said he'd seen thirteen deer that morning and hadn't shot even one. I asked him about his girls, and all his cousins I remembered. He asked about me. He said he had two daughters by two wives, but wouldn't marry again and wouldn't have more children. He said he'd done a lot of bad things, like shoot somebody's foot in a parking lot downtown (except he used a racist term for "somebody,") mostly when he'd been drinking, that he got crazy when he drank, and he hadn't drunk since July. He said he has a girlfriend he loves and he's been staying home. He raises a few chickens.

All the time—until we stepped around him and moved on, this time toward the food steaming at the end of the shelter—his eyes kept flicking across my face, inches away. For days afterwards, as the rain continued, I would remember that current, the weird feeling that came with it.

It was about eleven and we were deciding to leave, the rain falling harder. Others were thinking the same, moving out into the rain, men heading home. Claire and I were standing near the road end of the shelter, not looking out into the rain but back toward the men when the thirteen-deer man came by.

"See you," he said to me, because there was nothing else he could say. Glancing at Claire, I eased into the clot of folks leaving, moving backward and falling in step with him, passing through the dripping eaves and into the rain.

"I'll walk you to your truck," I said.

Almost instantly, his hand went to my waist, guiding us down Big Buck Shelter Road, which was muddy and thick with dark puddles. Then his hand was at my arm, then (rough, very rough, like holding a block of unplaned wood) in mine. We missed his truck in the rain and sloshed on down the road, toward the cemetery.

"I know I parked in front of that old barn," he said, and we turned back. I climbed in the truck ahead of him, moving his gun over. Almost immediately we were kissing, not gently but wet and hard and rough. He took off his glasses and laid them on the dashboard.

"I want you to know," he said, "there ain't a thing wrong with you," he said. When you grow up together in a town, you know each other's history, and people's histories are full of sadness and misunderstanding and the inexplicable. Fathers have died in car accidents, and others have been sent to mental institutions. Cousins have gone to prison and cities and war, and have not come back.

"Where are you sleeping tonight?" he said.

"At home," I said.

"I just want you to know, there ain't a thing wrong with you," he said. "You're all right."

Bucks come into rut a few weeks before the does, a natural history that prepares them for the chance of does coming into estrus early, and also so that they are sufficiently ardent and determined that many breedings will occur, insuring continuation of the genepool. The does flee, running low along the ground as if to appear smaller, clamping their tails between their legs.

The next morning was Sunday. I called Daddy early and told him about the meat, that I was hoping we could salvage some. It had rained all night and maybe some of the meat hadn't ruined. Daddy called the Sheriff, who said they were cleaning up, he'd meet us at the shelter.

We pulled the truck up next to a hillock of dead deer's heads and bodies and legs. All males, every one. Thick buckskins, wrought with fat and flesh, draped through the pile, and raw meat hung from nicked bones. The rain had stopped and the blowflies had begun to swarm over the pile of wild flesh, and the guts had started already to smell. Tim, the black man who worked for the Sheriff, was loading carcasses onto a small trailer, to haul them off to the middle of a field, for the coyotes and vultures.

"You're wanting meat to eat?" the Sheriff said.

"I hate for this to go to waste," I said.

"I don't believe I'd eat this," he replied. "I'll give you some meat." He walked away and came back with a three or four packs of wrapped venison. "You want meat, come doe season, we'll get you a doe," he said. "We always get more than we can use."

"That'd be great."

"You know, your Daddy's a good friend of mine," he said.

"I feel the same way about him," I replied, smiling.

"I can see that," he said.

Daddy and I helped Tim clean up the carcasses, heaving the bloody, gut-spilling bodies up in our arms and onto the trailer, gathering handfuls of dainty brown legs, raking up spilled guts, then emptying the trash barrel which had been filled with deer carcasses too, and the rain that had turned to blood inside it, and we poured that blood-water across the ground.

It is not the hunting. I too am willing to kill a deer, to sit in a tree a dozen feet above a canebreak that is overrun with two-pronged hoofprints, grass beaten down and sapling bark rubbed away by the antlers of rut-bucks. I am willing to aim for the tender haunch that hides the heart, and shoot there, and tear the soft hide away and take the meat. Not for the sake of killing, but for the sake of magic, because bucks are lords of deep woods of Appling County, Georgia and I am hungry for their knowledge—so hungry I will take scraps of it.

I almost never see deer. They stay hidden in a deeply magical place, until this day in late October that is suddenly like no other day before. So I, who am not privy to the secrets of whitetails, watch the hunters—merlins, with darkened faces and human odors disguised, dressed as trust, as leaves, as does—riding the back roads with guns behind their heads, entering the woods. Magicians, they enter forbidden realms and pull their wild tricks on beasts from another world, and they are ecstatic when their gun takes him down and they drag his secret knowing into our openness. They take him for his magic, and open his body to taste it, not because they are prone before its power, and respectful, but because they know no other way to have what they lack, except by death. And although they own the meat, it is, of course, bereft of magic, and they leave it.

"You can't call them hunters if they leave meat behind," my friend Rick said of it. "You have to call them the shooters or the killers. Or the men, or the humans."

"I wish you'd gotten the meat," he said. "I'm sorry. It's so good—neck roasts in chili, and the bright red scraps from the ribs and vertebrae, and the tough chewy tasty shank-meat that makes you able to work all day."

Once late at night I saw a doe running from the woods. The bright beam of her golden eye, caught in my lights, held everything she knew, everything that could be known. And the dead deer's eyes were like that, not lit, but profound and omniscient, haunting. They could see.

Which shows you can't trust eyes, but a few days later I got my brother to call the man who'd shoot you in the foot if he drank. We'll call him Lane. I kept remembering that he'd seen thirteen deer and hadn't shot one.

I was sitting over in the chair, quiet as a mouse but eyes feeling like marbles on fire, heart jumping, knees shaking up and down off my toes. The girlfriend answered the phone, as Dell explained later. They were eating supper but she handed the phone to Lane.

"How're you doing?" Dell asks. Quiet.

"I hear you're back at work—where're you at?" Quiet.

"Making good money, I guess?" (After a pause, laughter.)

"Any more openings over there?"

"OK, I'll check that out."

There is a longer blank space here where Lane asks Dell if he's seen their friend Paul lately and Dell says no, not much lately, he's always trying to see how quick he can get to the bottom of a beer can.

Another little space.

"Did you enjoy the Big Buck contest?" Quiet.

"My sister seen you over there." (Lane: "Yeah. I said we were friends.")

"She wanted me to get a message to you to call her sometime."

"Hmmmmm," Lane says. "All right."

"9463," Dell says. "She asked me to get it to you a while ago but I just haven't done it. Lane, I'll let you go. I'm headed out to my brother's. I just wanted to get that message to you."

(Lane: "What was it again?")

"Ninety-four sixty-three." Quiet.

"Talk to you later."

Before a doe comes into estrus, she starts to seek out a buck, if she is not being chased by one. The two may spend the day together. When the male approaches her she may not stand for him immediately, but may press her flank against his. He caresses her with his tongue. They nuzzle. She is only receptive for twenty-four hours. After copulation, which often occurs under cover of darkness and sometimes more than once, the buck may go off to seek another doe. If the doe conceives, she loses interest in bucks. If not, she will come back into estrus in another twenty-six to twenty-eight days, a lunar cycle. As the rut draws to a close, the now-gaunt buck loses interest in does.

I am not the doe nor I am the hunter. He is not the buck nor the hunter either. He can not emerge from a place he has never been. He can not tell me with his eyes or his body something he does not know.

I asked Dell about his chickens, if he raised them for the eggs, and Dell laughed.

"They're fighting cocks," he said harshly.

About a week later Lane called. Maybe I just needed to hear him say "There ain't a thing wrong with you" all over again and say that he'd seen another thirteen deer and still hadn't shot, or that he'd brought one down and spent all Saturday brain-tanning the hide.

I told him I wanted to talk, could meet him at the library, but he didn't say much, except he'd call when he wasn't working, and I thought how smoky his mouth had tasted when he was kissing me, and how roughly he'd done so. The weeks passed and he still had not called. When hunting season ended, the deer eased out to the shoulders of the roads, where occasionally in the dark I'd see them pause in their grazing, the funnels of their golden eyes a beam in the darkness.

—first publication

The Illusionary Distance
Between Pacifist and Warrior

Geneen Marie Haugen

There are many different levels of violence and non-violence....
If the motivation is negative, even though the external
appearance may be very smooth and gentle, in a deeper sense the
action is very violent. On the contrary, harsh actions and words
done with a sincere, positive motivation are essentially non-
violent.

—His Holiness the Dalai Lama

Like the skeleton of a shameful relation, the rifle had been hidden in the basement for ten years. I was contemptuous of guns, even more contemptuous of the barbarians who owned them. But this gun, *my* partner's weapon, was stored in *my* house. It was a bolt-action hunting rifle, to be sure, not a black market Uzi or a semi-automatic substitute for self-esteem. Still, like the multiple contradictions concealed within any life, the presence of the gun was one I couldn't rationalize or accept.

So instead, I ignored it.

As a coping strategy, disregarding the rifle's presence had worked brilliantly. Until another incongruity began worming the subterra of my awareness, a maggot born in the dark: I found myself contemplating the hunt, and my own unaccountable leaning toward it.

The possibility of hunting arose like an unwanted visitor from a *verboten* country. Like any truly distasteful guest, this one was disinclined to leave until it had cornered my attention completely. I was afraid it would rub off on me, contaminate me with social unacceptability.

Just as I feared, the idea of the hunt began to win me over.

What lured me to such an appalling thicket, a thorny wood that pricked and ripped and shredded a fancy quiver of beliefs? It was a clamor of feelings, ideas, experiences. The beat underneath them all—a jarring rhythm I couldn't tune out—sounded something like this: Why does someone who cherishes wildness no less than the human heart endure a facsimile of wild existence? I wanted to engage with the wild world in the oldest, most intimate manner of all.

I knew very little about the physicality of hunting.

I knew less than nothing about weapons. In truth, handling a gun was a barrier I doubted I was capable of crossing.

But my partner David knew how to shoot, and he owned the rifle I'd been zealously ignoring for a decade.

✺

We exhumed the weapon from the basement, carried it upstairs and unzipped the brown imitation-leather case. A vague impression of hunting sharpened into an alarming reality as I examined the rifle, whose walnut stock and crosshatched handgrips were both beautiful and menacing. The barrel was oiled and black, imprinted with the name, Ruger M77, and the caliber, 30.06.

David confidently drew back the bolt and displayed the empty bullet chamber. My heart pounded anyway when I picked up the gun. But the consequence of holding an unloaded weapon is hardly equivalent to firing a loaded one. Even the sight of my hands on the Ruger did little to convince me that I could fill the chamber with cartridges, aim and pull the trigger.

I shouldered the gun, feeling its dead weight, how hard it was to balance with my left arm upraised and partially outstretched. David—who'd owned the rifle for twenty years but never used it—advised me to lie down and aim. He had learned to shoot courtesy of the U.S. Army but had never hunted, and I was suspicious about his advice to lie down. How could I drop to my belly in the wild without alerting any creature I stalked? Flattening myself against the rug, I supported the Ruger on meditation pillows on the living room floor and peered down the scope. Cushioned, the gun's crosshairs were steady.

The Buddhist monks who had sewn the meditation cushions had never, I was sure, envisioned their zafus stabilizing a gun. Designed to assist a practitioner in cultivating peaceful awareness, my maroon zafu was a place to center, a portable sanctuary, an object whose purpose was distinct—not ordinary furniture, certainly not a gun stand.

The rifle juxtaposed against the cushions summoned a faint, disturbing image of the Chinese army's devastation of Tibetan monasteries. The weapon against the cushions gave rise to impressions of the destruction of temples and sacred sites throughout history, throughout the world. Thought to have evolved so far from savages, human beings still did not cultivate balance in the sacred-and-profane spectrum: the holiest leanings often gave rise to the bloodiest conflicts.

In the physical world, winners usually control the most deadly weapons. In the metaphysical world, winners and losers are less easy to define.

The Ruger was not meant for hunting humans, but hairier kin born of the same stardust. The gun was unloaded. Other than the written or spoken word, it was the most deadly instrument with which I'd ever had contact. The pen, it's been said, is mightier than the sword—such lofty words, issued from a writer, not a warrior. But if the pen can alter troublesome ideas, who can deny that the sword is a more efficient tool for quashing troublesome individuals?

Weapons ask no questions, and of themselves, require no accountability.

The gun conveyed a kind of power to me, but it hardly conveyed consciousness. How had I, a person who had long fancied myself on a "spiritual path," arrived at this strange juncture: practicing meditation with the intent of deepening my awareness of life, now entering a practice whose intent was taking a life?

ℰ

I had begun meditating some twenty years earlier, when I got my mantra and quickly forgot it. Sitting still wasn't my style. I meditated anyway, haphazardly, giving attention to my footfalls as I ran, to wind, to the sound of water.

Yoga worked better for a kinesthetic person like me, especially the flowing postures. But I was an erratic practitioner, a beginner for more than two decades. I never mastered full lotus, though I did learn to focus on breathing.

From chanting, I'd discovered the power of sound to induce ecstatic, near-visionary states of consciousness. I loved those highs, psychedelia without side effects. But as one of my meditation teachers once said, "Visionary states are seductive. But they won't help you be present in the grocery store."

I wasn't sure I cared about being present in the grocery store, but overall, I figured life is less painful for those who aren't trying to escape it. So through *vipassana*, I was learning about presence. The be-here-now thing. In reality this meant I was learning about the billions of ways I'm not here, there, or anywhere in particular.

Vipassana —or insight meditation—comes from the Theravada ("school of the elders") line of Buddhism, and thus said to be older than Zen, Tibetan and Soto, but its practice had only been brought to the West in the nineteen seventies. It's thought to be the technique practiced by the Buddha. The simplicity of *vipassana* pleases me: begin with the breath. When attention wanders like a willful toddler to memories, feelings or fantasies, simply note where it's traveled and return to the breath. The purpose: to erode the layers of inattention, and eventually, to discover the nature of consciousness and thus, the nature of reality.

So far, I had primarily discovered the chaos of my own mind.

One does not have to "be Buddhist" to practice *vipassana,* but during formal meditation instruction, I had taken the Buddhist vows of refuge. Taking the "triple-gem" of refuge in the Buddha (or possibility of enlightened mind), in the Dharma (teaching or truth), in the Sangha (community of practitioners) is generally all that's required for one to be considered Buddhist. But unlike Catholicism, Mormonism or Methodism, Buddhism—at least at the layperson level—is a pretty loose affair, and taking the vows of refuge did not necessarily make me a Buddhist. Neither did vowing to observe—as I had—the most basic moral obligations of Buddhism, the Five Precepts.

The First Precept: not to destroy life.

Many Westerners imagine that all Buddhists are vegetarian, and certainly many practitioners choose the veggie path. But on the high, dry Tibetan plateau, for example, vegetarianism is a luxury few can afford. Monks and others dedicated to the Dharma get around the first precept by accepting meat, as the Buddha advised, as long as it was not killed by them or for them—thus removing themselves from karmic consequence for taking the life.

The Jungian analyst, Jean Shinoda Bolen, once told me a story about the Dalai Lama wherein he was asked about eating meat. The Dalai Lama—who complies with his doctor's instructions to eat meat—said that, in the course of a lifetime, a human being might eat one cow (obviously, he was not talking about Americans). Then, with his customary chortle and smile, the Dalai Lama asked, "But what about a bowl full of shrimp?"

In the Buddhist tradition, the smaller creatures do not possess a lesser soul than the largest beings. When I relayed Jean Bolen's story of the Dalai Lama to a woman who would willingly eat fish—low on the food chain—but not mammals, I asked if considering the number of souls added another dimension to the issue. She paused, then said, "It changes everything."

But the Buddha's teaching does not appear ambiguous about the matter of taking a life, which begs a question: what karmic retribution befalls those who willingly stop the heartbeat of another creature? What of, say, the karma for the butcher who provides meat for His Holiness the Dalai Lama? Of the hunter who provides for less exalted family and friends?

It's particularly American to reinterpret Buddhist philosophy for the western hemisphere. I have lived in that mythic and peculiar subset of the western world—the American west—all my life. In terms of intact natural systems, my homeland is among the wildest left in the lower forty-eight states, perhaps even the world. Any vows of the spirit are meaningless if they can't be filtered honestly through the visible web of animal and plant lives I share.

Perhaps more than the other Precepts—not to steal, not to lie, to avoid sexual misconduct, and not to take intoxicants—taking the vow not to kill is easy to say, and virtually impossible to act out. Practitioners of Jainism—a religious system emphasizing asceticism and concern for all life—wear masks over their mouths to avoid accidentally doing away with flies. Some Buddhist monks do not dig in the garden out of respect for worms.

But I am not a Jain or monk. I'm hardly in line for Buddhahood. I do my best to live with care, but I'm not able to pretend there's no blood on my hands. Perhaps the toughest reckoning for those who attempt to hold all life in equal regard is this: the existence of every individual is fueled entirely by other lives.

It may be foolish and hopelessly unenlightened, but I'm willing to risk karma that consuming what's been killed by others does not guarantee a happier next-round than taking the life with intention.

And so I reinterpret the First Precept: to do least harm. It's an admittedly odd notion to ally with hunting—but I'll get to that.

Least harm may be more challenging than no harm at all, but it seems more honest. And perhaps what the Buddha intended.

                                               &

The shop that sells ammunition also carries nice clothing, shoes, beautiful pottery patterned with bears, trumpeter swans, elk and moose. The hunting department is on the top floor, in the back, and although I'd been in this shop dozens of times, I had never investigated the section devoted to weapons and camouflage. David strode ahead to request rifle cartridges and targets while I lurked on the edge, between the tents and binoculars, feeling furtive, rather illicit, as if I hovered in the shadowed entry of a porn shop. There was a wall of rifles, a case of handguns, stacks of videos with provocative titles: Bushwackin' Bulls. Playing in Predator Country. Fatal Calling (Learn to master the ABCs of doe talk! How buck body language will help you score!). There were displays of packaged cow elk urine. Packets of bull-rage, guaranteed to infuriate bull elk during rutting season. Scent-killers in pine and sage. Bear calls, moose calls, "Terminator" elk calls.

Exploiting the sexual behavior of animals is a popular hunters' tactic, particularly for trophy hunters. By imitating a bugling bull elk or scenting an area with bull urine, a hunter tries to lure another rutting bull—intent on protecting his harem—into the open. Hunters also scent with cow elk urine to seduce the normally-wary bull, now hormone-drugged like a teenaged boy in a girl's locker room. Although it's an ancient practice, the association of sexual behavior with hunting stirs deep resentment in me, brings to mind date-rape and other predatory human sexual behavior. If the bulls aren't bugling with the fever of the rut, the hunter's difficulty escalates, but is preying upon instinctual, reproductive behavior in the spirit of fair chase? It seems to bring out the worst in some people: a friend once suffered through an AA meeting where a hunter bragged that he'd killed a bull elk while the bull was mounting the cow.

The association of sex and violence, the eroticization of acts of violence (and violation of erotic acts) is endemic to Western culture, so widespread that we seem nearly immune to it. A hunter friend—someone I would call extremely sensitive to the ethics of hunting and killing—described to me the process of field dressing an elk in great detail. The purpose of this elaboration was to make sure I would know exactly what to do if I killed an animal without an experienced hunter along. My friend's instructions were mostly lost on me, though, when he described how, before making the gutting incision, I would need to roll the creature on its back and "spread its legs, just like a woman having sex."

But the link between sexuality and violence—or sexuality and death—is not just a freak of human culture. In The *Time Falling Bodies Take to Light,* William Irwin Thompson writes, "Sexual reproduction introduces death, for it produces new individuals that, by virtue of being limited and highly specific beings, must die. . . . Reproduction is the climax of life; in some species, the postcoital male immediately dies or is consumed by the female." In the insect world, the Black Widow spider is famous for her tendency to devour her mate. The

Carolina Mantid might eat her partner while still copulating. Anadromous salmon, both female and male, die after returning to their freshwater birth-river to spawn.

Bull elk spar to establish possession of the harem of cows, although, as David Peterson writes in *Among the Elk:*

> *[S]ince it runs counter to the survival and successful evolution of the species for prime males to kill and mutilate one another, conflicts between rutting bulls have evolved to be more symbolic than physical, including profiling, bugling, antler shaking, bluff charges, minimal-contact sparring, and the like. Still, on the rare occasions when serious physical violence does erupt, it can prove fatal to one or both contestants.*

There is little indication that bull elk direct violence toward the harem, although a bull may vigorously attempt to keep a wayward cow in line. Experienced cows will usurp young, unaware cows in the breeding line-up, shoving to be first. The harem hierarchy is perhaps less a matter of horniness than of survival for future generations: the earliest bred cows will also calve earliest, and their offspring will have the longest season to fatten before winter.

In elk, as in many animal species, male and female come together only during rutting season, when reproductive instinct overrides normally secretive habits. The animals' cyclic hormonal ritual causes a companion migration among hunters, who congregate in hunting shops to purchase ammunition, orange hats, packaged urine and manufactured elk calls.

⁖

Next to the rack of hunting videos, a boy stared with longing at the wall of rifles, then knelt in front of the handgun display and said, "Wow, Dad, come look at these." His father hurried over to kneel beside him. I broke into cold sweat, but summoned courage to ask the polite, young salesman if rifles come in different weights. I wouldn't have asked if he had seemed like a guy who drove around with weapons displayed in his truck window all fall—there's something about men with guns that can make normally conversant women unwilling to expose vulnerability. The salesman's polite manner did not change. Yes, he informed me, there is a range of weights, now that the stocks are made in synthetic materials as well as wood. I asked him how he keeps his aim steady; does he lie down? No, he said, he braces in different positions for practice shooting. In the field, he said, adrenaline gives him his aim. He laughed, squinted and slid a private, sidelong glance at the other salesman.

David asked me if I'd like to look at the rifles. I said no and we hurried toward the exit, carrying the paper targets in a bag and large boxes of 30.06 (thirty-aught-six, I could say that out loud like I knew something) cartridges in our bare hands.

When someone I knew nodded at me from the counter in the tent section, I flushed with embarrassment. What if she thought I was a gun enthusiast? Or a hunter?

&

On the public land bordering our home, chokecherries bowed with blossoms. Newly-leafed aspen rippled under the wind's light hand. A hawk screeched warning from a high bare limb, then arced against the blue, its auburn tail fanned and backlit. Mosquitoes were just coming to life. On the damp trail in front of my running shoes, silvery blue butterflies fluttered up like winged prayers. Masses of balsamroot bloomed, the first extravagant yellow of the season. The trail mud was impressed with deer tracks. Coyote musk stung my nostrils near a tree that marked territory. The ranchers who leased this land had just resurrected the barbed-wire fence from the ground where it lay all winter; the fence goes up in summer to contain cows, down in autumn to allow migration of deer, moose and elk.

Even though the trail was more a footpath than a road, four-by-four trucks and ATVs prowled it every autumn. In a meadow, near a spring that would be mostly dry by September, two enormous piles of automotive parts, broken beer bottles, crushed Budweiser cans and boards prickly with rusted nails were heaped and partially burnt. The debris was new since the end of last summer, dumped during hunting season.

Unease filled me like sudden sickness. In the brief early summer, after the snowmelt but before the reappearance of cows—well before hunting season—hardly anyone ventured here. For me, the land had been a nearby refuge. Now, like sanctuaries everywhere, it had been trashed.

Though surely no one watched from the shadows, my legs felt lead-heavy and I wanted to get away, wary of others who had traveled this trail. From the meadow every escape was uphill; I moved as if in a dream, loggy, slow, breathless.

I am afraid of hunters.

I am afraid to walk the National Forest in autumn, even while wearing a fluorescent orange vest.

I am afraid of encampments of men who might be high on blood and weapons and alcohol.

I am afraid that someone might take aim on my blonde hair, or on the reddish fur of my dogs, and squeeze the trigger before certain what's centered in the crosshairs.

It happens.

A few years ago a mule was shot in the leg by a hunter who apparently mistook the mule for a moose, then left it to die. On the National Elk Refuge, a man blew an elk call and when he heard a responding bugle from the trees, he aimed and shot his friend in the head. In Utah, it has been said that if you want to get rid of relatives, take them to the woods in deer season.

⅙

Even though I had never shot a gun, and in fact considered myself a peacemaker, I'd had a recurring daydream in which I hoisted a rifle with confidence and fired a few well-aimed rounds. The daydream had begun as a reaction to my first solo encounter with an armed man. One long ago spring in the Santa Cruz mountains, I walked the old logging roads until a nearby gunshot made me scramble into the brush.

I waited, heart thudding, until a man moved out of the shadows, his rifle raised to firing position, sighted on me. "Hey," I said, my voice barely a squeak, "What are you shooting at?" He put down the gun and talked me out of trembling cover to find out why I walked alone in the redwoods.

When I ventured solo in the woods again, a sharpshooting fantasy began to accompany me, though it was unspoken and hardly acknowledged. I was, after all, a gun control advocate and pacifist, at least in mind if not in gut reaction.

But if I cared to examine the shadow that accompanied me everywhere, I knew I was capable of violence. As a very young woman I had once flattened a drunk who'd hit me in the head and knocked me down a staircase. I pummeled him with my fists and feet until he was helpless. Though I seldom admitted it aloud, in my darkest heart I knew I could do it again.

In fact I was afraid I would do it again, punch out some child-slapping parent in the grocery store, or kick some tough in the balls if I saw him grab an unwilling woman. Even though such monumental stupidity could get me killed, I was afraid I'd act without thinking. Who wouldn't want to be a kickboxing master in these situations?

But to take possession of a weapon was another matter entirely, an elaborate new construction in the psyche. What happens to a woman's self-confidence if her proficiency with a gun diminishes a man's strength advantage?

The South Dakota rancher and writer, Linda Hasselstrom, has an essay, "Why One Peaceful Woman Carries a Pistol," that pissed me off enormously the first and second and third times I read it. She writes of confronting four men who were urinating and dropping beer cans on her property. The men responded:

> "I don't see no beer cans. Why don't you get out here and show them to me, honey," said the belligerent one, reaching for the handle inside my [car] door.
>
> "Right over there," I said, still being polite, "there and over there." I pointed with the pistol, which had been under my thigh. Within one minute the cans and the men were back in the car, and headed down the road.

This wasn't the only time Hasselstrom pointed her pistol at a perceived threat—an action that struck me as aggressive, not "peaceful" or even plainly defensive—and I had dismissed her as self-delusional and ridiculously naive to rely on a gun rather than wits. But I still clung to a younger, stronger and faster self-image, residual from years of traveling—even hitchhiking—alone. Outwitting predatory people (truth be told, I haven't ever encountered a woman that required outwitting) had been a routine hazard. But I never scared or threatened anyone, just managed my own escape.

Perhaps I was the one more naive.

ॐ

None of my women friends owned guns, to my knowledge, so I was startled when I found that some had been to the practice range. Connie, who claimed good hand-eye coordination. Susan, who said that, except for the noise, she had enjoyed target practice almost as if it were a shooting gallery at a carnival. My vegetarian sister, Lori, who had gone with her husband to fire both shotguns and handguns on more than one occasion.

Anyone who'd grown up with guns might not appreciate the weight that firing one bore on me. Weapons had been a lifelong taboo, imposed first by my father, and later by my own affinity for anti-war pacifism and left-leaning politics. As with many taboos, once the decision had been made to break it, I felt a rush of liberation as well as fear. Like a virginity no longer cherished but still held intact, I was glad to postpone the first shot a while yet, though I was anxious to cross that boundary.

ॐ

In my childhood home, there had been no hunters or weapons of any kind. My father had joined the Navy as a teenager; an early photograph of him in uniform shows a soft-eyed, soft-faced young man. The youth who volunteered to fight the war was not the man who emerged. Whatever his experience during World War II had been, he never spoke of it. All we knew is what my mother said: "Your father had enough of that in the war. He won't have any weapons in the house."

But in my mother's family there had been hunters. In an out-of-focus honeymoon photograph of my grandparents, my grandmother carries a rifle. Her mouth lifts in a faint smile. She could not have known what her future held: eight children and the Great Depression. My grandmother shot crows from the pantry window to keep them off the garden, and at least once, she shot a deer from the same location. The garden was well-tended and productive, but it was deer hunting that sustained the family of ten through the bad years. "We ate venison in season and out of season," my mother said.

If my grandfather knew of the boundary that my father had circumscribed on our weaponless home, he believed in hunting enough to violate it. When he sent my thirteen-year-old brother a .22 rifle—an initiation into manhood—the weapon disappeared quickly, as if there were something shameful about it, shameful about the man who had sent it.

But in 1968, when my musician brother turned eighteen and reported for his draft physical, my father was outraged when my brother's extraordinary hearing enabled him to successfully fake the physical and claim exemption from military service. For my father, weapons at home were not acceptable, but he—like many WWII veterans—viewed fighting unknown Asians in the jungle as necessary and honorable. It was an era of emotional extremes, a war that divided families.

ℒ

Summer solstice dawned mostly clear, with overnight dew evaporating like wild perfume off meadow grass and wildflowers. The longest day, for me, always signals the shortening of the light, just as solstice night in winter heralds not darkness, but returning sun. On June solstice, while others rushed outdoors to celebrate, I turned inward to prepare for the coming darkness. I gathered the meditation cushions and sat cross-legged, eyes closed, focused on breathing. In. Out. In.

Random, unruly thoughts skidded around the breath, bounced off, shuddered their way back in. It's almost always that way. To steady my attention, I practiced a *metta,* or "loving-kindness" meditation: *May all beings be happy. May all beings be peaceful. May all beings be kind. May all beings be safe.* The phrases strung together like rosary beads. *May all beings be happy.* In the eye of my mind, an elk herd broke free of a camouflaging forest. *May all beings be peaceful.* I imagined I prayed for them. *May all beings be kind.* Behind the meditative refrain, I had an unsought image of myself raising a rifle, pulling the trigger, an elk buckling to the leafy ground. *May all beings be safe.* I squirmed on the cushion, wanting to get up, to move about, shake the image away.

But this, I knew, was the contradiction I struggled to embrace.

ॐ

One June solstice years ago, I attended the Sitka Symposium on Human Values and the Written Word. It was held indoors, but I kept finding myself outside. Bald eagles rained from the sky, following fishing boats toward harbor. A pulp mill spewed waste into Sitka Sound. Whales breached and spyhopped in sight of shore. Glaciers careened between mountains, inching to the sea. At low tide, I walked the water's edge, picking kelp and eating it. I plucked ripe salmonberries too, and rugosa rose petals for tea.

Sitka's inhabitants included loggers and environmental activists, fishers, writers, people who played croquet after midnight, and others who drove ten miles to the end-of-the-road campground to see who'd just disembarked from the Alaska ferry.

It's a community and environment of contradictions, like most places, but I—who dwell in arid mountains—was lulled by Sitka's watery beauty. When I finally emerged from reverie I was stunned by how retro some of the symposium conversations seemed, as if I'd been transplanted to a smoke-filled midwestern coffee shop at dawn during deer season.

I came to and found the anthropologist and writer Richard Nelson— a resident of Sitka—extolling the hunter's life. The anthropologist, writer and filmmaker Hugh Brody claimed that, in his view, the hunter-gatherer era was the high point in human development. The anthropologists spoke of the Inuit and Koyukon belief that animals give themselves to the hunt. When James Nageak, an Inupiaq Eskimo from Barrow, Alaska told stories of whale hunting, the symposium seemed to tilt alarmingly toward a glorification of animal-killing, distressing several of the vegetarian-inclined, a few women like myself in particular.

Among ourselves, over cappuccino at the bookshop, we agreed that the men cleaved to an ancient male ritual; that hunting was no longer necessary for most people, especially those who live in temperate climates where plant food is abundant and varied. But weighted by the hunters' enthusiasm, we felt the weakness of our voices and bloodless arguments. We were defeated, until Linda Hogan stood up and offered a giant paw of a poem that swiped the hunters' assurance aside:

Bear

The bear is a dark continent
that walks upright
like a man.

It lives across the thawing river.
I have seen it
beyond the water,
beyond comfort. Last night
it left a mark at my door
that said winter
was a long and hungry night of sleep.
But I am not afraid; I have collected
other nights of fear
knowing what things walked
the edges of my sleep,

and I remember
the man who shot

a bear,
how it cried as he did
and in his own voice,
how he tracked that red song
into the forest's lean arms
to where the bear lay weeping
on fired earth,
its black hands
covering its face from sky
where humans believe god lives
larger than death.

That man,
a madness remembers him.
It is a song in starved shadows
in nights of sleep.
It follows him.
Even the old rocks sing it.
It makes him want
to get down on his knees
and lay his own hands
across his face and turn away
from sky where god lives
larger than life.

Madness is its own country
desperate and ruined.
It is a collector of lives.
It's a man
afraid of what he's done
and what he lives by. Safe,
we are safe
from the bear
and we have each other,
we have each other
to fear.

—Linda Hogan

The image of the bear bleeding, crying, covering its eyes in pain or fear matched no one's fantasy of a wild creature who had given itself to the hunt, nor did the madness of the hunter summon any illusion of a tender and mutual wounding.

It has been said by the mythologist Joseph Campbell that animals—unlike humans—have no knowledge of death. I do not believe this.

The Sitka Symposium stirred me up enough that I was prompted to return a couple of years later. Some of the same hunters and anthropologists attended as well. In the interim, I had developed a new theory about hunting.

Blood rituals pulse through women's lives, via menstruation and birth. Such regular engagement with blood gives women, I theorized, a deep and ongoing intimacy with the life force. Men cannot bring forth life from their bodies; therefore they are drawn to other blood rituals, perhaps maiming and killing as a way of engaging with the greatest mystery, life itself.

I had not tried to fit women hunters into my theory.

❧

Some called her a contemporary shaman. Janet Bishop practiced the Chinese healing art, *jin shin jyutsu,* and taught classes on contacting your angels. She made—and played—hoop drums. Such credentials might bring to mind hippie-granola heads, but Janet was also a hunter with over twenty years of experience.

"I don't hunt," she told me, "unless I have the dream." She paused, brushing her long hair back from her shoulders, then tipped forward from the waist, leaned closer. "I've never missed and I've never caused suffering." Janet did not blink. "I always get the license, but I don't always get an elk. Sometimes I've hunted with people who've asked why didn't I take the shot, but I hadn't had the dream. One year I hadn't had the dream and the season was nearly over. Then I dreamed the elk and in the morning my husband Benj was surprised to hear me say, 'We're hunting today.'

"We went out and walked a long way—you have to be willing to walk a long, long way—until I could hear elk and smell them. I crept along on my belly and raised my head and there she was, a cow elk looking at me. Presenting herself, like in the dream. I took the shot. She trotted off about a hundred yards and went down. I got up and walked toward her, singing. I sang and her soul went—" Janet raised her hands to the sky—"and she died."

Janet rocked forward and nodded, slightly. Her eyes never left mine, and in them I recognized something old as fire. "Yes, that's how it was," she said. "That's how it is."

To ease my preparing-to-kill conscience, I would have liked to believe that animals present themselves willingly to the human hunter, but I doubted it, just as I couldn't imagine relinquishing my own body without a struggle to grizzlies, wolves or maggots. But I wondered how my beliefs would transform if elk dreams came to me in the expanding darkness of autumn.

ॐ

David and I drove south on Highway 89 to the gun club and followed the posted instructions to check with the range tender before removing the rifle from the car. We paid three dollars each and carried the Ruger in, unloaded, chamber open. The only other shooters were at the edge of the range, aiming at the sky.

The range tender set us up at shooting stations, gave us sandbags to brace the rifle barrel on. He called, "Cease fire," through a bullhorn, and the man and woman shooting clay pigeons unloaded and laid down their weapons while David and I walked onto the range and placed our paper targets on stands at the twenty-five yard line. Tucked between the splayed flanks of the higher slope, the firing range was V-shaped, with the farthest targets in the crease of the mountain. I couldn't imagine shooting a target two hundred yards away or more, but this, I'd been told, was what I would eventually aim for, the average distance between hunter and kill. The range tender drew on a pipe. I found the tobacco smoke strangely reassuring, a smell that I've—stereotypically, of course—associated with philosophers, surprising in an atmosphere where I'd expected another stereotype: gunslingers spitting tobacco juice.

He told us to take a few shots at twenty-five yards, then a hundred. Then, he said, we could sight the gun.

David slid a brass cartridge into the chamber. We covered our ears. Janet had suggested that he shoot first, with me holding his shoulder and biceps lightly, to sense the rifle's kick. I stood behind him and placed my hands on his body. He aimed. With a crack, David's arm and shoulder jerked back and the dirt exploded about 150 yards away. There was no delay between events; they occupied the same loud, crowded moment. Thinking he'd missed the target—thinking: if he has missed, how will I hit it—I asked, "Where did it go?"

"Just about dead on," the range tender said.

David shot again, an inch to the right of center. The boom reverberated like thunder trapped in my ears. He handed me the rifle.

I sat on the small bench at my station and fumbled a cartridge into the chamber, drew the bolt closed. My heart thudded as I adjusted position, squinted down the scope, tried to keep my elbow on the table. I reached around the heavy sandbag that padded my shoulder to crook my index finger over the trigger. Crosshairs lined up center target and I breathed. In. Out. In. I shook with fear, made myself breathe steady. In. Out. In.

I held my breath and squeezed slightly—I didn't feel the trigger move before the bullet exploded, the butt slammed my shoulder, the distant dirt whirled up. "What happened?" I asked David.

"I think you missed the target," he said. "Try again."

Re-loading, my eyes watered up. Blinking, breathing, holding my breath, I fired again. When the rifle kicked, the scope slammed my forehead. "Where did it go?" I asked.

David studied the target. "Let me look through the scope," he said. "I think you hit the bull's eye."

"Cease fire," the range tender shouted through the bullhorn, even though the clay pigeon shooters had left and no one else had arrived. David opened the chamber, left the rifle on the stand, and we walked out to relocate the targets. On mine, dead center: two overlapping, blackened bullet holes, a sideways figure-eight, an infinity sign.

"I guess I didn't miss," I said to David. My eyes filled up again.

I could kill somebody, I thought, unprepared for the sensation of horror colliding with pride, annihilating the distance between pacifist and warrior, uniting Gandhi and Rambo like overlapped bullet holes, closing in on the fierce range of the creator/destroyer goddess, Artemis.

Nothing had prevented me from firing the gun. No anatomical barrier, no crisis of conscience, no staying hand of the peaceful goddess. Afraid but willing, I had loaded the rifle and pulled the trigger. And I would do it again.

David and I re-positioned our targets at one hundred yards and returned to the shooting stands. The bull's eyes gave me a bizarre courage to throw off anonymity, and I introduced myself to the ranger tender. Puffing smoke with inscrutable calm, he told me his name was Blake.

"Ever fired a gun before?" he asked.

"No," I replied.

"Gonna get an elk this year?" he wanted to know.

"I hope so," I said without flinching, as if "getting an elk" was not a dramatic departure for me. I couldn't believe I said it so calmly. After seventeen years of eating no red meat at all, no mammals, I'd tasted elk for the first time only a year and a half before—wild elk from Janet's freezer. I had been prepared to hate it, to be revolted by it; instead, I found the elk nourished some estranged and desiccated place inside me. I had chewed slowly, imagining the elk's muscle, her tongue and teeth, so like mine yet missing the sharp canines of a carnivore. I took plenty of time to contemplate the elk's life. Through her, I ate the sun and rain and plants my own body could not digest.

She tasted faintly red, of iron and flowers.

&

At one hundred yards, I stared down the scope at the concentric circles of the paper target. My peripheral vision registered motion: a herd of animals running onto the firing range? But when I turned toward the movement, the long grass rolled under the wind like a silver-and-dun pelt undulating across the hillside. I gave my attention to the crosshairs again, aimed and shot slightly high, slightly left of target center, three bullet holes within one inch of each other: a lethal triangle. My shoulder burned. Even after removing my ear protection, I could hardly hear David and Blake. Laying his pipe on the table, Blake adjusted the rifle sights.

When I asked David if everyone with a good scope shot close to center, he said probably, but he thought it unusual for multiple bullets from a first-time shooter to hit so near one another. Blake handed me the rifle to fire again. The bullet pierced the right side of the target. The next time I took aim, I winced, unconsciously anticipating the kick, and found myself about to squeeze the trigger with my eyes closed, ready to flinch, guarding shoulder and forehead. I forced my eyes open, concentrated on breathing.

"I'm scared," I said, "I'm starting to cringe before I pull the trigger."

"It's scary," David replied.

I aimed, squeezed and the bullet blasted instantly, no perceivable delay for the sequence of ignitions—the firing pin sparking the primer which ignites the gun powder whose expanding gas launches the bullet like a miniature rocket. The bullet tracked slightly right again, and Blake stared through the spotting scope and said he believed he mis-sighted the gun.

"The 30.06 might be too big for me," I said.

"If you're not gonna be shooting this gun, you should quit before you learn bad habits," Blake said. "Let me know a few days ahead when you're coming again, and I'll get something smaller for you to try."

Relieved, I stood the rifle in the rack to let the barrel cool.

Near the shoulder joint, my upper arm swelled and turned blueblack, a self-inflicted, temporary tattoo, a mark of violent passage. Inexplicably proud, I soothed it with arnica liniment that evening and displayed it to Janet Bishop the next day.

But such hollow pride was riddled with shame, and loss. Crossing the boundary from sharpshooting fantasy into a real gun experience extracted a toll in innocence. I couldn't deny that I'd just opened the gate to harm or kill. To stalk and kill, in particular, a beautiful, wild creature who embodied an instinct to live, just as I did.

ॐ

I took up a firearm on a journey to do least harm.

The contradiction was so immense that—like my father who wouldn't allow weapons but who would have preferred a soldier son— I could hardly carry it whole. It nearly sunk of its own weight into unconsciousness. The mind could only exhume one end at a time, running back and forth to extricate fragments. When the bones were laid out, stained but bare, I identified the warrior skeleton as mine.

Pacifist and warrior inhabit the same body, like opposite ends of spinal vertebrae, each with unique purpose, each necessary to the functioning of the whole. When one overpowers the other, it's a trip to the chiropractor.

Yogis infuse each small bone, organ, muscle of the body with awareness.

Buddhas turn from nothing, stay present for the terrible and sublime.

Artemis brings forth life and takes it without regret.

Balance requires nothing less.

I didn't know if learning to shoot would tilt my behavior toward the violent end of the spectrum.

I did know that meditation had not, of itself, rendered me more peaceful. Seated on my zafu, focused on the breath, observing the rising chaos of my own feelings and ideas had only begun to illuminate how much is numbed, buried, suppressed, ignored.

Perhaps the greatest harm we do ourselves and others is not recognizing that we each encompass the full catastrophe, the total spectrum of behavior. How would we ever know compassion if all possibility is not contained within each human heart?

"Everybody's scandalous flaw," Rumi wrote, "is mine."

I was one of the barbarians.

—from *Tracking Artemis*, a work-in-progress

Surprised by the Sacred

Pattiann Rogers

Driving on a paved road not far from my home last summer, I saw an injured snake, hit by a car, stuck by its open wound to the road. It was curling and writhing, struggling to free itself. I stopped and went back, thinking to move it from the hot, bare road and into the shade and shelter of the weeded ditch where I felt it would eventually die, yet possibly suffer a little less.

As I reached the snake, lying on its back, twisted around its wound, and bent to move it, it took one very sharp, deep breath, a gasp so deep I could see its rib cage rise beneath the ivory scales along its upper body, and, in that moment, it died. It lay suddenly without moving, not at all the existence it had been, inexorably altered in being. And its gasp and the dying were simultaneous, the breath stopped, held within the narrow width of its dead body forever. I was stunned in that moment by an awareness of order and union: the snake at my fingertips had been a living creature, drawing breath as I draw breath, taking air into its body. *Living*—the word was suddenly expanded for me in meaning, in impact. It now embodied a compassion of connection wider, more undeniable than any I had perceived before.

One definition of sacred is: declared holy. I would declare this moment to be a sacred moment in my life, and I would declare the elements composing this moment—the struggling snake, its life ceasing, the vision of its breathing, the unrelenting summer sun, the steady buzz and burr of the insects in the weeds around us, the fragrance of dry grasses—all these elements I would declare to be holy in their bearing of essence and divinity.

A similar moment of enlightenment, also involving a snake, is described in a poem by D.H. Lawrence. On a hot summer day the speaker of the poem comes upon a snake drinking at his water-trough.

> *He sipped with his straight mouth,*
> *Softly drank through his straight gums, into his slack long body,*
> *Silently. . . .*
>
> *He lifted his head from his drinking, as cattle do. . .*
> *And flickered his two-forked tongue from his lips, and mused a*
>   *moment,*
> *And stooped and drank a little more.*

As the speaker watches, he believes the snake is poisonous and that he should kill it.

> *But must I confess how I liked him,*
> *How glad I was he had come like a guest in quiet, to drink at*
>   *my water-trough*
> *And depart peaceful, pacified, and thankless,*
> *Into the burning bowels of this earth?*

The underlying unity of life is revealed in that moment. All life—beautiful or reprehensible, dangerous or benign—takes sustenance from the earth, all lips that drink, all throats and bodies and roots that seek water.

And all forms of life are one in their tenacity, in their determined grip on existence, in their unfaltering will-to-be, exhibited so obviously in the sow thistle rising through any crevice forced or found in cement or rock; in mayweed and burdock thriving along roadsides, among rubbish and waste; in the unrelenting persistence of birds—sparrows, crows, warblers—up at dawn, even after a sudden spring storm of sleet and ice, a long frigid night, calling and scrabbling in the cold, there to survive, crisis or no. "Urge and urge and urge/Always the procreate urge of the world," Walt Whitman writes in "Song of Myself."

This kinship of being, of devotion to life, once recognized, demands respect for each living entity in its place. Another definition of *scared* is: venerable, worthy of respect.

My family moved to a farm in Missouri when I was fifteen. Along with the purchase of the farm, we inherited a herd of sheep, just at lambing season. It was a painfully cold, late January, and when twins were born, it was often necessary to bring one lamb into the house to keep it from freezing while the ewe mother took care of the other. Even today, many years later, I can see those newborn lambs, whiter and cleaner than the snow they lay on at birth, each so immediately out of the warm, wet womb into the wide winter cold, the unfathomably deep, grey skies, the world wholly new to their eyes just opened, and, hanging from each lamb, the drying string of a bloody umbilical cord.

I've never felt anything again so soft as the fleecy silk of those young lambs, silk so soft it was barely discernible against my fingertips, the sensation enhanced by the feel of the thin, warm body beating beneath. I remember having one of my fingers accidentally mistaken for a nipple and taken quickly into a lamb's mouth, the surprisingly strong sucking and gripping power of that tongue and throat on my finger. Life is this final, the altogether everything, this crucial.

We seem to be creatures who need physical sensation, tangible objects to imbue with the abstractions that mean so much to us as a species—innocence, compassion, peace. Each of the newborn lambs we cared for during those early years of my adolescence has come to be for me the very feel, the sound, the living body of faith, of purity and hope. These are the same virtues many people in the past believed were presented to God in the sacrifice of unblemished lambs. "Behold the Lamb of God," John the Baptist announces when he sees Christ walking toward him out of the crowd.

The newborn lambs of my adolescence entered the world bearing this history in their being, in their bodies—stories of the sacred. And they were dear to me, their presence enhanced, because of the stories they bore.

The surprise of encountering unusual juxtapositions can also bring awareness of the amazingly divine carnival of life, this sacred circus that surrounds us—the juxtaposition of a tomcat sleeping with a fallen forsythia blossom on his head, a toad found in the toe of a rubber boot, the disappearing and ephemeral form of surf blown against implacable rock, the wild abandon and indifference of nature seen against the static of the man-made. . .

> *Out from the hollow*
> *of Great Buddha's nose—*
> *comes a swallow.*

—Issa

or the vast and the far seen clearly against the small and the near. . .

> *A lovely thing to see:*
> *through the paper window's hole*
> *the Galaxy.*

—Issa

Once, in a muddy, ill-smelling chicken yard noisy with cackling hens, I held in my hand one half of a fertilized chicken egg accidentally broken. In the center of that half shell filled with golden yolk, a small dot of bright blood pulsed regularly and steadily into a threaded network of spreading red webs so small and fine they were hardly visible in their reality. Heart and its pathways.

For a moment I was lifted out of that scene. Everything around me disappeared, and nothing existed except that vibrant red instant of complex life proceeding, though doomed, with astonishing trust. The miracle of it, a hallowed miracle. Who could think otherwise?

"A mouse is miracle enough to stagger sextillions of infidels," Whitman, again, from "Song of Myself." And I agree.

I've often experienced a moment of deep happiness when watching someone sleeping, and wondered why. I think what occasions that joy is an awareness of the truth that the body itself is totally innocent, flesh and bone unquestionably fine, justified, and without blame. All aspects—feet and legs, the intricacy of the ears, the grace of the neck and the arms—all are sculptures unsurpassed in beauty of line and function. And the hands, solely in and of themselves, are astonishingly perfect and inviolate. Jacob Bronowski writes in *The Ascent of Man* (Little, Brown, 1976): "I remember as a young father tiptoeing to the cradle of my first daughter when she was four or five days old and thinking, these marvelous fingers, every joint so perfect, down to the fingernails. I could not have designed that detail in a million years."

When the human body is sleeping we can see clearly, without interference or confusion, that the body is indeed sacred and honorable—a grand gift we hold in trust. It is sublime and chaste in its loveliness and as unbothered by greed or violence, by deceit or guilt, as a brilliantly yellow cottonwood standing in an autumn field, as the moon filling the boundaries of its white stone place. If there is sin, it resides elsewhere. "The man's body is sacred and the woman's body is sacred. . ." Whitman, "I Sing the Body Electric."

I believe the world provides every physical image and sensation we will ever need in order to experience the sacred, to declare the holy. If we could only learn to recognize it, if we could only hone and refine our sense of the divine, just as we learn to see and distinguish with accuracy the ant on the trunk of the poplar, the Pole Star in Ursa Minor, rain coming toward us on the wind; just as we come to identify the sounds we hear, the voices of our children, the creak of the floor at the lover's footstep, the call of a finch unseen in the top of a pine; just as we can detect and name the scent of cedar or sage, wild strawberries or river mud and rotting logs.

Might it be possible, if we try, to become so attuned to the divine that we are able to perceive and announce it with such ease too? And perhaps the divine, the sacred, the holy, only come into complete existence through our witness of them, our witness for them and to them. Perhaps reciprocal creation, as I observe it operating in my own writing—creating the poem which simultaneously creates me which simultaneously creates the poem coming into being—just as the marsh wren created by the marsh simultaneously creates and dreams the marsh of its creation and therefore creates itself—is the same phenomenon occurring in regards to divinity. Maybe the existence of divinity in the universe depends in part on us. We may be the consciousness of the universe, the way by which it can come to see and love and honor itself. If this is so, then our obligations are mighty and humbling. We are cocreators. We are servants.

I believe we move through the sacred constantly, yet remain oblivious to its presence except during those rare, unexpected moments when we are suddenly shocked and shaken awake, compelled to perceive and acknowledge. During those brief moments we know with bone-centered conviction who it is we are; with breath-and-pulse clarity where it is we have come from; and with earth-solid certainty to what it is we owe all our allegiance, all our heart, all our soul, all our love.

Footnotes

1. D. H. Lawrence, "Snake," in *The Complete Poems of D. H. Lawrence,* ed. V. de Sola Pinto and F. Warren Roberts (New York: Penguin, 1964), 349.
2. Walt Whitman, "Song of Myself," in *Walt Whitman: Complete Poetry and Collected Prose* (New York: The Library of America, 1982), 190.
3. Issa, "The Great Buddha at Nara," in *An Introduction to Haiku: Anthology of Poems and Poets from Basho to Shiki,* ed. and trans. Harold G. Henderson (Garden City, N.Y.: Doubleday Anchor Books, 1958), 139.
4. Issa, "Heaven's River," in *An Introduction to Haiku,* 148.
5. Walt Whitman, "Song of Myself," 217.
6. Jacob Bronowski, *The Ascent of Man* (Boston: Little, Brown and Co., 1973), 417, 421.
7. Walt Whitman, "I Sing the Body Electric," in *Walt Whitman: Complete Poetry and Collected Prose,* 122.

—from *The Dream of the Marsh Wren,* a work-in-progress

A Banishment of Crows

Lisa Couturier

One for sorrow
Two for joy
Three for girls and four for boys
Five for silver
Six for gold and
Seven for a secret never to be told
            —Counting Crows, "A Murder of One," a
            variation on the English magpie-counting rhyme

Toward the end of a rainy December day I decide to follow crows
flying to their nightly roost. This means driving with my eyes on the
dusky sky, looking for the birds, rather than watching the traffic along
Rockville Pike, a congested, commercial, mini-highway in suburban
Maryland.

   I once knew where the crows roosted. In December of 1995, when
my daughter Madeleine was three months old, my husband and I
brought her to visit our folks for Christmas in the Maryland suburbs
of Washington, D.C., where we both grew up. One windy day of that
vacation we grabbed a video camera and took Madeleine beyond the
housing developments to a field of dried and broken cornstalks where
hundreds of crows had gathered. I edged toward the birds with my
baby sleeping against my chest, hoping that when she opened her eyes
the flight of hundreds of crows would leave an early etching of
movement, freedom and mystery on her newborn mind. We wanted
the video to document her awakening among the birds, creatures who
had, in a sense, been with her since the day of her birth.

Although Madeleine's birth was difficult, I waited out the first fourteen hours of labor at home, on the fourth floor of an old red brick house on East 89th Street in New York City. During those magical hours, my husband and I watched the time between contractions and watched crows through the slim iron security bars over our open kitchen window. Five birds regularly visited the trees and vines in the backyard of the house, where our kitchen was an inner-city tree fort opening straight into an oasis of green, and into the crows' lives.

It was impossible to know if the same crows came around all the time, although we sensed they knew each other well. One preened another. They followed together, hopping and sprinting from branch to branch. One voice answered another. I'd lived in Manhattan nearly ten years by then, and this kitchen window was the first place that the sounds of the city—the annoying car alarms, horns, boom boxes, and endless white noise—didn't drown out the cawing, gurgling, rattling, cooing sounds of crows, birds I didn't know I missed until I heard them again.

As far as I was concerned it was a family of crows that flew in and out of my days that summer, my belly big with my first child. I knew the popular symbolism of their appearance: a portent of evil and death. But as they distracted me from my pain, their blackness reminded me of the dark cradle from which my baby would soon descend.

Black. It is often the color in which we choose to make love. It is the color of conception. Within utter blackness our brain, skin, bones, our body, grows. Our eyes first open into it. Life begins in black.

A few days after we made our film of Madeleine and the crows, I was at a busy intersection two blocks from Rockville Pike, along Montrose Road, when I heard through the car window a persistent noise that wasn't man-made. I opened my window to the darkening sky; the noise melted over the car. Flying above me was a stream of crows—hundreds and hundreds, thousands—flowing toward some tall and densely packed deciduous trees in one of the few older wooded areas in Rockville. Before I'd moved away fifteen years ago, I rode by this little forest countless times to drop off, pick up or visit my mother, who worked for a government health program nearby. Funny how places in your hometown become so deeply embedded in you that you no longer really see them.

The crows continued in. They flew above Rockville Pike and dropped into the bare branches along Montrose Road by the dozens. Their winter chorus grew. This was their roost, in 1995.

₷

Rockville Pike, or "the Pike" in Maryland vernacular, is an old road. Stories tell of big historical figures like Benjamin Franklin, George Washington, Andrew Jackson, James Polk, and troops from both sides of the Civil War using Rockville Pike as a strategic travel route during Colonial times. Back then, the Pike wasn't much more than the dusty Seneca Indian trail it began as. The trail started at the mouth of Washington D.C.'s Rock Creek, a stream that flows into the Potomac River, and led northwest toward modern-day Rockville. One historian described the area in the late eighteenth century:

> *Large tracts of timberland were cleared for farms and the dense woodland began to thin out due to the building of homes. . . . Many of the Maryland settlers enjoyed lucrative incomes from the crops which flourished in a fertile soil and moderate climate. . . . [Yet] within a short time after the entrance of the white man into this wild life sanctuary . . . the buffalo, bear and wolf became extinct in the county. At that period bounties were paid for wolf scalps. Bobcat and deer, which had been plentiful, decreased in numbers. . . . With the disappearance of the old trees and forest boundaries, many birds and wild fowl migrated to safer havens. . . . In 1800 the farm lands began to deteriorate. . . . The county was regarded as so sterile and unproductive as to be frequently referred to as 'the Sahara of Maryland.'"*

From *Western Gateway to the National Capital*(Rockville, MD) by Noma Thompson, 1949

Today, agricultural land along the pike is sparse. The road is, rather, one of immense wealth and commercial success, a retailer's religious experience. There are twenty-three shopping centers along just six of its forty-two miles, as well as restaurants, apartment buildings, office towers, gas stations, hotels, and car dealers. It is, said a Washington Post article in 1997, "one of the East Coast's premier commercial thoroughfares," a place where, "per square foot, retail sales are greater than on [Beverly Hills'] Rodeo Drive." Still, more construction is planned for this suburban artery. An explosion of new development. By 2005 there may well be ten million more square feet of commercial projects built as well as thousands of new homes. "Those projects will pave over scattered grassy fields and the last farm along the way," says the *Post*. "When it's all done, there will be few remaining spaces . . . ."

℮

It wasn't until 1996 when I discovered that development had destroyed most of the crows' roosting site on Montrose Road. Although, as I would later learn, they would attempt to return. On my annual Christmas visit I drove to see the tremendous movement of a train of birds across the sky, coming in from as far as twenty miles away every evening between October and March. They gathered for the warmth generated by thousands of bodies and for what we might call safety in numbers. Their gravest predator is the great horned owl, who lives and hunts in woodlands, deserts, even city parks. It is a silent night stalker, craving the taste of brains and seizing its prey without warning.

Except for a small parcel of trees left at the easternmost corner, one block from the Pike, the roost site had been razed. Old trees sat snapped in half. Tractors waited in mire. A sign advertised: *EXCLUSIVE TOWNHOMES TO BE BUILT HERE SOON. Exclusive.* Casually, I'd come to associate the word with its secondary definitions: stylish, fashionable, maybe a little snobby. When I was in the magazine publishing business in New York, I asked writers for exclusive rights to their work. Exclusive was special. Looking at the land, I realized how absurdly honest the sign actually was: the possession of these woods was now limited to humans. Had anyone known about the roost, I wondered? Had anyone cared?

"People often have strong opinions about crows," says Cornell University professor and crow expert Kevin McGowan in *The Washington Times*. "Some are fond of them, perhaps because the crow's apparent intelligence makes it more human-like than most other birds . . . . Most other people generally hate crows."

In his unforgettable words, Edgar Allan Poe said such birds were "Grim, ungainly, ghastly, gaunt, and ominous." Modern America seems to agree. In his study "Perceptions of Animals in America," Yale professor Stephen Kellert found the crow to be one of America's least liked animals, sharing the title with roaches, rats, rattlesnakes, vultures, and lizards to name just several. "In much the same way the absence of legs makes the snake unappealing," says McGowan, "the physical appearance of crows—big, black and evil-looking—makes them unpopular."

Unpopular enough to be hunted for sport. "People shot crows by the hundreds, by the thousands in Buckeystown, north of here," an old Rockville native remembered. "So many of them, the sky black full of them in the sixties and seventies. Crow shooters by the hundreds shootin', just to get rid of the birds. Probably still do today."

Not too far from Buckeystown is Darnestown, Maryland, where an adult female crow was recently found dying from a wound inflicted by a beebee gun. "Maybe a teenage boy," said one of the naturalists, when I called to arrange a visit to see the crow. The shot shattered the crow's wing, which had to be amputated. On my way to see her, I absentmindedly sang along with an old Earth, Wind & Fire tune on the car radio: "Child is born with a heart of gold / Way of the world, makes his / heart grow cold."

Although crows are protected under the migratory bird act, there is a hunting season on them in specified, mostly rural, areas of the state. Rockville is not among them. Perhaps conveniently, the hunting season coincides with the crows' roosting season.

&

Crow. *Corvus brachyrhynchos*. Corvus is Latin for crow and brachyrhynchos means "short beak." Crows belong to the Corvids, a Latin name for the family which also includes ravens, magpies and jays. As a group, "corvids are the top of the line in avian evolution, among the most recent and successful of modern birds," writes Candace Savage in *Bird Brains*. And one of the most intelligent. Naturalist Tony Angell writes in *Ravens, Crows, Magpies and Jays* that, in the lab, the American crow is "superior in intelligence to all other avian species tested." Other research has determined that corvids are first on the list for overall avian brain size. "Their brain-to-body ratio," says Savage, "equals that of dolphins and nearly matches our own."

Which might help explain the strong family bonds of crows. Take, for instance, Edgar Allan Crow, who was rescued by a naturalist in Rockville after a truck hit the bird. When the naturalist ran to help Edgar, a group of crows began mobbing her in an effort to save him. While fighting them off, the naturalist noticed that some of the birds had spots of white (partial albinism) on their feathers. Left flightless and unable to fend for himself after the accident, Edgar became a crow ambassador in a nature center, to where "his family moved with him," the naturalist said. "It's clearly his family. Some of them have the same white-spotted feathers. When no one is around, they visit him. They sit on his outdoor cage. He throws food to them."

Unlike most birds, crows mate for life. And McGowan's decade-long research shows that, like humans, the birds live in extended families. The parents welcome their young to stay in the home territory, which they occupy year-round and for life. This can continue into the offspring's adulthood, until they establish their own territory either close by or on a piece of the parents' land. In spring and summer the crow family spends its days and nights near home, tending to family life. The young from one or more previous years help the parents feed and guard the newest brood. In fall and winter, the home area is used during the day but by late afternoon the family and the larger community of crows migrates to the communal roost.

ஃ

Before I began my drive down Rockville Pike to look for the crows, I asked an Audubon Society official, Jane Huff (who had once affectionately said: "crows are too intelligent for their place in life and so they get into mischief") if any environmental impact statements were done before construction destroyed the Montrose roost I'd seen in 1995. "People knew it was there," she said, "but crows aren't an endangered species, you know."

Why is it that we take for granted all but what we are about to lose?

There had been complaints about the Montrose roost, complaints about the noise and that such a large roost—nearly five hundred thousand birds, maybe more—could present health hazards. By 1997, the birds had moved to a new spot—the trees in the parking lot of White Flint Mall, a large, upscale shopping center less than two miles south of Montrose Road. "But," said Huff, "I don't know where the crows are now."

I remembered the crows at White Flint Mall, perched in trees not far from Lord & Taylor and Bloomingdales. After a movie at the mall during my Christmas visit in 1997, I walked to my car, around 9:30 pm. A couple hurried by arm in arm, their faces down. At the head of my car was a parking-lot-sort-of-tree, a bit fragile, short and lonely; and sitting in it were at least two dozen crows. Being diurnal birds, they should have been sleeping but instead many were dipping through the night sky, startled by, and perhaps startling, shoppers leaving for home to roost in their own human sort of way. Perhaps because folks felt a frightening Hitchcockian flavor to the parking lot at night, the mall began a "roost harassment" program. Loud speakers blasted crow distress calls into the night in an effort to move the birds away from the shopping center, eventually "bombing" the roost with firecracker-like sounds. This land, too, was to be exclusive.

Would there have been more tolerance for birds like the beautiful cardinal or robin? Must beauty require prettiness?

With a little empathy, a little anthropomorphism, you could imagine a bomb waking you, shattering the night. Imagine the great growing of fear twisting through your muscles. Imagine the dread of fleeing into the peril of the owl at your wing tip.

"Anthropomorphism" writes James Hillman, the Jungian psychologist, "recognizes that humans and animals participate in a common world of significations. We can and do understand each other despite the arrogant philosophies that would preserve consciousness as an exclusively human property."

In the scientific world anthropomorphism is a crime. Condemned. Laughed at. If I commit any crimes during my life let them be crimes of passion on behalf of the nonhuman world. My life is in need of such sin.

&

I am no longer an annual visitor to Maryland. From my home in a small, old community just over the border of Washington, D.C., I watch great blue herons fly above the Potomac River. Beaver, deer, opossum, and raccoon trek through the river's wooded shoreline. A five-lined skink lives in the stone stairs of my front porch.

In New York, the streets were fat with the future—the next great play or dance or idea or job or assignment for me to discover. But Maryland represents to me what the Celts called a "thin place": a geographical location where a person experiences only a very thin divide between past, present and future. I grew up in and around Rockville; and I will probably die here.

Outside in the mornings, Madeleine and I hear the cawing of crows, at first far away, echoing through the woods along the river. Slowly they close in, spot us throwing corn, bread, sunflower seeds into the grass, and land in the tall trees around our house. Once, a high mound of upturned earth two houses away drew hundreds of crows searching for garbage. They covered the roofs of several homes and lined the trees' branches. I squinted through the sun at them, black scarves in the wind, and walked with Madeleine along our stone path to feed them. They fell silent as we moved below them, a mountain of eyes. It was one of those moments when suddenly you feel you've crossed over the edge of your civilized world and into quite another. It's when the tables turn and you are not doing the turning. If you surrender to it—to that moment when perhaps the wild and the tame are one—there's an incredible lightness, an openness there on the edge, as you wait to see what verdict the world will serve you. We were granted four more seconds there, clutched by the crows, before a neighbor walking a dog passed by and the birds retreated into the sky.

"You will find yourself again only in the simple and forgotten things," Jung wrote.

I have a clear picture in my mind of when I was twelve. I wore a yellow coat, held a pad of paper and a pencil, stood by a wood fence, and watched crows from not more than ten feet away (a distance so close as to be absolutely unthinkable now). Day after day the crows came to search the grass for insects and seeds. I imagined I could tame the birds if I stayed near them long enough, not knowing that perhaps the only reason they stayed at all was because I had yet to be tamed myself.

"A given landscape permits and prohibits how one perceives, what one is literally able to experience," writes Sallie Tisdale in Stepping Westward. In returning to Maryland, I have returned to a landscape that sustained not only a roost of thousands of crows but a girl who fell captive to them.

⚘

When I think about it, my past consists of hundreds of trips up and down Rockville Pike. In a way, the road maps my childhood and adolescence; the details are delineated along the side streets, in the parking lots, shops and restaurants. For instance, the one and only McDonald's in the area was, years ago, on the Pike. My parents used to take my siblings and me there for dinner and then to the now defunct Rockville Drive-in. We watched the children's show before sleeping through the main feature in the back of our white station wagon. The Pike is the road on which, in a grocery store, my brother gave me, a two-year-old, an oversized gum ball on which I immediately choked. My mother, eight months pregnant with my sister, hung me upside down and pounded the candy out of me. It is the same store where, in the parking lot, just before I left for college, I denied my mother's entire existence by cockily announcing that I couldn't imagine anyone actually wanting to be a housewife and spend her entire life in Rockville. I am now a mother and wife. This is a thin place.

My drive along the Pike to search for the crows begins at 4:45 p.m. at Congressional Plaza, just a stone's throw north from the Montrose roost site of 1995. The main attractions at Congressional Plaza are The Gap and Starbucks Coffee. But I remember summers there filled with ice-cream sundaes and surreptitious glances with the first boy who ever unsettled me by inadvertently touching my leg with his under a coffee table. We were fifteen. He was the same boy with whom I played basketball and football. In the winter he taught me about ice-skating on the ponds and lakes along Rock Creek. He told me I would be safe as long as I listened to the ice. The cracking of it, he said, sounded different depending on its thickness, its location, the time of day. I believed him and learned to think of ice in terms of its voice— thunderous, brittle, deep, feathery, squeaky.

Congressional Plaza used to be Congressional Airport, across from where an eighty-one-year-old man, Mr. Porter Welsh, worked at a general country store in the 1930s. Porter, who now lives in Florida, is one of the few people Rockville historians consider part of the city's living history. Some say that Rockville is where "way down South" begins, and you would believe it listening to the genteel lilt of Porter, a man who knew the crows way back when.

"Of course in the ol' days we didn't think of crows as a problem, just put up with 'em more than you younga' folks. When I was a small child I knew the sounds of them comin' and goin'," Porter remembered during our phone conversation. "Would imagine they've been here for eons. I saw them, dense numbers of 'em behind the old airport. I watched them go out in the mornin' and come back in the evenin'. At night the woods back there were thick with 'em. The land along what is now Montrose Road and Congressional Plaza, jus' off the Pike, was forest and farmland way back. That's where I saw them, in the thirties and forties. They utilized all that area. I would know. I lived there for some years."

Are there crows out there with a secret allegiance to the woods their kin have breathed in and out of for, if sixty years, why not a hundred, a thousand, or more? Crows with a homeland? I search for the birds believing that they have a sense of place and, by consequence of roost harassment and unceasing suburban sprawl, perhaps a deep sense of impending placelessness as well.

By 5:00, as I walk out of Starbucks with my favorite coffee, it is nearly time for crows. But I see nothing like what my hairdresser described as a "black sea above my head." There are a few small groups of crows flying with purpose through the wind and rain, but no black line to their destination that I can easily follow. I get in my car and head south, anyway, passing strip mall, strip mall, strip mall.

Each stoplight is a chance to look up for a minute or so and think about the birds. Has the weather caused them to disperse? Is a count of twenty or so crows a sure bet to the roost? They fly over the traffic in groups of six, ten, eight. I set off after a group of twelve, which of course I lose after another stoplight. In the traffic it will be impossible to follow a particular group. I park by Toys-R-Us to watch for any rhyme and reason to their flying. If more than one group appears to be flying in the same general direction, I'll drive in that direction too, without the birds as guides.

I end up on a less well traveled road that intersects the Pike across from White Flint Mall. It feels wrong but I go anyway. As I zoom over the top of a small hill I think I see birds in trees. But I'm driving too fast. I pull a quick, illegal, U-turn in the middle of the road and head back. Near the trees is a parking lot with a chain slightly raised over the entrance. I know I shouldn't cross over it, but, like the U-turn, just another small sin. I drive in. A white van with a flashing yellow light pulls up next to me. A darkened window rolls down. I have this tiny criminal feeling that is weirdly exciting. The boy behind the window is with the White Flint Security Patrol. What am I doing here, he wants to know? Am I an employee for White Flint? This is the special employee parking lot during the Christmas season.

I lie. Another sin. I tell him I'm a biologist studying bird flight patterns, especially those of crows, which is partially true.

"Oh crows!"

I am in luck. A boy who knows the crows. "Do you know where they are?" I ask.

"Hear those firecrackers, they come from a gun on the roof of the mall," he proudly tells me. "It's to scare the crows. That's why they're going in all directions."

I listen. "I didn't think the mall was still bombing them."

"People don't like the bird droppings on their cars. We start bombing at 5 pm. But I'm usually on the early morning shift. That's when I see the crows flying out. They come," he says, "from down there," as he points south.

I drive out of the proper exit to "down there," a quiet street that parallels the Pike and which is lined on one side with a small slice of deciduous trees and on the other with office buildings that, so close to Christmas, are fairly deserted. Everyone's shopping. The blazing red-scripted sign of Lord & Taylor, at White Flint Mall, is visible from the corner where I park. Rolling down my window to listen for the bombs, I quickly notice the heavy sound of scraping feathers. I hear guttural "gwals," "ops." I hear scattered screeches, wood-pecker-like rattles. Where are the birds? Beside my car are four white pines I am ignoring, thinking that the birds would go for the deciduous trees. But the crows appear. Some wing their way into the pines, while others shoot out, performing aerial gymnastics. The "gwals, "ops" and "caws" intensify. Inside the trees the birds are identifying and greeting one another, seniors are overthrowing juniors for the interior branch spots, they may even be, some ornithologists say, exchanging information about area food supplies. All those years ago I had learned to think of ice in terms of its voice. Something similar could now be said of trees.

From that point on I drive with my window down, to listen for what I cannot see. There are maybe only several hundred birds in the trees around these office buildings; this must not be their final roosting site. The bombs stab the air on no apparent schedule, probably because the birds would be smart enough to recognize a pattern, which might lessen their fear. I decide to leave this little war-zone in search of the bigger roost. It is 5:23.

By 5:30 I am back in the Toys-R-Us parking lot. I scan the sky and see nothing. Time to give up and go grocery shopping. For speed's sake, I take the Pike instead of the side streets. This turns out to be a good idea. Stuck in traffic at one of the busiest intersections in Rockville, that of Montrose and the Pike, I hear a raucous crow symphony. If the day before you had asked me about trees living at this intersection, I would have said not. But there they were, ornamented with thousands of crows, on maybe a half-acre of land owned by the State Highway Administration. The sky is as dark as skies get in huge suburban spreads with mega-sized lampposts. I decide to call this spot roost #1 and turn the corner to find a parking lot from which to watch the birds. It is 5:43.

I pull into a smear of asphalt surrounding a historic Rockville site, the Montrose School, built in 1909. A friend of Porter's went to school here. The building must be a vestigial image from old crow culture—when it was a dot on the land. There are crows in the sprinkle of trees around the school. In fact, there are birds flying from roost #1 to this spot, what I call roost #2. It is strangely quiet here. Just a few rattles and caws. Even the traffic seems far-off, which it isn't. The spring-like smell of the December rain washes over me and I am stained with a sadness for these birds, for their losses.

At 6 p.m. I look behind me toward the harshly lit parking lot of the store wherein I choked on the gum ball, and am startled to see seagulls flocking in the night sky. When I was a kid, gulls lived at the shore. They were a highlight of summer vacations near the Chesapeake Bay. Never in Rockville. But as in most urbanizing areas, seagulls and pigeons settle in. As I put the car into gear, I see crows leaving roost #1 for roost #2. When they fly into the bright beams of the parking lot lights, their undersides radiate white. I had seen a white sparkle of crows, not gulls. White crows in a black sky. Once again the tables have turned; for a few seconds crows are angels; the world is inside out.

I am back at the intersection by 6:04. Above the red, yellow and green lights are yet more crows. They do not scatter but move together, across the Pike. I follow them to another parking lot. They are dropping quietly into the few surviving trees of the Montrose roost. The easternmost corner. Traffic drones on around them. I notice construction trailers, temporary fencing, a sign for ADC Builders and PBM Mechanical. These will be the last months of the existence of what may be the crows' historic roosting site, their place. I smell butter and fresh bread and realize I am near a bakery, "La Madeleine."

The crows, my daughter. My daughter, the crows. I get out of my car to walk through the twisting rain and dark, empty parking lot alongside the madness of the birds' lives. With their final banishment from this spot so also will disappear any secret allegiance that they may have had to this place. Of course they will find a new roost, but they will not land here when Madeleine is old enough to understand the significance of their soaring to and from a sacred homeland.

Meanwhile, Madeleine will learn to count, "One for sorrow, two for joy, . . . seven for a secret never to be told."

—first publication

Moving Water

Kristen Vose Michaelides

Four women, two green canoes. When we wake the first morning, we follow wispy tendrils of mist to the water's edge. While we slept, water vapor condensed onto small particles in the air to form a thick fog. Now, the rays of the sun reach in with warm fingers to knead the risen opaqueness into constant motion. Ever so gently, morning light begins to overtake the cloudy expanse, infusing it with the golds and oranges of daybreak. Moments pass, and more moments still, as the light plays on the soft moving forms of vapor. The rays instill the fog with an ephemeral radiance. As we watch, breathlessly expectant, the white mist swirls and evaporates, revealing a vast expanse of lake, near hills, distant mountains, and wide sky.

On the shore beside us, the canoes lie huddled just beyond the breeze-blown water's reach. The heavy presence of their humped backs, stranded on the rocky, sloping land, hastens our preparations. Soon their hunkering forms become transformed by lake-water contact into graceful floating vessels, enticing us to enter.

Pushing off and swinging down into the now familiar curved seats causes four hearts to flutter for a moment in exhilaration. Few things in life speak Freedom more than leaving land and becoming an unrooted island on northern waters. Floating is akin to flying: both display the same innocent dismissal of gravity, naïve to its universality. The earth's mass would like to pull you down through the waters towards its core, but the canoes skim sweetly across the surface waters unawares.

These backcountry trips are like that: they seem to dimiss all the complex universal laws of man for the duration. All the formulae for living and interacting in an advancing human society produce irrelevant, nonsensical results in the free expanses of the natural world. On the northern waters, in the northern woods, amidst the wild places of this earth, we become reminded of a simpler, more lucid state of being. Look. Listen. Touch. Smell. Taste. Float.

Throughout the summer, while guiding numerous backcountry trips for the Appalachian Mountain Club here in the north woods of New Hampshire, I have observed the unfolding process of many people, the speed of which is determined by the number of weighty layers of importance they have come to bear. People shuck away these unnecessary layers, and meticulously remove the thin fibers that restrain them, until their inner beauty is revealed. Once their true selves come out, the trip truly begins. The formulae are discarded, replaced instead by the joyous infinities of a living planet.

There is something of a new and powerful quality to the trip I am now in the midst of. The moment we four women met at Pinkham Notch yesterday morning, a gentle force nudged our spirits towards each other. We each felt the pull, and gave ourselves up to it fully.

Just yesterday. It is difficult to believe I have only known two of these women for the length of a single day. At this moment yesterday, Beverly and Macky were just names atop standard trip medical forms. My co-leader and myself, both in our early twenties, were engaged in making preparations for the trip: sorting gear and repackaging food, filling water tanks and loading canoes onto the van. We moved efficiently, in the patterns well-established after many months of getting trips ready to depart.

Then we carefully read over the medical forms of the participants who had registered for this senior all-women's canoe trip. Last-minute cancellations left two forms in my hands, and I looked them over carefully to try to discern who these people may be, and what to be prepared for. Their names were Beverly and Macky, ages sixty and sixty-nine. One with very little canoeing and camping experience, one with a bit more. While neither seemed to bear any extreme medical conditions, we both knew that we would have to take extra care on this trip not to push our participants too hard. We knew very little about the two women, and we did not want to risk putting too much strain on their backs or hearts. We were both unsure of what to expect, and hoped that winds would favor a calm upriver approach on the Androscoggin to Lake Umbagog, our first day's destination.

Soon Beverly and Macky arrive, spilling over with an energy I had not anticipated. There is a great spirit coursing through these women and it sweeps me in the first moment that I greet them. If I hadn't read the medical forms, it would have been impossible to guess their ages correctly—enthusiasm invigorates life and maintains one's youth. Unlike most people, they have no unnecessary, concealing layers to discard. They come to us as women who know who they are, certain of their strengths and weaknesses, and glad for each category equally. They greet each other warmly and bustle about in their own preparations. A feeling of contentment imbues my being, as we each take in the faces of seemingly old friends. We are all excited to depart, and soon our van is moving to the waters.

After arriving at the put-in, we go over strokes and canoe safety on shore. Beverly has never held a paddle properly before, and her pretend strokes on land are in their beginning stages of moving air, let alone liquid. That doesn't stop her from enthusiastically clambering into the canoe and working her paddle in the waters at the first opportunity. Six decades of life to my two, and still possessing the spirit and joy of a young child bound on a new adventure! I bubble up at the sight of it all.

Macky in person upends the image of a stocky, hard-working man with grease-lined hands that the name on paper evokes. She is a petite and delicate woman, whose inner vibrancy matches that of her bright, inquisitive eyes. My own eyes watch as her age spills away with each graceful entrance into the canoe, and each powerful, well-guided stroke. Macky had heard these waters were beautiful, and came to see for herself.

&

This morning, the ephemeral fog, rustled by the intimate touch of sunlight, surpasses beauty and enters into the sublime. Such exquisite and gentle motions on a lake's grand scale tantalize one's spirit, alluding to a sensible being weaving the cosmos. The human spirit, deep in contemplation, ponders the infinite splendors that must exist beyond this lake, beyond this earth, beyond those stars, simply because this morning's display seems a fragment of something grander. This expanded sense of scale, out here on wide open waters under a sky that stretches blue infinity in every direction, is humbling. This is nature's finest act: to humble a species whose sense of dominance has increased exponentially with every newly-evolved neural connection. Only nature has that power.

From my stern position in the second boat, I look at the forms of the three women sharing this lake's morning movements with me. I realize that this is what draws us to each other so easily: we each possess a heightened receptiveness to the humbling forces of the natural world. The zig-zag motions of water striders and the long shadows of high mountain peaks evoke equal awe. Nothing is too small nor too common in nature to be denied our utmost respect and appreciation. This carries through to the deep respect we hold for one another. We four women, blissfully alone on this lake, enter into an intimate friendship with the waters and with each other.

We paddle along the water's shore in the soft early light, exploring one small portion of the Lake Umbagog national Wildlife Refuge, which encompasses sixteen thousand acres here on the Maine-New Hampshire border. The lake itself is bisected by the state line; on this trip we keep to the western New Hampshire shore. Our whims rule our course, which meanders with our imaginations around islands and through marsh grasses within secluded coves. There are other campsites scattered along the shore, but seldom does one come upon more than one or two other occupied sites on any given stay. Very few permanent habitations exist on the lake, and it evokes a sense of the pristine in its composition. The refuge contains a diverse array of wildlife habitats, from forest to aquatic communities. It became protected only six years ago, in a national effort to conserve wetlands for the benefit of future generations of living creatures.

A bird rustles. The binoculars are quickly raised, simultaneously. The two older women's friendship quickly deepens as they work together to identify bird species on the lake. The diversity of birds on Umbagog is a constant reminder of the abundance of life found within the ecosystems of this region. Many species of both water and land-dependent birds utilize the refuge for breeding and migration. In the upper reaches of a large, debarked tree, dead but still standing, sits an enormous nest. The tree grows out of the wetlands located north of the headwaters of the Androscoggin on Lake Umbagog. Within the nest rests New Hampshire's only breeding pair of bald eagles, and their fledglings. Their plumage is magnificently textured, and their size, even from a significant distance, is awe-inspiring.

Then there are the loons. Their dark heads dot the lake's surface. The dots then dive, searching for food, before resurfacing in a distant expanse of water. At times they are under for so long that it seems certain that something must have gone asunder in the lake's interior. On those occasions, the loon inevitably pops up in close proximity to the canoe, appearing to mock the folly of humans for measuring the world by human standards of breath-holding.

I wonder often if loons sleep. All day long they dive for food, without seeming to tire. And at night, just as sleep begins to lull the mind and body wrapped in the zippered warmth of the down bag, they begin to cackle. Their cries are the most wild of any I have ever heard. The chatters and shrieks carry out across the water, echoing off the hillsides. The first time those sounds reached my ears I felt certain the word 'lunatic' must have been derived from 'loon'. Beverly used to read a story to her now grown children at bedtime in which the cry of the loons emitted through the pages. "Ha Ha Ha HA!" For years she dreamt of hearing that wild cry. Last night the loons bestowed upon her ears the sounds she had only previously known through a written description. The true sounds thrilled her, and us all. It was nature's birthday gift to Beverly.

We learned early on that Beverly's birthday, one past sixty, lay on this second day of our trip. Furtive exchanges were made amongst the three of us remaining, plotting a small celebration. As we paddle, Beverly in the bow, she tells me how her husband passed away a few years back. She decided then that she would go on a trip every birthday, giving to herself what her husband would have given her if he were still able. The birthday trips would be adventures in new places. So here she is, in a canoe paddling around a region of the north country she's never been to before, holding a paddle she's hardly ever felt before, sleeping in the woods overnight (which she's never done before), with people she's never met before. There is no self-pity in her voice when she speaks about her husband, just a great fondness, and this trip brings her great joy. Beverly is a woman of a character so strong and real that I, just at the point in life where I can call myself woman and believe it, strive to keep the quality of that strength aflicker inside of me.

To give everyone a chance to improve their skills, we switch bow and stern pairs often. To give everyone a chance to learn from each other, we switch partners as well. Now Macky sits in the stern of my boat, and we engage in a quiet conversation about our lives. I listen as she tells me about various environmental organizations she's been a part of, and different conservation projects she has worked on, from New York to her present residence in Maine. We both share a passion for educating people about conserving and protecting natural ecosystems. I've devoted much of the recent years to the biological sciences and environmental education, and felt I'd done quite a bit, but listening to Macky elevates my aspirations to higher standards of achievement. As we exchange thoughts on the design of recycling programs for elementary students, I develop a new appreciation for the harmonious blend our lives create: beautiful ideas come from mixing youthful creativity with the wisdom of Macky's experiences.

At times we all grow quiet, and let the soft sounds of paddles brushing gently through the waters ripple through our persons. The canoes glide serenely, and our motions achieve a harmony that resonates to our souls. Our intrinsic connection to the water and the air is realized in every liquid pull and deep inhalation. We search the sky for birds, the waters for fish, and our spirits for the bounty of life. We have found our place in nature; we enter a state of deep contentment.

In these fluid moments I become mesmerized by the rhythms we create with the waters. My mind lingers on the connection we are drawn by. Our kinship to each other comes in part from the simple fact that we are all women. Of many ages, diverse backgrounds, and varying experiences, we are linked to each other and all women by our innermost perceptions of our surroundings. We hold in us the ability to nurture unselfishly, and we look at our surroundings with this same sense of compassion and commitment. Our emotions run true and vibrant, rooted in a core of strength whose energy surfaces when that which we love most deeply is either near us, or in danger. In tune with the pulses of the natural world, we commune with wild places and with each other in the deepest form.

ș

Late in the afternoon we draw our canoes ashore at our site, laying our weary forms down for a good night's rest. We eat dinner on an exposed bit of rocky shore, overlooking the waters that filled our day. Then, with Macky working to distract Beverly, it's off to the depths of the woods with stove and brownie mix and Bisquick in hand. A large stack of chocolate pancakes grows on a plate, and is decorated with raisins glued on with peanut butter, spelling "Happy B-Day Beverly." We creep back through the forest and burst into song.

Beverly is fully surprised, never expecting a birthday cake out here in this distant wild place. The joyous singing, here in the midst of this beauteous landscape, draws us all down to the same excited, wondering, exploring age of a young child. Out here, existences are ageless, and life is carefree and reinvigorating. Lifetimes of experiences and the energy of youth are mixed into each person equally. We are wonderfully alive.

ș

As the light begins to fade over the waters, I reflect on what it is we are celebrating. Today we celebrate the life of a woman, rich in experience and vibrant as the sun that warmed the napes of our necks at midday on the lake. We celebrate the joys and the sadnesses and the infinite emotions that have deepened her perceptions and infused her life with color. We give thanks for her creation.

That woman's life does not exist alone: it is finely interwoven into the lives of many others, and now we three who sit beside her have gladly become part of the intricate fabric. So today we celebrate women, and the unique friendships that form between this half of our species. We celebrate the depth of trust and respect women are able to form for each other, and the inner strength that we all share somewhere inside us.

We women do not exist alone: we exist within the wonderful infinities of the natural world. So today we celebrate nature, and the many ways that it inspires us to strive for a more harmonious existence. We celebrate the power the wilderness has to humble our beings and invigorate our spirits.

In this wild spot we have become kindred spirits, all women, all lovers of natural places. I am overwhelmed by the internal beauty of the people in my company, and the wild infinity which surrounds us. It feels as if all that exists in the world is we four women, two green canoes, and the wilderness.

—first publication

Grizzly Bear

Susan Marsh

Hours after the members of our backpacking group said good night and headed for their tents, I lay awake in mine. I blamed my sleeplessness on a full moon, the lumpy ground, and my out-of-shape fatigue. But something more kept me awake. I imagined rustling and twig-crunching outside. Each time I convinced myself the noise was only the creek or an intermittent wind washing down the mountainside, it sharpened, snapping me alert. This was my first backpacking trip since I moved from Oregon to Montana, where campers shared the night forests with grizzly bears.

That morning, on a mild Saturday in June, we had gathered at the trailhead in the Pioneer Mountains northwest of Yellowstone for a weekend excursion sponsored by the Montana Wilderness Association. A couple from Butte was already there when my husband Don and I drove in. We shyly introduced ourselves.

The trip's leader, a burly blond man who called himself Wag, skidded his Dodge pickup into the parking lot beside us. One beefy hand grasped the steering wheel. In the other he held a bottle of Henry Weinhardt's. An old tattoo smudged his arm. He looked more like an aging Hell's Angel than a Forest Service landscape architect.

A Subaru with Bozeman plates was the last to arrive. The woman at the wheel peered at Wag from behind her dark mane of hair. Cautiously she approached, and rolled her window down an inch. "Is this the Wilderness Walk?"

We nodded. I could not tell if her weak smile signaled relief or disappointment. "I'm Ruth," she said.

She immediately began questioning Wag. "There aren't any bears around here, are there?"

Wag smirked and drained his beer.

Ruth pushed on. "I know it's silly, but I am scared to death of them."

"There's bears. Probably won't see one here, though. Not a grizzly, anyhow."

"I hope you're right."

Wag reached into the bed of his truck and pulled out another Henry's. "Don't worry about bears. They're damn near extinct. Only about two hundred left in the whole state."

Ruth and I exchanged glances, hoping for reassurance in each other's eyes. Newcomers from opposite coasts, we had signed up for this backpack trip to meet people, see new country, and pitch our tents where a bear was unlikely to wander through. None of the maps I had seen of grizzly bear range included this part of the Beaverhead National Forest.

Wag concluded, "Last October was the last time we got a report of grizzlies around here. We'd be lucky to see one."

Now, awake in my tent as the full moon shone through the fly, I imagined a bear behind every tree.

The few wild bears I had encountered usually sprinted away before I realized what I had seen. Only once, in Wyoming, had a bear failed to bolt. Don and I nearly ran into it on the trail. It followed as we retreated to a talus slope and scrambled up the largest boulder. The bear circled, closing in until it was only thirty feet away. It stood on hind legs for a better look, raised its nose in our direction, and ambled a few steps closer. Its face was broad and concave, characteristic of a grizzly. We clapped our hands and hollered. Don blasted a dog-training whistle, making the bear wince and flatten its ears. Finally, it lumbered down the trail in the direction we planned to go.

We quickly changed our plans. We marched back up the canyon and across a high plateau. At dusk we arrived in the grove of spruce where we had camped two nights before.

As I lay awake in Montana's Pioneer Mountains, I remembered that bold bear. Bold, but not aggressive. It had only been curious, looking for handouts. But its lack of fear had instilled fear in me.

✌

I did not realize I had slept until I sat up, suddenly awake. Something felt wrong. With bears still haunting the back corners of my mind, I listened again for noises. Nothing stirred. I stuck my head out of the tent's zippered door to check on the food bag, hung high in a lodgepole pine.

I glanced around for landmarks. The meadow, the draw where the creek ran, and the talus slopes above all lay in their proper places. But the moonlight drained them of familiarity and benevolence, rendering ghostly images in black and silver. Under my straining eyes, shapes at the far edge of the meadow appeared to jerk and twitch, as if an animal moved among the willows. The moon's position above the western skyline told me it was long into the night. Through the treetops the Big Dipper teetered on its handle. Ursa Major—the Great Bear. I hoped the only bear I saw that night was the one that hung above me in the sky.

I closed the tent flap and slid back into my bag, filled with a vague sense of dread. Don's watch, dangling from a mesh pocket in the side of the tent, read 3:00. Too early to get up, I pressed my back against my husband's warmth and catnapped until the light that hit the tent fly came from the rising sun.

✌

On Monday morning I arrived at my job at the Forest Service headquarters in Bozeman. A note lay on my desk, pencilled in my boss' hasty scrawl. "Gone to West. Investigating bear incident." I ran downstairs for a newspaper.

The headline leapt at me. *Bear Kills, Eats Camper.* At Rainbow Point, a popular campground on the outskirts of the town of West Yellowstone.

Mid-afternoon when Ross returned to the office, I stood at his door. His body sagged, his face was drained. He slumped heavily into his chair and sighed.

"You don't have to talk about it," I said.

He handed me a stack of photographs. A ripped tent. Pine saplings smeared with blood. Ross sighed again. With his eyes fixed on a point across the room, he stared past the half-eaten chocolate doughnut that had lain on his desk since early morning. I looked at a few more of the pictures. Dizzy and nauseated, I handed them back.

"The guy was doing everything right," Ross said. "No food in the tent, even his toothbrush was stashed away. The campground was full of people."

"Did they find the bear?"

"No. But we've got all the campgrounds emptied and closed. Every motel room in West Yellowstone is booked."

"When did it happen?"

"Saturday night. Around 3:00 in the morning."

I whistled softly. The same hour I sat up in my tent in the Pioneers, not many miles away.

Biologists found the bear sleeping off its meal in the cool mud of a willow bottom near the Madison River. It was killed and brought to Bozeman for examination. What had prompted an apparently healthy grizzly bear to enter a crowded campground and pull a man out of his tent as if selecting a sandwich from a vending machine? The biologists had no answers for the newspapers.

"We couldn't find anything wrong with the bear," one researcher said. "But this is unusual behavior. Bears will avoid people unless cornered or injured."

While the biologists scratched their heads, the Forest Service armchair experts offered theories. Most agreed that Yellowstone grizzlies had become aggressive because they were not hunted.

"We need a season on these bears so they'll remember to be afraid of people," one of my colleagues growled. "I never go out without my rifle. It's too bad they didn't clean out the bears a hundred years ago."

My friend Joe, an ardent conservationist, was angry over the bear's death. "This was their home first. With the roads and campgrounds and open dumpsters all over town, it's a wonder there are any bears left around West Yellowstone. We ought to stay out and leave them alone. Without the grizzly bear, there is no wilderness."

For what was left of June, paranoia nearly kept me out of the mountains. I stayed far north of Yellowstone, peering into the forest and listening. As I crept, rather than hiked, the strong opinions of friends and coworkers played over in my mind. Many people expressed great passion for bears, and a fierce desire to protect a creature that could kill and eat them.

I learned what I knew about bears in places less wild than Montana. The bear looming in my mind, fed on legends and lies, was surely larger and more fearsome than the Yellowstone grizzly. But even in Montana, where people claimed to know better, bear lore consisted of tall tales. No one ever came home from an encounter saying, "I saw a grizzly bear today," as if it were a bluebird. There was always a narrow escape, a harrowing scramble up a tree. Hearing these stories made me consider any bear a threat. Now one bear had confirmed my deepest fear. For days after, the light-headed nausea that swept over me when I flipped through Ross' blood-smeared photographs still clung like cobwebs in a darkened closet. I might be eaten.

When Don and I moved to Montana, a friend sent us a book, *The Grizzly Bear*, written in 1909 by William Wright. One evening after the attack at Rainbow Point, I took the book to the backyard hammock and opened it with new interest. I read until twilight.

During his twenty-five years in the company of wild bears, Mr. Wright evolved from trophy hunter to naturalist. He wrote, "I studied the grizzly in order to hunt him. I came to hunt him in order to study him. I laid aside my rifle."

Wright began his career by hunting what he saw as a ferocious predator, the bear of the imagination. After years of observation, he discovered a creature worthy of respect. He ended his book with the conclusion that grizzly bears were defensive, not aggressive. They did not go looking for trouble, but avoided it if they could. The same thing the biologists were telling us now. What would Mr. Wright have made of the bear at Rainbow Point?

Grizzly bears seemed intent on proving the experts wrong. The summer had scarcely begun, and already they had mauled hikers in Glacier National Park and raided dumpsters in Cooke City. They were killing sheep by the dozens in the Absarokas. And now one had pulled a tourist from Wisconsin out of his sleeping bag for a meal. If these bears weren't looking for trouble, what were they up to?

Like people, bears were unpredictable. I did not know them well enough to tell the shy ones from the killers, so my reaction was to assume the worst about them all. Yet they fascinated me, emblems of the wilderness I loved. Wherever I found signs of bears, I knew the land would be big enough, wild enough, for me. But I still wanted to be at the top of the food chain, able to walk down a trail without fearing for my life. The grizzly bear made me consider what I was really asking for, when I asked for wilderness. The only parts of Montana without grizzlies were those from which they had been eliminated. My preference for hiking in those bear-free zones made me wonder—did I agree more with my coworker, who thought all grizzlies should be shot, than I did with my conservationist friends? Did I want a forest cleansed of dangerous predators, made safe and sanitized? I did not think so. I liked seeing old claw marks on the trees, piles of scat full of berries. But I wanted to keep my distance. I hoped the bears would keep theirs too.

In my hammock, and at the university library, I kept reading about bears. The grizzly resisted my attempts to comprehend it. It retained its mystery even to the experts, despite the radio collars and maps of its migrations around the Yellowstone region. The grizzly was a singular, different sort of creature, ready to disprove whatever we concluded about it. Still people sought human-like, or at least understandable, behavior in the bear. What we hoped to find was kinship. I recalled from photographs that a bear, when skinned, looked especially human, curled like a sleeping child. It looked too much like us not to share some of our traits.

Grizzlies once seemed like big friendly dogs, begging doughnuts from tourists and sidling up to the garbage-dump "lunch counters" in Yellowstone. In those days, we knew the bears as simple creatures looking for a free meal. With the dumps long closed, the bears were wild again, ineffable. The one I had encountered in Wyoming stared with tawny, inscrutable eyes. In them I tried to read familiar urges and emotions. I concluded it was curious, investigating the possibility of a candy bar. When the bear turned around at last to leave us, its gait suggested nothing so much as boredom. But my attempts to read its gestures did not alter the reality of the bear, a bear beyond my knowing. For many moments I stared down the trail to where it vanished, before I slid off the boulder and ran the other way.

I began to read beyond biology, searching for the bear of myth and literature. I found that the grizzly bear had starred in stories as ancient as humanity. Surprisingly, the storied bear was often depicted as a transformative healer, the giver of life. The bear, in its hibernation, brought forth new life each spring, a creature of beginnings and rebeginnings. A creature signifying resurrection.

The bear, with its symbolism of rebirth, implied a prior death. With its power to kill and to bring forth new life, perhaps the bear offered a model for profound change. Who, after all, did not feel changed after a close encounter with a bear? The one that had me scrambling up a boulder in Wyoming remained vivid in my mind for years. A creature that could brand its image upon me asked a question—what part of myself was I seeking to avoid? What inner transformation did I fear?

By encountering bears in the forest, in the newspapers, or in the ancient myths I was transformed from a blithe recreational hiker to wary potential prey. Because of the bear I began to see the forest with new eyes, eyes that had reason to stay alert. From now on I would notice the snap of twig, the dark shape in the shadows, and understand what they implied.

            🐾

After the hike into the Pioneers, I joined the Montana Wilderness Association. As a membership gift I received a belt buckle. I opened the box to find a bronze grizzly bear looking back at me. Around the bear's face curved the words, "Montana Wilderness." As Joe had said: The bear, the wilderness—one and the same.

Included in the box was an invitation to a potluck for new members in Bozeman.

When I arrived, Ruth waved from across the room. I found a plate and helped myself to a brown, savory biscuit. As I sighed with pleasure at the first warm bite, a bearded man with sandy gray hair grinned.

"Like those?" he asked.

"They're wonderful. Did you make them?"

"My specialty. Grizzly biscuits."

"Why do you call them that?"

"After the secret ingredient. Grizzly bear fat."

I smiled. Surely he was kidding.

"Dan guides for an outfitter in the Yukon," my hostess whispered. "They hunt grizzlies. He brings back enough lard for a year's worth of potlucks."

I began to eat the biscuit more slowly, though not with any less pleasure, trying to discern the taste of grizzly bear in the rich, sweet flakes. Eating of the bear, like some forbidden fruit, inspired both thrill and guilt. I forgot about the other items on my plate, absorbed in each bite of grizzly biscuit.

Did eating of the bear lend me any of its spirit? I did not feel braver or stronger after one biscuit, so I reached for another. Somewhere in my body there were cells absorbing bear grease, molecules of grizzly becoming part of my own mantle of fat. Would the next bear I encountered in the forest sense that I had eaten grizzly biscuits? Would it be angry, or afraid?

I worried that eating of the bear might make me its enemy. Television nature programs from my childhood, with their footage of lions running down gazelles, had instilled in me the idea that predators were always the enemy of prey. Remorse began to intrude on my enjoyment of the biscuit. I did not want to be the enemy of grizzly bears. I wished the hunter in Canada had missed his shot, and that this bear remained a bulky shadow in the forest.

⛀

In August I walked through a stand of lodgepole pines a few miles west of Rainbow Point. Knowing I was trespassing in bear country, I practiced an absurd combination of stealthy walking and loud singing. Many of the pines around me wore long vertical gouges left by claws. I wore my bronze belt buckle like an amulet, as if this display of solidarity with the bear might offer some protection.

Though I would have felt more comfortable among trees with fewer claw marks, I walked that trail for reconciliation. This was the bears' home before it was mine. This was wilderness, complete with all its predators. Under the canopy of pines roamed lynx and fishers, wolverines and grizzly bears. Wolf tracks had been seen on the plateau above. Somehow, we had to hold this complete, priceless wilderness together.

Like the wilderness, the bear survived because enough people sought to hold it together. Though we feared the grizzly when it came too close, we feared more our power to extinguish such a creature. Through inattention or willful destruction, we had already extinguished too many other creatures, too many other wildernesses. In Yellowstone our voices gathered: *Don't let it happen here.*

From myths and science, knowledge and experience, a new picture of the grizzly bear emerged. Each image was an overlay, a transparent sheet through which I could see the others. When I peeled back the vision of a brute on hind legs swinging its head menacingly at me, I found a gentle bear sitting on its haunches eating berries. They were the same bear, threatening and benign, feared and revered. The Yellowstone grizzly minded its business, resisting the human intrusions at its door.

In 1909 William Wright lamented, "When my grandfather was born, the grizzly had never been heard of. If my grandson ever sees one it will likely be in the bear pit of a zoological garden."

Wright's grandson could still see a grizzly bear in Yellowstone. The old man would be pleased to know this, I thought. As I continued through the forest, I paused at each marked tree, fingering the pitchy scars. Like beacons they announced, *Here wild bears still thrive, to dig roots and catch spawning trout, to mate and den and bring new cubs into the world. To feed our imagination and dreams.*

Living in bear country tapped a tattoo into my brain: even at the outskirts of Bozeman I kept our garbage can in a shed and glanced toward the apple trees and garden whenever I walked outside at night. I paid attention, walking in forests like this, knowing that I trespassed, knowing I might be observed. Like a lodgepole pine with parallel grooves running down its trunk, my life was marked by the presence of bears.

Wag had said only two hundred grizzly bears remained in Montana. Every year there were more people. Though part of me feared them, I knew the bears had more to fear from us.

The crack of a twig jerked me alert. I froze in place and strained to hear, boring into the shadows with owlish eyes. From an alder-choked gully in front of me came the snap of branches breaking, the thud of heavy footfalls. My pulse pounded in my throat. I glanced around at the trees in case I needed to climb one. None had a limb I could reach. What if I had chanced upon a cub, whose mother was nearby? How stupid of me to be walking in this place, out of earshot from anyone who might come to my rescue. The thrashing in the alders continued, but I could not catch a glimpse of a moving branch or the blur of a running animal. It's probably just an elk, I said aloud, while images of half-eaten bodies and saplings slick with blood flooded my head.

I stood still as a doe until the sound vanished into the forest. I never saw the bear.

—first publication

White Water, Dark Future

Carol Ann Bassett

From its source in the Chilean Andes, the Bío-Bío River drifts gently through pine forests and wheat fields before picking up speed on its long journey down to the sea. More than a hundred rapids appear throughout the canyon—great churning holes that rival even those on the Colorado River in the Grand Canyon or the Zambezi in Africa. Yet from our camp the first night in a bowl-shaped valley, the Bío-Bío (pronounced *BEE-o BEE-o*) did not appear to be the tumultuous cauldron we had heard about. Instead, the water was so calm we could nearly see our reflections as the moon rose high above the canyon.

There were seventeen of us, ranging in age from twenty-seven to fifty-seven—including an architect, a botanist, two doctors, a muralist, and a judge. A well-traveled group, we had sailed the waters of the Galápagos, kayaked in China, climbed the Himalayas, and even photographed sharks from an underwater cage. That left the Bío-Bío River, the Olympics of white water adventure, whose class V rapids— the highest class runnable by commercial outfitters—place it among the ten wildest rivers in the world. We had come to challenge its rapids but also to mourn them: Six massive dams are planned in the heart of the canyon. Although the dams will generate electricity throughout Chile and Argentina, they will also flood the river, its rapids, and the homeland of Chile's most traditional culture—the Mapuche Indians.

Our journey began near Lonquimay, a small ranching town in the foothills of the Andes, a little more than four hundred miles south of Santiago. For five days, we would descend the river in two rubber rafts, a paddleboat, and three kayaks. On the first morning, we launched our small fleet of boats into the current. There were no rapids here, only ripples pierced by the slow swing of oars. We floated down past snow-capped volcanoes and tree-studded cliffs. The mossy banks, the hanging ferns, the black-stained seeps, seemed a giant tapestry woven into the earth.

In the afternoon we passed by Chilpaco, a town born overnight during a gold strike in 1932 and now abandoned. We stopped for lunch on a broad, sandy beach, then hiked through meadows to an alpine lake called Laguna María y Jesús. It had been a dry year, and Chile was in a drought. In the last few weeks the sapphire waters of the lake had dropped more than twenty feet, and once-submerged logs now littered the shoreline. We dived in anyway and bobbed around, observing the tortured shapes of the granite peaks, the scarring left by glaciers, and the araucaria pines that seemed to sprout from the mountains like hair.

Scientists believe that the araucaria, which can live more than a thousand years, once existed from Brazil all the way down to Antarctica. They also believe that South America was connected to Africa and New Zealand, and that a land bridge once united Chile and California. The Bío-Bío itself is thought to have changed direction in a cataclysmic upheaval, flowing north instead of south, when tectonic plates collided beneath the continent.

The river originates in Lago Galletue, high in the Andes near the Argentine border. If flows for nearly two hundred miles before emptying into the Pacific at Concepción. It can be rafted only during the Chilean summer, when melting snowpack contributes enough water for boats to descend safely. We would travel about seventy miles of the Bío-Bío, about sixteen miles a day, stopping for lunch along the shore and camping in the pines.

Although it was February, the sun didn't set until 9 p.m. That gave us time to explore our camp near the ranching town of Troyo. David, our botanist, roamed the area identifying summer wildflowers along the banks of the river: Queen Anne's lace, purple irises, bright red fuchsia. Throughout the afternoon, *huasos,* Chilean cowboys with silver spurs, passed by on their horses and smiled at us in amusement. When the sun had set, we uncorked a bottle of Chilean wine and settled down to a dinner of corn on the cob, salad with white cheese and olives, and a rich beef soup.

We had come here with a small Chilean rafting company, Altue Expediciónes, owned by a young entrepreneur named Francisco Valle. Francisco would carry our gear in his jeep, high and dry along a primitive road that follows the river, meeting up with us each night at camp. We would brave the rapids with our guides. Our lead boatman was Sergio Andrade, a ponytailed artist and carpenter from a small community near Santiago. Sergio had a strong, dark face, yet there was a softness to him—the way he quietly hauled water up from the river and chopped the wood for our campfires. I knew he would set the tone for our journey, and I decided to travel in his raft. Alex Astorga was captain of the paddleboat. Tall and lean, with muscles the color of burnt sienna, he could run over boulders while carrying a kayak in a single hand. Whale was a hulk of a man from Arizona. A typical river rat, he roamed from country to country, rowing the Colorado in the summer and the Bío-Bío in winter. Whale rolled his own cigarettes and drank bourbon from a flask. He loved telling campfire tales, and on this particular night he was talking about some gruesome mishaps in Lava South rapid—a leg pierced by an oar, a jaw shoved clear into someone's cranium. Lava South lay only a few days away. Rather than listen, I rose from my place near the fire and followed Sergio down to the river to look at the stars.

The sky was full of unfamiliar constellations: Achernar, Altar, the Turkey, and the Ship. Hydra resembled a serpent. The Southern Cross floated like a kite. By comparison, the northern skies seemed all but starless. The wind picked up and rumbled through the pines. It had grown colder, and I pulled my knees to my chest for warmth. "Can you tell the difference between the sound of the water and the sound of the wind?" Sergio suddenly asked me.

I pondered his strange koan and admitted I could not.

"One is constant and gentle," he said. "The other is wild and capricious."

Which, I wondered, was which?

In the first twenty-five miles the Bío-Bío passed through moss-covered forests before cutting across a broad plateau. Turquoise waterfalls plunged a hundred feet into the river. Runoff from the melting snow coursed down side canyons. As we rounded a bend, Volcán Callaqui appeared large and majestic, a plume of smoke curling from its perpetual snows. We were passing through the roots of the Andes. *Nalca* plants, "poor man's umbrella," rose from the rocks with elephant-ear leaves. The blossom of a vine called *copihue*—Chile's national flower—dangled from trees like small red trumpets. From time to time, a flock of slender-billed parakeets wheeled across the river. It seemed strange to see parrots this far south, and, gazing up at them, I thought I heard something like a waterfall.

"Rapids," said Sergio, standing on the wooden platform in the raft and peering downstream.

Suddenly we were plunging through a maze of rocks called *el culebrón,* "the big snake." Down we went through a serpentine maze. Cold waves washed over us in the front of the boat as we bounced off rocks. Before we could finish bailing, we entered *el abretón,* "the big squeeze," a narrow chute between a house-sized boulder and a vertical wall. If these were class II and III rapids, what must lie ahead?

With no watches, no calendars, and no schedules to follow, we found the days slipping by without our noticing. We began adapting to the natural rhythms of the canyon. The women in our group grew less self-conscious and more beautiful; the men stopped shaving. One morning, while bathing in the river, I saw a black-faced ibis, large as an emu, standing on a rock, presumably hunting for insects or frogs. Startled by my presence, it rose with a great flapping of wings, sending out a metallic call as it disappeared up the canyon.

The bird life on the Bío-Bío was extremely rich. There were spectacled ducks, mountain gulls, and *chucaos*—robin-like birds considered soothsayers to the Mapuche Indians who live in the canyon. It is believed that if the warning call of the chucao reaches the listener's ears from the left, danger will befall him. So strongly do the Mapuche believe this that upon hearing the bird they will turn in their tracks and go home.

On the third day, we began to enter the homeland of the Mapuche (also known as Pehuenche and Araucano). "Ah-hoo!" called Sergio, cupping his hands to his mouth. Voices called back from wheat fields high above the river. Oxen appeared with crude wooden carts, and smoke spiraled from the chimneys of log houses. A young goatherd paused on the shoreline. Our ragtag appearance, the odd movements of our boat, made even his small flock of goats stop and stare before dashing off to safety.

We must have looked like a ship of fools. Never once would we see a Mapuche on the river. Local legend says that those who drown spend the rest of their days in *chenque*—a watery cave far below the river. The Mapuche were not foolish enough to tempt that fate.

How so mighty a river could have so diminutive a name remains something of a mystery. Bío-Bío is a Mapuche word for the song of a small green flycatcher, the Chilean elaenia. The word Mapuche means "people of the earth." When the Incas pushed south in the 1400s the Mapuche held them back with bows and arrows. The Spanish fared no better in the centuries that followed, colonizing Chile but leaving the Mapuche, after a few bloody battles, to lead a quiet subsistent life, gathering pine nuts, worshipping the spirits of the mountains, and hunting the rich fauna of the cordillera. Still, contact with the outside world has brought change. Gone now are the *guanaco* (a relative of the llama), the *guemal* (a long-eared Andean deer), and the *pudu* (a smaller deer that once flourished in the southern forests). Some Mapuche wear Nikes and T-shirts with such statements as JAMES DEAN'S ALIVE, unfortunate gifts from rafters. The week we passed through, the wise men of one village were decked out in red ESPN baseball caps; a television crew had visited not long before and thoughtlessly awarded the hats as souvenirs, thus wrecking the cultural pristineness they'd come to document.

The Mapuche reminded me of the Tarahumara Indians of Mexico's Sierra Madre. They had learned to adapt in the harshest of regions, growing their crops on steep hillsides and surviving six-month-long winters. Despite their limited contact with the outside world, however, the Mapuche exhibited an openness not often found in so isolated a culture. Many have even learned Spanish in addition to their own language, Mapudiingii.

One day, while exploring the countryside along the river, I met an old woman walking down the road. Her tattered skirt had been mended a dozen times and was held together in some places with safety pins. She wore hand-knit socks and shoes of brown and white speckled cowhide. Her waist-length hair was bound beneath a kerchief, blowing in the wind as she approached with a small ceramic bowl.

"Hello," I said. "Where are you going with that bowl?"

"Down to my house. Do you want to come look at my weavings?"

I followed Olga, for that was her name, down a dusty path leading to her house high above the river. It was harvest time, and her family had already cut their wheat. In a circular-shaped corral, a man and two girls cleaned the wheat by tossing it high into the air with wooden shovels. Once the wheat had been separated from the chaff, they would load it onto ox-drawn carts and haul it down the road to be ground into flour.

Olga motioned for me to sit at a long wooden table. Her husband and son joined us. Then she disappeared into her shack and returned with a bowl of wheat kernels soaked in water. She placed it before me and smiled with approval as I began to eat. Where do you come from? she asked. Is it very far away? Does it snow in your country? Do you chop firewood like we do?

Olga had only one small weaving made from the wool of her sheep. I bought it, not because I needed it, but because it was beautiful. She said she had lived in the canyon all her life. Three generations of her family had been born in this very house—her husband, their children, their grandchildren.

I asked if they knew about the dams.

"We've heard about them," said her son, José.

"Will you have to move?"

"We're not sure yet, but if we do, they will have to buy our farm and give us money to survive. We can't leave our home without money to begin somewhere else, and we don't have any money."

"Where will you go if they flood your land?"

"Farther up into the mountains," he said, waving his hand toward the tallest peaks. "But it's very cold up there, and it will be much more difficult to survive."

The wind ripped across the yard, stirring up dust devils as I followed the road back to camp. Far below, the Bío-Bío turned blood-red in the falling light. It seemed extraordinary that after all these years Olga's family and an estimated two thousand other Mapuche would be displaced by the development of dams by the Chilean company ENDESA. Not once, the Indians said, had an offer been made for their land, nor had any new land been set aside for them. Though the Mapuche had been successful in holding back earlier invaders, it was unlikely they would be able to defeat the new *conquistadores*—the dam builders.

Near the community of Quepuca, Mapuche women greeted us on shore, selling weavings and hand-knit socks. We changed into dry clothes and set up camp in a large clearing above the river. Francisco, the owner of the rafting company, wanted to prepare a traditional Mapuche dinner, so I followed him and Sergio up the road into the trees. We must have visited three houses before we found what we were looking for.

At the home of Juana and José Alcán, Sergio purchased a young black goat and tethered its legs with rope. Juana's son, José, laid the goat on a table and sharpened his knife. Then gently grasping the animal's snout, he pushed the blade deeply into its throat. As Juana collected the blood in a shallow tin pan, she whispered something to the goat in the soft sounds of the Mapuche language. Later, when the blood had coagulated, she would make *ñache*—an uncooked soup with onions, chili, and lemons.

Back at camp, José roasted the goat over red-hot coals. He stood squarely in the dirt, one hand on his hip, the other resting on a long metal poker. In the glow of the flames, he seemed almost lost in thought as his friend Juan appeared. "Mari-mari (hello)," said Juan. "I see you're doing the cooking tonight!" We invited the two to dinner—a feast of sizzling goat with corn and potatoes, cheese, bread, and salad.

Around the campfire that night, the conversation centered on the dams. Smoke billowed through the trees as Juan threw another branch on the fire. "Imagine," he said, "all of this land, the very land we're standing on, will be flooded. We will lose our homes, our animals, our wheat fields—all we've ever worked for our entire lives. We need to become more organized, to pressure the government, yet there are people throughout this canyon who aren't even aware of the dams. Where do we begin when we are all so spread about, from Quepuca to Temuco?"

When the fire had died down, I climbed a small rise to my sleeping bag and watched the stars. I felt a kind of power in this canyon, something ancient yet vaguely familiar. Maybe it was the sacrifice of the goat, but that night strange visions entered my sleep. I dreamed that a large black buffalo carried me on its back through a sun-drenched canyon. Onward we galloped through a shallow stream, the water spraying from its hooves like prisms. The coarse fur of the beast against my thighs, the wind in my hair, seemed so real that I could not tell whether I'd been dreaming or not.

I awakened to the slow ringing of an axe: Sergio chopping firewood for our morning coffee. I rose, slipped on my shoes, and climbed a hill where someone had erected a cross. Three young hawks rose from its crossbeam. I sat on a rock observing the mists that had settled over the Andes. Range upon range dissolved into blue until I could not tell where the earth ended and the sky began.

By afternoon, the sun beat down, burning our faces as we entered a dark basalt gorge. It was our fourth day on the river and tension was high. No one said much; even Whale had grown quiet. Just ahead lay the class IV and V rapids everyone was dreading: Jugbuster, Milky Way, Lost Yak, and Lava South. We made it through the first three without mishap. Then we pulled in to scout from boulders high above the river. Lava South was one of the worst rapids I'd ever seen. The water was dangerously low. Sharp, glistening rocks protruded. Stomach-churning holes appeared everywhere. Our entry was critical; if we veered too far in either direction we'd be doomed.

Down we slipped on a silver tongue into the throat of the rapid. Sergio pulled hard to the left, his muscles straining as we jammed into a boulder. "High side!" he yelled. We shifted our weight toward the rock and slid free again, but before we knew it we were spinning into a giant hole. Water pounded us from every direction. We clung to the lifeline until our knuckles turned white. At last we were flushed out again—alive, in the lapping current.

In an eddy we bailed and awaited the others. Near the first big hole, Whale's raft teetered dangerously on a rock and nearly capsized. Then Alex's boat appeared, its seven paddles digging wildly in the air as it bounced over boulders. We waited a long time for the kayakers. Two of them made it through; the third had decided to portage.

At Las Termas de Avellano, Francisco greeted us with cold champagne. We spent the rest of the afternoon mindlessly soaking in hot springs and diving into the river until the moon came up. Later that night, strange objects began to appear in the sky. Every few minutes, meteorites whizzed over the canyon. Then something much larger and brighter appeared. It was moving fast, and its long green tail lit up the sky for at least twenty seconds. In the morning we heard on a shortwave radio that a Soviet satellite had reentered the earth's atmosphere and crashed in Argentina. It had passed almost directly over camp.

The morning was crisp, clear, and calm. Torrent ducks sunned themselves above blue-green pools, and cormorants flew ahead of the rafts. We proceeded through a narrow lava gorge, its rocks so tortured that in places they appeared to have been squeezed from a tube of paint. We hit some minor rapids—A Hundred Waterfalls, Obelisk, and many without names. "What's this one?" we asked. Sergio thought for a moment and said, "The Carousel." As we entered, he spun the raft in circles, pulling hard on the oars until the sky was spinning above us. Peals of laughter rose from our boat. But the back-to-back Royal Flush rapids, the river's most challenging, lay just ahead, and we sobered up fast.

We had magnificent runs through the first two, then pulled over to scout One-Eyed Jack. Could a rapid be worse? An enormous boulder rose from the center of the river, splitting it in two. Eighteen-foot waves crashed against rocks and tumbled down huge chutes. One-Eyed Jack wasn't a rapid; it was a waterfall. One false move and we'd be joining the watery denizens of chenque far beneath the river. "It looks wicked," said Whale as he scrambled back down to his boat. "We're really going for a ride."

The water carried us on its back through the heart of the rapid. We glided over rocks and dived through waves. The bilge brimmed with water, yet every move, every stroke of the oars had been carefully orchestrated by Sergio.

A perfect run—we had made it down the legendary Bío-Bío River. In the calm waters ahead, on the final stretch of our journey, Alex played an Andean song on his bamboo flute, its high lively notes echoing off the canyon walls. Whale passed around his flask of bourbon. Sergio laid down his oars and let the river carry us. Sunlight danced on the water in coronas. We had grown unusually quiet. It was as though we had just emerged from the womb of the canyon.

Then the first signs of the dam appeared. As we rounded a bend near Ralco, construction workers could be seen on a cliff high above a water-gauge station where someone had spray-painted the slogan *LONG LIVE THE BIO-BIO*. Men perched like locusts on an electrical tower reaching halfway into the clouds. Across the river, bulldozers had made enormous claw marks in the canyon walls. Entire hillsides had been cleared of trees. Now, muddy water drained into the river near floating logs, and bright orange markers indicated where the shoreline of the lake would be. I wanted to know more about the dams, and later I paid a visit to the field office of ENDESA, high above the river.

At the entrance to a sheet metal building, a bright poster proclaimed the Bío-Bío *A REGION OF OPPORTUNITIES*. Tiny boats sailed on future lakes. New hotels and ski resorts appeared in the mountains. Cattle barons and loggers dominated the imaginary landscape. Alejandro Mercado, chief engineer of the Pangue Dam project, greeted me at the door and led me down a hallway, past workers busily hunched over maps.

"We don't get many visitors here," he said. "What do you want to know about the dams?"

Chile needed more electricity because it had failed to keep up with the growing population, Mercado said. When the six dams are completed, they will provide more than ten percent of the nation's energy. Unfortunately, he admitted, they will also affect white-water adventure on one of Chiles most famous rivers. "The river will continue to pass through [parts of] the canyon, but the dams will interrupt the journey of rafters."

Once the dams are built, the ecological loss will be greater than that. The *lleque* tree, a rare fir that grows along the river, will disappear. So will parts of the araucaria forest, which the Mapuche depend on for survival because of the nutritious seeds produced by the tree's large cones. Ecologists consider the araucaria pine an endangered species; the Mapuche consider it sacred. The destruction of the forests will in turn affect the habitats of such large mammals as the puma, the Andean fox, and the wild boar, all of which have been observed along the Bío-Bío in winter. Bacteria, silt, and a lack of oxygen in the man-made lakes will also kill trout and salmon for considerable distances downstream. The rare bronze-winged duck, which cannot survive on lakes, could also be imperiled. So could the Andean condor, the slender-billed parakeet, and the gray-headed goose, the latter of which the Mapuche domesticate as a food source.

And what of the Mapuche themselves? Given their history and close connection to the land, I could not imagine them assimilating into the dominant culture of Chile, nor could I envision them abandoning their homes without a struggle.

Near our final camp in a broad, grassy field, bulldozers screamed across the land, clearing trees and blazing roads to the dam site. As we unloaded our rafts that afternoon, it was difficult to believe that the Bío-Bío will no longer flow wild and free. Choked off and harnessed like so many great rivers, it will lie beneath an artificial lake where motorboats smoke and whine on waters defiled by litter.

By destroying the natural world, were we not also destroying something in ourselves—the freedom of the human spirit, the need to dream? These thoughts weighed heavily on us as we packed our gear into a bus the next morning and followed the dirt road out of the canyon. Far below us, the Bío-Bío glinted silver in the morning light.

—from *Condé Nast Traveler*

A Map for Hummingbirds

Ellen Meloy

Montana's wild geese migrate in family units. They navigate by memory
and topography—the shape of a mountain, a curve of river—and by
an internal compass that responds to the earth's magnetic field. The
point bird in the distinctive V-shaped formation is usually a gander,
although the geese change position frequently. Updrafts of air behind
each wing in the V reduce drag for all but the leader, which must drop
back to rest. Think of the V as a single creature: aerodynamically fluid
and energy efficient, adjusting its flight pattern by loud honks.

Borne by sturdy bodies and powerful wings, the geese stay aloft for
hours. The peoples of old did not underestimate the endurance of
migratory birds with large body mass. They also observed, correctly,
that hummingbirds migrate but presumed that such tenderly small
creatures—birds that must eat constantly to fuel a rapid-fire heartbeat—
could not fly long distances on their own without dropping dead. Thus,
according to folk belief, big Canada geese would carry tiny, fragile,
hitchhiking hummingbirds on their backs when they migrated.

A cold front can trigger migration in the fall, although the precise
moment of departure is never predictable. Not all goose families are of
like mind about staying or leaving or when. One minute they might
be nibbling succulent plant bits in a serene valley, the next minute they
rise into the clean blue air above the Montana-Idaho border. Below
lies a rumpled cordillera of rocks and ice and a pickup winding along
the Interstate highway. Inside the truck are two humans, also migrants,
also at odds about staying or leaving or when. Cranked on for the first
time in months, the truck heater smells like melting chihuahuas. The
man drives. The woman, who never wears socks south of Pocatello,
takes off her battered desert sandals, pulls on a pair of woolies and

shoes, then stares down at her feet as if they were freshly embalmed mummies. Paths cross. The distance between sky and road, wing and tire, diminishes sound but not a vague sense of air flowing in opposite directions. The southbound geese comb our northbound hair.

Birds respond to changes in their environment by migrating. In temperate North America the best strategy is to move south for the winter to warmer terrain, where better menus flourish, and to return north in the spring, where the mild season and longer daylight hours favor mating, nesting, feeding, and growing up. Nature, of course, never quite sticks to the grid. Some birds head south when they should head north. My ornithology book defines reverse migration as bird movement that proceeds in the direction opposite the one expected for the season. If a storm or heavy winds sweep them off course, for instance, the birds fly back to the beginning or to a point where instinct reorients them to their preferred lane of passage.

Reverse migration is the metaphor of my life in Montana. My husband's seasonal work as a backcountry ranger and a home we built in southern Utah keep us in the desert during the hottest months, from early spring until late fall. Our slightly delirious Utah life, spent largely outdoors, unfolds in the sensuous red-gold light of a heat-scorched, tense, skinless earth fissured with deep canyons and upthrust in sandstone monoliths. Each winter I haul my lizard pelt and desert soul back to our Montana home, blue-starved. For months I have not seen so much light at this end of the spectrum: thick conifer forests the color of malachite, steel-gray peaks creased with cobalt shadows, lofty cornices underlined with blue-violet cusps of snow. Montana is a sojourn in northern light.

The truck moves through an indigo dark. The geese push onward to open water and a rest. At this point in our migration all other vehicles have fallen off Idaho, whose edge meets an abyss into outer space—or so it seems. Our vehicle slips solo up the massive plateau that hovers above the rest of the continent like Coleridge's Xanadu ("That sunny dome! those caves of ice!"), a distant, glittering place undercut by something dark and alluring. The night beyond our high beams obliterates all horizons, all distinction between land and sky. The lights of scattered ranches become stars. Nothing but the ground beneath me tells me that gravity exists. Away from towns spread like islands in Montana's vast space, few travelers are immune to the floating sensation caused by this blanket of darkness.

Geographers often describe Montana's size with the how-many-states-can-fit-into-it measure. Nearly three Connecticuts. A couple of Vermonts. One slightly distended West Virginia. Stretch the analogy further: overlay Massachusetts onto southwestern Montana, where I live. The Crazy Mountains impale Boston, tossing half a million people downslope into a rude heap. Cape Cod's curled finger tickles a paltry number of sage-freckled acres west of Twodot, and the Connecticut River disappears into the Missouri like a lost noodle. The Berkshire Hills form a dust cover to the Scapegoat Wilderness. Cowboys from Deer Lodge sell Housatonic gentry a few sizable cattle outfits. The city of Butte pierces the overlay, startling everyone in New Bedford with a giant open-pit copper mine. Yellowstone National Park, however, now sits conveniently in their backyard.

Montana easily fits Gertrude Stein's remark, "more space where nobody is than where anybody is." The journalist Joseph Kinsey Howard called Montana "the space between people," implying that a vehicle and a few tanks of gas are needed merely to bring you close enough to see if the other person's eyes are blue or brown. So much space fosters deep introspection, philosophic distraction, fierce independence, and narrative inventiveness—desirable traits for writers, cowboys, and that up-and-coming New West prodigy, the golf pro. Under the Big Sky, human and landscape exist in the right proportion to one another; comfort is found in one's own insignificance. As a young, insignificant woman I believed that Montana's humbling and informing scale would provide the proper vessel for my terminal restlessness, my notion that home could be found in movement itself. I felt that rootlessness might find root in a place of this size.

Some birds, notably young gulls, herons, and egrets, do not always migrate in predictable seasonal directions. Juvenile wandering can be linear—the young birds head north as the rest of the colony heads south—or explosive: they move in all directions and at considerable distances from their hatching area. When immature birds cannot compete successfully for food with older birds, they must wander until they find an adequate food supply for themselves.

Years ago I came to Montana as a juvenile wanderer, a native westerner exchanging one rural home for another. Behind me I dragged previous lives—student, lifeguard, hermit—and ahead lay a buffet of new ones. I made a living in technical illustration, churning out laboriously stippled pen-and-inks of bones and feathers, detailed diagrams of geological strata, and the cell divisions of anxious amoebas. The medium enriched my knowledge of science and gave me thumb calluses, thick reading glasses, and the revelation that my art, so meticulous in nature, was also extremely uptight. For relief I painted barns.

In the Rockies' brief growing season I jump-started my garden inside a junked farm truck, its cab and windshield facing south, its windows adjusted for ventilation. This greenhouse yielded seedlings for tons of unlikely tomatillos and one cantaloupe the size and flavor of a used tennis ball. Montana's weather crossed Seattle with the Yukon: one storm covered the land in humid, brooding skies, the next in brittle, frigid air that burned the skin like poisoned needles. Contrary to predictions, winter didn't kill me. I boldly crawled under the house to thaw my pipes with a blow dryer. When a more severe cold snap froze every molecule of liquid in my house except a tumbler of whiskey, I drank the whiskey. I survived winter's cold but not its length; each year I fled to the desert to cheat it.

In Montana I married a man who called his sleeping bag "Doris" and lived three blocks from where he was born. At the time of his birth, in the early fifties, the neighborhood boasted a hospital, a convent, modest family homes, and one active and at least five former brothels. On one of our first dates he took me to a bird refuge in a remote intermontane valley, where he shot a duck and served me its tiny butchered breasts for dinner. Before I could decide how I felt about dead duck, he told me its name: bufflehead. We were eating bufflehead breasts.

In Montana I learned to fly-fish, row a river raft, belly dance, and herd sheep. I frost-nipped my feet on cross-country ski trips in moonlight and rearranged my knee cartilage on treks across mountains with a heavy pack. The land seemed so vast, each season so deep, adventure became irresistible, even if moments of exquisite beauty had to be earned by extreme pain. These years matched youth to place, reckless energy to a land that does not yield easy living to anyone.

Perhaps the southbound geese that flew above our northbound heads picture their winter grounds as an enormous open-air restaurant; their primary occupation is to eat. On my feeding grounds on the upper Missouri River, I exchange the lusty, brainless, overheated, intimately physical life of the desert for winter's distinct mood of reflection. I trade summer's harlotry of color for what Melville called a "fixed trance of whiteness." I trade the wild for shelter.

My street abuts a million acres of timbered high country along the Continental Divide, possibly the last street until the next town nearly ninety miles away. Here, edge of town means a distinct, palpable border. On the tamed side of the wilderness, below our house, lies the old redlight quarter and, wedged into a narrow gulch, a dense cluster of commercial buildings with ornate facades of sandstone and granite. Montana's innards—gold, silver, copper, lead—paid the bill and fed the town's aspirations to worldliness. A delirious mix of architectural elements borrowed from the Italian Romanesque, French Renaissance, midwestern American Gothic, and mining-camp Baroque doesn't quite hide a frontier soul. Similar opulence is found on the downtown's other flank, merely a gulch away from the whorehouses, in a neighborhood of stately mansions built at the turn of the century by mining magnates who followed a cardinal rule: The dirtier your mine, the farther you live from it. They lived here, close to their banks.

What could be more western than an endemic confusion of virtues? As towns like mine outgrew their frontier motleyness, civic pride called for churches, schools, and other refinements. Visitors from the East wanted mud and bugling elk and virile men who mumbled about posses and punched each other's lights out. As the nation paved its highways in the thirties, Montana, short on funds and long on need, stretched its blacktop budget by building its highways as narrow as possible. Not that it mattered; traffic was negligible and everyone drove all over both lanes anyway. These days *los ombres de global economy* dress like Wyatt Earp on weekends but demand a four-lane to the ski lift. Everyone wants Montana to be not a state but a state of mind.

The downtown district recently sprouted a thick crop of espresso bars. From my house I can walk this gauntlet and arrive overcaffeinated at my favorite bookstore. The cafes, and weekly calls from realtors hoping to wrest our house from us, portend Montana's demise as a faraway, hostile, possibly coffeeless place. The great interior West is filling. Hoarding the limelight are white supremacists, golf pros, a ranch-hungry Hollywood elite, and nearly everyone else from California who saw the flyfishing movie. The state's soul, however, perches precariously between pieces of its own myth as a paradise of raw nature and a backwater of rural primitives in love with sheep and assault rifles.

In winter Montanans become a hearth people, content to shut the door against the howling wilderness. The season exacerbates an insularity in the Montana character, an ease with keeping to oneself without diminishing one's community. A few cope by shooting their refrigerators. Others embrace the pleasure, if not the necessity, of friends and neighbors, one of whom might someday pluck them from a snowdrift. Ranches a tenth the size of Belgium keep a lot of people far apart. Early homesteaders often built their houses on adjacent corners of their sections and lived close to one another. Before long they moved to the other side of their holding, ostensibly because their chickens got mixed up together. Something about this extraordinary land accommodates a desire for privacy without loneliness, seclusion without solitude.

The winter solstice marks the midpoint of our stay in the far north. This calendar suspends me in the purity of a singular season; winter's most evocative qualities freeze-frame in a landscape that wears them to perfection. Days unfold in preternaturally bright sunlight or under a pewter sky weighted against snowy hills with its impending storm. Nights are sudden and complete, with a faint glacial scent. The moon is lilac as it rises, silver at its zenith. I never see the seasons change in Montana, I never see the green, only its scheduled death. For me Montana is always cold, the original and ultimate state of the universe.

January brings the coldest days, bone-chilling polar air that leaves no slack. Every surface freezes so hard it would rip your lips off if you kissed it. Car exhausts spew dry-ice fumes. The air crackles with helium, ozone, neon, argon—air that can be 108 degrees colder than me—yet somehow I remain liquid. Not counting my bathtub, the aquariums in the local pet store have the only open water for miles. Winter's worst grip sends me there for the solace of gurgling water and a fecund, tidal humidity. The same Arctic front sends the derelicts to the library. Some sit cozily next to the heat vent in their baggy parkas and unlaced pac boots. Another sleeps at a table, snoring face down on *La Technique: Cooking with Jacques Pepin*.

Despite the pervasive lethargy of hibernation, things get done. Ravenously hungry after the cold spell, cedar waxwings—tawny birds with black bands across their eyes—strip my crabapple tree of its frozen fruit, then fly off like masked bandits. My husband cleans the basement. Someone resuscitates all those Bostonians heaped at the foot of the Crazies. According to the news, the Romanians are selling their excess bears. I order two. The legislature, which meets here every two years for ninety days, undoes the laws that the previous session repassed in response to laws depassed by the session before that, making everyone so dizzy, we wish they would meet every ninety years for two days. I send out postcards with photos of typical Rocky Mountain ungulates and letters that note a ski trip to the valley of the bufflehead breasts, the length of icicles, the blizzards and the chinooks, the shock of exploding color from arriving seed catalogues, an epidemic of imploding marriages among friends—all the riches and wrecks that mark life as *Homo sapiens* on a wobbly, spinning planet that tilts its northern hemisphere away from the sun.

Then the season turns and the light slowly climbs the orb.

Before migrating a bird must eat a great deal, storing energy in the form of subcutaneous fat. The bird must also become predisposed to migrate by a metabolic state called migratory restlessness. In spring this condition is controlled by the pituitary gland, which in turn is stimulated by periodicity, or changes in day length. Fat, restless, and physiologically prepared, the bird now needs only the external stimulus of a drop in barometric pressure, the moist, southerly air of a warm front, before it loads those little hummingbirds on its back and takes wing: northbound.

For me the migratory impulse manifests itself in too many trips to the pet store aquariums. The geography wars, the tension between allegiances to two places, escalate. One day I will press my face against a window that frames Montana's crystalline winter purity and I, too, will long for hummingbirds. Fat, restless, and physiologically prepared, aching for the desert, I will turn winter's bend with the geese and take wing: southbound.

—from *The Place Within*

Out in the Desert
Four Views of a Western Town

Kate Boyes

❦

1. Wide angle

August. In the desert. I kneel on blistered asphalt, try to pick the lock on my car door, and wonder why we don't have a word for "August in the desert." We need a word like that, one that describes how heat and distance and dryness work on the mind, leaving it always slightly addled.

If we had such a word, the researchers who sent me to this town might have remembered it when they planned their project. The project schedule seemed reasonable enough back in the office: summer—gather data; autumn—analyze results. But every time I step out of my air-conditioned car, the plan's major problem hits me in the face, borne on the parching wind. It's August, and I'm in the desert.

The town's one police officer pulls over and parks behind me. He sits for half a minute in his patrol car watching me fiddle with my car lock. He doesn't ask if I need help; neither of us needs to waste breath for him to figure that out. When he's seen enough, he pulls a strange tool out from under his front seat, walks over, and starts picking the lock like a professional. Says he confiscated the tool from a minor doing 110 miles per hour in a "borrowed" car. Dropped charges when the kid showed him how to use the thing.

In seconds the door is open. I pick up my keys from the dashboard, drop them quickly, and leave them where they've fallen on the floor. "Never locked myself out before," I say, as if that explains why I would pick up keys that have been sitting for two hours on a dashboard in a closed car in August in the desert. The officer nods, almost smiles, and then looks out across the dry land between us and the mountains. We watch a dust devil funnel up and swirl over the flat. Then he nods again, walks back to his car, and drives off. I don't embarrass us both by thanking him. He's doing his job, making sure I don't die in his territory, but anyone in town would have done the same.

I retrieve my keys, start the car, and let it idle while the air conditioning kicks in. Sweat beads on my temples. A drop trickles down across my cheek and falls on my forearm. For one moment the drop shines there on my arm, startlingly clear, and then . . . nothing.

Lack of moisture sets the desert in fine focus. As I drive toward my next appointment, I see the town's outline knife-edge clear against the bare mountains beyond. The clarity is like that of an insistent thought that wakes you in the night. A thought that vanishes by morning.

What word describes this town? I pull up to the next house on my list, gather my questionnaires, and try to sort my scattered thoughts. Mirage? No, mirage doesn't seem like the right word. A mirage only reflects reality. This town is real. In the few days I've been here, I've met people whose kindness and honesty and trusting make them seem more substantial than people I've met anywhere else.

I struggle over words in the desert. This place encourages brevity and demands clarity. Saying many words wastes breath and the moisture it contains. Saying the wrong words for the desert—wasteland, devil's garden, moonscape. hell—leads to abuse of the land and the people who live here.

What word names this town? I know that word, but I won't say it. If you knew the name and came to this place, you would see that these people have been hurt time and time again. You would want to protect them as much as I do. I call the town "Willow Creek," but that name is a mirage, words for a real town that reflects the experiences of many towns in the arid West.

The desert preserves; crackers stay fresh forever, buildings don't rot. Bodies buried for centuries in desert caves can look almost alive. One was discovered a few years ago not far from here. The men who discovered the body stole it from the cave, dressed it, drove it around in their pickup truck, even bought it a drink at the local bar before authorities stopped their macabre night out. Social customs—kindness, honesty, trusting—are preserved in the desert, too. Sometimes those customs hang on long after we think they're dead. They become reminders, desiccated but recognizable, of what we've lost.

2. Time lapse

The Willow Creek town hall is my oasis. Outside, cottonwood trees shade the small square of green grass. Inside, I find every town facility: police station, records office, library, pioneer museum, town newspaper, rest rooms. Walls with three layers of handmade adobe bricks keep the inside temperature about fifteen degrees cooler than the temperature outside. Between appointments, I come here.

When I wander for the first time into the town hall, the woman in charge of records greets me by name. We talk about the possibility of rain, and then I ask how she knows who I am. She says she overheard the police officer talking about rescuing me on the road outside of town. Unlocking my car was the only event on his police blotter that day. My rescue will be reported in the "Police Beat" section of the town's biweekly newspaper, the Willow Creek Gazette, when the paper comes out in another twelve days. "Won't that be exciting?" she asks. And because my research will be done here and I'll be gone before the paper hits the town's three streets, I say, "Really."

Downstairs, in the library and museum, I search through stacks of newspapers and journals dating back to the town's founding. For twenty or thirty minutes at a time, whenever I have a chance, I gather fragments of the past. I turn pages that crumble at the edges no matter how gently I touch them, pages frail and sallow as mummified skin, and try to figure out why I feel a sense of dread in this town.

"God sent me to this green place." Most of the early journals begin with some variation of that phrase. Mid-1800s: lush, natural grasses fatten the cattle, and orchards and gardens grow easily along the waters of Willow Creek. After crossing vast stretches of sage and rabbit brush flats, this place was Eden. Settlers fed themselves and sent meat, fruit, and vegetables to the large city a few days' wagon ride away.

A saw mill opened to make lumber for that growing city. Trees that took hundreds of years to grow in this dry climate were clear-cut. Coming from the East, settlers couldn't know the trees would grow back slowly or not at all. They must have waited for new forests to spring up, watched the slopes, prayed. Two generations later, when the folks who had seen tree-covered slopes around town were all dead, the people here told each other, and believed, the hills had always been bare.

Mining fever broke out in the late 1800s. Today, only relics of mining remain. Deer die when they browse on leach fields abandoned for fifty years. Children fall down mine shafts. Two years ago, during a heavy spring snow melt, mine tailings washed down the mountain and poisoned town wells. But in those early days, copper and gold dug from deep within the tree-bare hills made money.

Through the time period of these changes, the journal entries remain positive, even cheerful. Townspeople were happy to help cities in the West grow. When the transcontinental railroad came through, they greeted it as a chance to contribute to the growth of the nation as a whole. They dug irrigation canals to water even larger sections of farm land. Sure, old-timers wrote letters to the editor complaining about the sage that was replacing natural grasses in the valley. And some folks wondered if they should change the town's name since Willow Creek, drawn on heavily for irrigation, often dried up before it reached the outskirts. But most people trusted that what was good for the nation would be good for Willow Creek.

One day, I stare at two pictures in the basement hallway while I wait for the library to open. The pictures are studies in gray, one with a triangle in the upper left corner, one with a regular series of objects strung across the center. When I look closely, I realize the triangle is a roof peak and the regular objects are the tops of fence posts. Dust clouds swirl in the air; drifts of dirt cover the rest of the house and fence. At the bottom edge of both pictures, there's an inscription in white ink and shaky Palmer Method handwriting—"Willow Creek." The Dust Bowl, here?

When the librarian arrives, red-faced with the heat, I ask to see old agricultural reports. Back to the brittle pages. Crop yields, livestock production, 4H awards. Finally, a report from federal experts who visited Willow Creek in the 1930s. Their verdict: A combination of poor land use—primarily the overgrazing of grasses that might have held topsoil in place—and drought in an area that receives less than fifteen inches of rainfall a year led to disaster for Willow Creek. Their prediction: "Beyond a doubt it is only a question of time until the town . . . will have to be abandoned."

Turn the pages of the newspaper. Look at the faces. Grim, determined. In journals, I read, "We came here to live and we came here to stay." The townspeople misused the land, but they knew now that they'd made a mistake, and they were prepared to live with the consequences. They would do better; they must do better. But how, some asked in their journals, could they make a living now that the grasses, trees, minerals, and even the good land were gone? How could they live on nothing?

Nothing, as it happened, was just what the federal government needed. Drawn by the open, uninhabited space around Willow Creek, the government began siting military facilities nearby. Within a few years, cheerful headlines announced the opening of a U. S. Army installation. Then a test site for military aircraft began operations. A storage site for outdated chemical weapons mushroomed south of town. Everyone who wanted a job had one. Willow Creek, a town the experts thought would die, had been saved.

Of course, the new jobs had problems—explosions, chemical spills, radioactive contamination. Obituaries over the next forty years sometimes included the cryptic note that a death was "work-related." But newspaper editorials show that residents still held strong trust in their government through these years. Work for the military was difficult and dangerous, but the people of Willow Creek were proud to do it. Even when front-page headlines announced that rumors about leaking chemicals from old weapons were fact, announced that investigators discovered the military had for years simply dumped toxic waste on the ground around town, announced that chemical analysis proved wastes from multiple dumpings had combined to create toxins more lethal than anything officially produced by the government facilities.

No wonder that when cities across the nation began having problems disposing of hazardous waste the waste dump companies thought of Willow Creek. They needed a place good for nothing else, and the military had made much of the land here just that. Even more important, they needed to find a town either friendly enough or gullible enough to accept such a project without waging a lengthy, expensive siting battle. According to full-page ads paid for by waste dump companies, the companies would provide residents with free health screenings, train volunteer fire fighters to handle toxic spills, and even give scholarships to local students who wrote the best essays on ""Technology and Progress."

The people of Willow Creek considered these offers. The military was cutting back, and some people thought jobs at the waste dump might make up the difference. But the people didn't trust cities now, and they were beginning to doubt the government. The people here had begun to suspect that what was good for the rest of the country might be disastrous for Willow Creek.

No thanks, they said to the waste dump.

Willow Creek said no, but economic development agencies clamored for a county-wide decision. In the resulting vote, the only large town in the county—the one farthest from the dump site—said yes. And soon cities all over the country were shipping hazardous waste to Willow Creek, forking over the dumping fee, and still paying one tenth of what it would cost to dump waste in their own state. The county economic development agents were delighted. They looked at proposals for several new dumps. They considered vying for a waste burning facility. Maybe two.

And the military, which was indeed cutting back, now proposed biological weapons, much cheaper to develop, as an economical mass-destruction alternative. The people of Willow Creek shouldn't mind a biological weapons plant close by. As if in exchange, the military promised to rid the area of those leaking chemical weapons near town; the Army would build a chemical weapons incinerator right here, up wind of Willow Creek, and blow the smoke of nerve gas over the town and off into the brilliant blue desert sky.

3. Snapshots

The head of the county economic development agency invites me into his office, located not in the county but in the state's capital city. Everything is gray in this windowless room—the furniture, the light, his hand when he shakes mine. No, he's not from Willow Creek; no, he doesn't live there; yes, he visited the town—once. But he says he really feels close to those people "out there."

He shows me the brochure he gives businesses looking for a place to relocate. The pages emphasize the educated, willing work force of Willow Creek and mention the fact that there is no union influence in the area. He says the county has almost closed a deal with a major company. The county will pay for new roads to the company's plant, will run utility lines to the plant at no cost, and will give the company land on which to build. The county will also waive the company's taxes for five years.

Then he shows me brochures he sends to the state's tourist office. Glossy pictures of the mountains around Willow Creek, with bicyclists in the summer scenes and cross-country skiers in the winter scenes, cast a dull shine in the artificial light of his office.

He takes my hand again as I leave, smiles broadly, and says, "Tourism, weapons, waste—Willow Creek can have it all."

↪

I'm resting under a shade tree outside the Willow Creek town hall, not asleep but not awake, and I'm aware of a car driving past me several times. The car slows on its final pass, and the driver tosses a note through the open passenger-side window before speeding away.

I wake up enough to realize I'm late for my next appointment, so I stuff the note in my pocket and read it later that night. The note says she's single, raising four children. She was waiting tables at the truck stop near town—near in the western sense, that is, a fifty-minute drive away—but she couldn't afford to buy her kids what they needed. And she was tired of having her rear end grabbed. She's making good money now at the weapons plant. Instead of signing the note, she writes "I'm sorry."

↪

He's wearing a Harley Davidson cap low over his face. His ten-foot home is in a trailer park that grew here when the hazardous waste project came to town. Mobile homes sit at every angle, wobbly on cinder block supports. Roads are any uncluttered space wide enough for a car to squeeze through. Trucks haul in potable water; sewage is hauled out the same way.

The comic books scattered over his floor are the first books I've seen in any of these trailers. He says he likes to read when he comes off his graveyard shift at the waste dump. So I ask him to read and fill out the questionnaire. He looks through page after page of questions about the quality of this town's public services, about economic development, about hazardous waste, about biological and chemical weapons. He reads each question slowly, using his finger to trace sentences across the page, shaping words with his lips.

Then he shakes his head and hands the pages back. "This stuff don't have anything to do with me."

&

Her husband died a few months ago, and she's painting their storm windows alone for the first time in over forty years. She doesn't ask me to help, just hands me a paintbrush and keeps working while I dab white paint on the wood and explain why I'm here. Yes, she'll fill out a questionnaire, but she hopes I'm not one of those environmentalists. Her husband never liked "that kind of people." He worked for the military his whole life, and he never believed stories about what the military did to this town.

We clean our hands with turpentine and she invites me in for a glass of cold lemonade. The top of her piano is covered with photographs, and I ask if that's her whole family. After a few moments of silence, she tells me these are pictures of family members who have died. Her first. grandchild, born deformed, dead at ten months; her youngest son, brain tumor, dead at 22; her sister, cancer, age 34; her brother, cancer, 51; her nephew, cancer, 19; her husband, cancer, 64.

She tells me again that her husband always said the military didn't do anything wrong around here. Then she looks at the pictures and whispers, "But sometimes I wonder."

She does volunteer work in each of her three children's classrooms at least one day a week, teaches church school, and leads a girl scout troop. She's too busy to fill out a questionnaire, but she calls me one evening and we talk for a while over the phone.

She was the first person to suggest that the people of Willow Creek ask the military what toxic chemicals it had dumped near town. Later, she told her neighbors what she'd discovered in her research—the proposed waste dump might not be as safe as company representatives and county economic development people said. When the biological weapons facility and chemical weapons incinerator proposals hit the papers, she organized the opposition. She's learned a lot about politics and power, and she doesn't like what she's learned.

It's time to put her children to bed, but she wants to tell me something more. I hear her ask the little ones to leave the room. When she comes back on the phone, she tells me Willow Creek is going to be punished because the people have desecrated God's temple. "I'm not leaving, of course. My husband and I, even our kids—we've all got to stay right here and take our punishment, just like the rest of the town. But I live every day knowing in my heart that He's going to crack the earth open and let it swallow us all."

4. Aerial shot

Willow Creek sits in a valley crossed by geological faults. If you fly over in the morning, you see dark lines that seem etched into the land. The lines are shadows cast by up-thrust sections along faults, sections higher than the desert floor. The faults run their own course, driven by forces we can't control. From above, you can see that the town was laid out with no regard for faults. What we can't control, we try to ignore.

The state's geologists say the faults are active. In fact, if they ran through a major city, and if there were an earthquake, they could create enough damage to make the 1989 San Francisco quake look like a civil defense drill. However, the people here know what happens when the earth shakes: a few houses sag, trailers slide off cinder blocks, century-old windows crack. So far, no one has died. Quakes are a fact of life, like rattlesnakes, but not a big problem.

Faults weren't a public issue when the hazardous waste dump, the biological weapons facility, and the chemical weapons incinerator were proposed. But during a state-wide push to improve earthquake awareness, a television program broadcast the map of active faults in this state. It didn't take a cartographer to see that the faults ran near sites chosen for dangerous projects, projects that could leak toxic substances into the water or spew biological or chemical death into the air if disrupted. The people of Willow Creek, who had accepted quakes as part of life, now lived in fear of them.

"Well," one elderly man said, "its like as if them rattlesnakes that's been living under my shed for years began chasing me around, trying to get a bite. Like them coming into the house and slithering up into my bed."

Some people in Willow Creek formed a group to oppose additional waste dumps and the weapons projects. They expected that as soon as the county economic development agency and others in power saw maps with the fault lines marked in red ink, the projects would be scrapped. What they discovered was that folks in power had known about the faults before they approved the first dump.

As residents were recoiling from the shock of that discovery, the Environmental Protection Agency named a manufacturing plant near Willow Creek one of the worst air polluters in the United States. Newspapers announced, incorrectly, that the EPA had called the area around Willow Creek one of the dirtiest in the nation. Cleanliness is still next to godliness here. The people of Willow Creek were appalled.

Then the third blow fell. A shipment of toxic waste moved across the country for several months while its owners tried to find a dumping place. Four states turned the shipment away, all in front of television cameras that captured weary drivers, adamant state health officials, harried company executives. Where did the waste find a home? Willow Creek.

The bitter run-off from these decisions poisoned goodwill in Willow Creek. When I knock on doors now, not long after these events, the people want to talk. Older folks try to convince me Willow Creek used to be a clean, safe place to live. People who feel used by the county government, the military, and the big cities need to explain that feeling to me. Workers at the weapons facility and the waste dump tell me about living in fear that they will contaminate their children.

Everyone looks anxiously at the sky. A young woman finally explains why. She says death will come from above, from air that looks clean but is carrying invisible particles from chemical weapons. "Everybody here fusses about dirt," she says. "My mom's a cleaning fanatic. But we all know it's not the dirt that's going to kill us."

I'm an outsider here, but the people of Willow Creek talk to me because the town's police officer has already nosed it around that I can be trusted. He understands that his friends and neighbors need to tell someone what's happening to their town, and he hopes the project I work on will encourage people elsewhere to sympathize with Willow Creek. He believes some good will come from what I do.

I'm not allowed to share my feelings while on the job, so I can't tell him I think my work will do no good. The questionnaires I hand these people aren't written in words from the desert, but in words from offices and conference rooms. How can their answers have real meaning in such a foreign language? What the people say to me has real meaning, but hearsay won't be included in the data analysis. I can't tell him this project is another case of Willow Creek giving something vital—data— and receiving nothing of real value in return. I can't tell him I justify my presence here by telling myself I "at least do no harm."

A man who grew up in the big city near Willow Creek told me he and his friends often drove out here in the 1960s just to stop at the ice cream stand and flirt. They even modified a Beach Boys song, hoping it would convince some of the local girls to go parking with them in the mountains outside of town. "Oh, the Willow Creek girls they are most, from the Rocky Mountains to the coast . . . . Yeah, we're out here having fun in the warm Willow Creek sun."

The girls still flock to the ice cream stand in the heat of August, and they are as kind as ever when I stop by for a cool drink. They laugh and tell me about their boyfriends and their dreams. They are as honest as the children I meet while passing out questionnaires, children who tell me their parents aren't home and then invite me inside to watch cartoons. What I see is the open, friendly way people here had always lived, the way they thought they would live forever.

But I have also seen the people of Willow Creek respond to other outsiders—from the big cities, from the military, even from the large town in their own county—who do not live by the maxim "at least do no harm." Then the townspeople's smiles—like the water in Willow Creek—evaporate. Sparks of kindness go cold, leaving the people's eyes dark and empty as mine shafts. Fault lines cross their frowning faces. And I begin to understand the word "trust" when I see what dies when trust is betrayed.

—first publication

Selected Poems

Penny Harter

A Baptism

In the old tin box with a hinged lid
out by the back porch,
the empty milk bottles gathered,
rinsed of all but a slight residue,
waiting for the next morning's milkman
to carry them away.

But the children got there first,
filled them at the side-yard tap
and took them to the curb
where a dead squirrel needed baptism
and was prodded with a broken branch
along a faintly milky stream
into the storm drain.

Put back into the milkbox,
its lid left open to the setting sun,
the bottles filled again,
the night sky with its stars
entering them slowly
as it does all vessels that wait
for the milkman to come.

Another Forest

Sometimes when we look above the mountains
there is another forest by the sea
on another mountain where ghost pines float
in the twilight, their needles trembling
in that fog that muffles everything.

And sometimes we climb that farther hillside,
our tears joining clouds that smell of brine.
Beneath blurred branches, we recall
how the harbor gulls can never get enough,
and how in that restaurant on the pier
the lobsters with rubber-banded claws
still think they have a life.

Ascension

The dead mule stiffens on a blaze of snow,
its bent neck obedient to the boulder
that broke its fall down the mountainside.

The vultures that circle
before a swift descent
to their most holy task
are angels,
fallen down an ache of air
into the warmth of blood,
the shrine of meat,
where they will feast
until the nave of ribs
is open to the sky,

and they have raised the dead into the light
that shines from their black wings.

In the Distance

A fire glows in the distance.
The road we travel winds
through the foothills;
now we see flames,
now only a smudge of smoke
above a ridge.

The road climbs, carved
into the mountainside,
taking whatever shape it can
at the edge of the sky;

we see the fire more clearly
from this height, until we turn
to face the deeper mountains.

Out there
wind disperses the smoke.
We are all moving
toward the same horizon.

The Hinge of Pain

Each half fits the other,
held by a pin.
How many angels?

The hinge of the jaw
does its good work
until the winding cloth,

and the hinge of the eyelid
blinks away our dust
until the close.

Tonight my bedroom door
creaks on its hinge
as it slowly swings shut,

but a stone from the mountain
holds it open
between you and me.

The Migration of Stones

The local migration of stones has begun.
They move by wind and water,
            the loosening of dirt,
                        the mountain letting go its young,
to rhythms old as the Earth's journey
among galaxies.

This afternoon I carried one,
a small brown animal,
its back warming in my palm,
then dropped it into different dirt
and left it there.

Tonight I think of stones
moving through the soil,
of countless meteors inflaming the dark,
and of the long migration
of our breath.

Translating Stones

We walk toward the Rio Grande
on a tapestry of stones
embedded in the mud between rains.

Look how they have found one another—
the frictions of flood and wind,
the curses of heat and cold,
forcing them to touch, to rub together,
planing the jagged scarps where once
they were torn from a larger whole,
a nearby mountain or a lava flow.

We walk toward the Rio Grande
on some stones smooth as eggs,
and others that have lived long enough
to become hearts,
　　　　　or triangular Buddhas.

In rain again, these stones
shine like an altiplano.
We want to possess them all,
study their patient language;
when we reach the river
we are mute.

Turning

It is time to turn our faces from the stars
to look at one another.
Our cheekbones are horizons;
the whites of our eyes,
small moons.

The single star that feeds us,
that feeds on us—
leave it for a while;
then all that might have been
tries to blow our hair back from our skulls
into the inevitable dark, where we remember
that we must go on warming one another
by those small fires we kindle
at the edge.

Gastropoda

Make a song for this fossil,
for the mollusk who died here,
for the tiny spiral it has left
open to water or stars.

Hear the snail's tracks
as it slides across your cheeks,
moves across the planes
of your skull, mountains
on its way to the sea.

Sing the thread of slime
it binds you with, silver
as the moon that is still
bound to the Earth, strong
as the grasp of the sun.

The Milky Way

Imagine the hair of a woman
so long it's knotted with stars,
its luminous clouds pulling
her body through the dark
as she spirals, obedient
to the cadence of galaxies
who also do not know
how they will die.

Outward

Always the thrust is outward—
green leaves from the dirt,
sperm from the cool interior,
fire from the core of a star.

The piñon bears candles
each spring, new green needles
reaching for the sun.

Even our foetal palms
sprout fingers
as we bloom in the dark.

Some say the universe
was born like this—
an incandescent blossom
fertilized by its own
unfolding light.

Reading the Pine

There are galaxies in the grain
of this pine, atoms whirling
like dervishes, their dance
etching rings as they make
the sturdy trunk, the distant limbs.

Enter the river of bark,
its knots spiraling
in dark crevices;
smooth the peeled branches,
pale as ripening sunlight,
glistening with growth.

Now touch this table,
illusion of stability,
its whorls and streams
moving so slowly
they leave you behind.

River

Slowly grinding sandstone,
layers of shale and limestone
that have known other waters,
this river has worn its way
down to black plutonic rock,
once molten magma
fused deep in the Earth.

Those who see river spirits
tell us that these waters
know what they are; know
that their job is to carve
canyons, dark mouths telling
endless stories of silt;

and to move these mountains
piece by piece, teaching
that all of life is simply
letting go.

—from *Lizard Light* and an untitled work-in-progress

In the Name of Restoration

Marybeth Holleman

Evening light sifted golden through tall spruce and hemlocks, illuminated cascading water. The white gauze of water poured toward me, tumbling over boulders, pulsating through a narrow rock passage. As the tide continued out, the waterfall steepened, dropping as much as ten feet, rushing to make the water level in the lagoon equal to that of Ewan Bay. When the tide turned and began filling the bay, the waterfall reversed, pushing water through the tight passage into the lagoon.

As I stood in a skiff too large to fit through the passage, I remembered another time when I had glided on the incoming tide from still water in the bay to the quick pull of waterfall to still water in the lagoon. I drifted in the oval lagoon, gazing up into dense forests concealed with thick-trunked trees draped in broad platforms of moss and long strands of old man's beard. Then, flowing with the outgoing tide, I poured back out into the bay.

This virgin forest, nearly sixty thousand acres of North America's northernmost rainforest, was now protected from any large-scale human development—especially clearcutting. Chenega Corporation sold it for $34 million, part of the $1 billion natural resources settlement managed by the *Exxon Valdez* Oil Spill Trustee Council. I was there with a guide, Roger Stowell, and a photographer, Jim Lavrakas, to write this silver-lining story eight years after the oil spill.

Now it is ten years after the spill, the mark of a decade upon us. The Council, a group of state and federal agency representatives, has had as its sole purpose the restoration of land and wildlife along the fifteen hundred miles of shoreline damaged by oil. With that $1 billion, they were not to compensate people who had been harmed by the spill—a separate civil suit covered that. The money was for the place and its wild inhabitants. To restore the wild. Reverse the damage.

The forest around Ewan is newly protected, but most of what has been funded has not been restoration. It has instead, as *Scientific American* phrased it, been a "scientific fiasco." We have not acted in the best interests of the place, but have instead fallen prey to short-term self interest.

℗

"Ground zero": first and hardest hit. The purchase of Chenega lands protected the heart of the spill from darkening. The vast majority of the forty thousand tons of oil came ashore here, where most of the Sound's salmon pour into in spring, where thousands of birds migrate through, where residents of Chenega Bay, a small Native community, have struggled to rebuild after the 1964 earthquake's tsunamis washed away their village, taking with it twenty-three of their people. Twenty-five years later, also on Good Friday, oil spilled, once again threatening the existence of their village.

Roger took us past tsunami-swept Chenega on our way to Sleepy Bay on Latouche Island. In a protected cove, the old village faces Whale Bay, Icy Bay, and the Sargent Icefield. Icebergs from Tiger and Chenega glaciers poured toward it, and I recalled flying over it, watching from above as three humpbacks glided through the ice field. It's beautiful, a good place for a village—until the tsunami hit. Now it's abandoned, only the schoolhouse, high on a grassy hill, visible from a distance. Now the remaining fifty-six villagers gather there once a year for three days to remember the dead. Not that remembering is hard.

"You know Don Kompkoff?" Roger said as we passed, "His brother, when he saw the wave coming, grabbed his two kids, the boy by one hand, the girl by the other, and started running up the hill. He held tight, but they were yanked from his hands. They were never found. He took to drinking, died a couple of years ago, I think." Roger bowed his head. "It's sad, so many of them lost family, especially kids, because they were all playing down on the beach when it hit."

At Sleepy Bay, a northfacing curve of beach on Latouche Island, the scene made me bow my head. Multicolored booms in three parallel half-circles cordoned off a beach. A dozen people, dressed in bright yellow raingear though there wasn't a cloud in the sky, milled around on shore, wielding buckets and long pipes and odd-looking mechanical devices. The intensity of human activity and technology, contrasting completely with all other beaches we had passed, was all too familiar. In 1989, nearly every beach looked like this, so wrong in this wild.

I was not surprised oil still stuck to this beach. Three months earlier, we'd found some on nearby Green Island, just turning over a rock. I knew of other beaches on Knight and Chenega as well. I was surprised, however, that we were still trying to extract it, that after billions spent on cleanup we still believed in the power of technology this much.

On shore, we were immediately approached by three white men wearing hard hats and jeans. At first they acted guarded, asking us who we were, what we wanted. But then they warmed to us and, lured by the promise of a picture in the paper, began showing us the latest oil cleanup technology, a new kind of drill pipe that was supposed to get the oil out from beneath the rocks, oil eight years old, oil that months of hand-scrubbing, summers of cold and hot water washing, years of biochemical treatment, had not budged.

Sleepy Bay has endured all attempts to get the oil out. In 1990, I watched bulldozers move rocks, digging into the beach to uncover oil for hot water to wash away. The beach wasn't cleaned so much as rebuilt, left scrubbed and sterile. And still it held oil. In the summer of 1998, when other wild salmon stocks finally returned to the Sound, the stream at Sleepy Bay was empty. It should have held hundreds of spawning salmon.

These men were proud of their technology, one patting the inventor on the back as he told his story of discovery. But the real story was behind them. Ten Natives of Chenega Bay, once again dressed in protective gear, once again trying to clean this beach so close to their home that, before the oil, they routinely came here to collect mussels and kelp, fish for salmon, hunt deer. They were silent. Only one spoke briefly, turning over a rock to show me oil glistening beneath, as fresh as if it had washed up yesterday.

I thought of what Roger had told me as we passed the old village, of how oil spill workers defiled the old village site: the plaque with the names of the dead chipped away; the old schoolhouse spray-painted with "Oil Spill Cleanup 1989" like some high school senior prank. But still they were here. Was it the money they were making, or the promise of an oil-free beach?

When we left, I looked back and saw the villagers sitting in a row on beach logs like cormorants on a rock ledge, eating lunch, staring out to sea. The image came unbidden: kneeling in a row in church, praying for forgiveness, for an end to suffering. This beach cleanup was not restoration, but only an imposition of will onto the land. We cannot will the oil, no matter how we strong-arm it with technology, to leave the beaches. It is an arrogant delusion, one born of a philosophy in which humans reign supreme over nature. When those villagers looked out to sea, did they see a better way to restore the Sound? Or were they as uncertain as I?

↊

I was glad to leave Sleepy Bay behind, eager to go to our next stop: Jackpot Bay, where memories were joyful. I remembered boating through a series of bays, each connected like a string of pearls by narrow passages. I remembered rowing our inflatable up the creek, then walking up further, two-year-old Jamie in tow, to a meadow brushed with wildflowers, where we bathed in the stream and ran naked through the meadow, my sweet toddler laughing in a voice as clear as the stream's water.

What we found, though, dismayed me. Near the mouth of the stream, a small settlement had risen: three large wall tents, a couple of buoys on the water, a gas can on the beach, a bright blue tarp covering three fuel barrels, and trails crisscrossing the small headland. This was a research camp, Roger told me, peopled all summer.

We boated ashore and were met by a young man in T-shirt, shorts over long underwear, and baseball cap. A graduate student, Phil was here for the summer helping with the pigeon guillemot project. He introduced me to two others, Pam and Bill, and I asked about their projects, funded by the Trustee Council as restoration work.

The pigeon guillemot is a small black and white seabird devastated by the oil spill. These researchers studied a colony of them on Jackpot Island, a small hummock in the middle of the bay. Every morning, these researchers climbed the island, found tunnels in which the birds nest, and reached their hands way down in them, up to their shoulders sometimes, groping for eggs. They counted them. Later they would capture and band the chicks that hatch. They did all this in the morning, when the adults were out feeding on the waters.

They weren't able to tell me what they hoped to learn from the project, or how their work might help the bird recover. They wouldn't venture to say whether the land purchase might affect the birds or their project. They were uncomfortable with us, edgy. Another boat appeared, and Phil said Dave, the project director, was aboard. Pam took the skiff out and didn't return, though I asked her to see if I could talk with them.

"Dave is probably giving her a hard time for talking with you," Phil told me. It was all very strange, as if they were hiding something.

Later I figured it out: they hid nothing. That's the point. They had nothing to show for their work, no clear benefit to the birds, no restoration. Just data and banded birds. Every day on that trip, we saw several research boats. Six years ago, I saw none. Before the spill, only a few researchers worked in the Sound. Now, though, with funds from the settlement, a cadre of scientists study pigeon guillemots, river otters, sea otters, mussels, harlequins, herring. All a result of the spill, of the $1 billion natural resource settlement. And, except for a few projects, none have helped the animals.

That evening, I lay in my bunk thinking of the last time I was in this place. Yes, it was four years after the oil spill. Yes, I was aware that there were fewer seals, sea otters, birds. But I believed it was healing. It was peaceful; only a few sport fishers were about. Wounds take time, undisturbed time, to heal. I thought that, after the frenetic first two years' $2 billion cleanup and several-million-dollar damage assessment, the Sound was now getting that undisturbed time to heal.

What had changed? The Trustee Council began disbursing money. Eight years after the spill, more research went on in the Sound than did four years after the spill. Now, instead of damage assessment, it is called restoration. Now dozens of projects employ hundreds of people during the season. Now there is a pot of money to fund it. The spill spawned a new industry whose center is here.

But it is not restoration. They are not working in the best interest of the wildlife, the wildlife that exists here and now. They are instead picking at the wound, keeping it open, creating new wounds. Yes, we know more about these animals being counted and darted, poked and prodded. But what good is that knowledge? They aren't more protected from oil spills; their lives aren't better, safer. Toxic oil still seeps from beaches; pink salmon and herring still don't produce normal offspring; of dozens of affected species, only one, the bald eagle, our nation's symbol of freedom, has recovered.

Their lives are, instead, harder for all this research, for so much is intensely intrusive. Harlequins, strikingly-marked sea ducks, have suffered severe reproductive failure since the spill, and no one knows why. So we have funded the "harlequin roundup": in the spring, when the birds are molting and flightless, researchers in kayaks circle a flock of swimming ducks and herd them into nets. Once caught, they have radio transmitters implanted in their bellies, and are released. So far, most have died.

Others have died in the name of science as well: sea otters, salmon, scoters, harbor seals. Harbor seals and Steller sea lions were declining before the spill, likely from diminished food sources due to overfishing. Oil-slicked haulouts exacerbated matters. Shortly after the spill, nearly two dozen seals were "collected" so their stomach contents could be studied. Many others have since been captured and burdened with large radios and antennas on their backs.

We define restoration as restitution for a loss, as returning to a previous and more desirable state, as renewing, giving back. These research projects, these vivisections, not only fail to do that—they make things worse. But, like the high-technology beach cleanup, we continue to put our money—the Sound's money—into it. As one letter to the editor said, "Research should not be the legacy of the spill; Prince William Sound should."

Unfortunately, intrusive research isn't the most blatant misuse of restoration money. There's the Seward Sealife Center, an aquarium touted as a research facility where tourists can see puffins and river otters and harbor seals. How does confining animals count as restoration? Of the $50 million it took to build the aquarium, $38 million came from the settlement. Each year, millions of dollars of settlement research money will support it. For one research project, healthy river otters have been captured and caged, and are being fed oiled food, after which their blood is tested—this to give researchers a benchmark for interpreting the blood samples they've already collected from otters in the Sound. In response to a letter to the editor denouncing this project, a researcher wrote that "we don't know whether oil affects river otters." Of course we do.

The money has been used to fund other buildings; in fact, nearly every community in the spill zone has a new facility from these funds. In Kodiak, it's a multi-million-dollar industrial technology center; in Seward, a commercial shellfish hatchery. This isn't restoration; it's a pot of money, and everyone wants some.

In the latest round, the Trustee Council has set aside $140 million for a "Restoration Reserve," money which can be stretched to last for decades to, as one Trustee Council member said, "fund research projects by scientists who aren't even born yet." They ought to be honest. They ought to call it the Research Reserve.

Many who clamor for a piece don't even link their request to restoration. An esteemed former leglislator is pushing to use the reserve for science education throughout the state. Letters from University of Alaska professors asking for an endowment ignore restoration as well; one professor says only it "would serve the state well, now and in the future. . . the university lags behind state development." It's about tenure and job security. It's about self-interest, and short-term self-interest at that: show me the money. It's not about the health of the wild.

What do we want? Do we want to just know more about harlequin ducks, to read some glossy-photo story about them in *National Wildlife* or *Audubon*? Some story full of interesting factoids about the lives of harlequins, which inevitably ends with the sad facts of their decline, their imminent extinction, as if it is beyond our control, inevitable as the phases of the moon? Is that what we want?

I don't think so. We're just not given the whole story. Many of us want to help the harlequins, to restore Prince William Sound, to fix the damage of the oil spill. And we think this money will do that, these scientists and technocrats will do that. What we're missing is how far afield it's gone, all in the name of restoration. What is hard to accept is that we don't always know how to help, that the best way to help may be to do nothing.

&

At a national Environmental History conference last August, sponsored by the University of Alaska Anchorage, a panel discussion ensued about the *Exxon Valdez* oil spill. Walt Parker, who has worked in oil transportation safety issues since the inception of the Trans-Alaska Pipeline, said the risk of an oil spill in Prince William Sound is greater now than in 1989. While much has been spent on response, little has been spent on prevention. The pipeline is older and less sturdy; the crews haven't improved; no new ships have been brought into the Valdez trade. Although the Oil Pollution Act of 1990 established new tanker standards, including double hulls, none have been built.

"It was an old fleet in 1989," he said, "and now it's even older. The North Pacific are the roughest waters in the world. These tankers have been operating in them now for ten more years."

The best thing we can do for Prince William Sound is to do everything possible to prevent such a spill from recurring. We're not doing that. Instead, we're sticking our hands in burrows, rounding up and capturing and implanting radio transmitters. Instead, we're flushing beaches. All this science isn't restoration. It's science.

At the same seminar, Stan Senner, science coordinator for the Trustee Council, said, "Most of the recovery has and will come from natural processes."

This is clear admission that science can't fix it, that humans can't fix it, from those who are responsible for restoration. So, what good is the science? What good are the buildings, science projects, beach cleanups paid for with restoration money?

Senner justifies the research by saying it "provides information that will enable us to sustain the ecosystem over time." But we have no proof that we can "sustain the ecosystem." The bald eagle recovered without any help from science. And few restorative management decisions have come from ten years' worth of research. Senner admitted that less than 10 percent of the research would be useful for management decisions.

What's worse, those made are often baffling and contradictory. In this past year, the river otter was moved to the "recovered" list even as six were captured and caged in the aquarium for research, even as river otter trapping in the Sound was limited.

Perhaps the best restoration is to simply let it be. Perhaps we should limit the numbers of people in the Sound, the numbers of boats and campsites. A permit system, as we have in Denali National Park. I'd be willing, even if it meant I couldn't go out there every summer. In the name of restoration, I'd be willing.

But things are heading in the opposite direction. We're building a road connecting the highway system to Prince William Sound at Whittier, only forty miles south of Anchorage. It's estimated that the numbers of boats and people in the Sound will increase from a hundred thousand to more than 1.4 million a year. There will be more boats than river otters, more people than pigeon guillemots.

The Trustee Council did not make a move against this road, though only four lines in the road's Environmental Impact Statement were devoted to effects on the Sound, though even the researchers in Jackpot Bay said the road may do more damage than the oil. Despite their charge to restore the Sound, the Council did nothing to prevent the next disaster.

It is so hard for us to accept limits. Limits to what we are allowed to do, limits to what we are able to do. This is why it's so hard for us to see that so much of what goes on in the name of restoration does not help. And the scientists, whose careers depend on the research money, it's even harder for them to see.

&

The next morning, before we flew back to Anchorage, we boated over to a small beach on Chenega Island. We walked into the forest, following a small stream crossed with fallen logs and bending branches. Jim moved quickly up and through the brush, looking for a photogenic old-growth tree. I moved more slowly, abandoning the stream and following an animal trail—deer? river otter?—around two large boulders and up a steep bank. Sounds were muffled by thick moss: at my feet, on the branches, on the trunks around me. Every limb I touched felt mossy soft, wet and green. Walking was slow, for moss hid a tangle of fallen limbs and rocks; my clumsy feet found them.

I looked up at shafts of light pouring down upon small patches of the forest. So little light and sound in the middle of the day. One tree, larger than the rest, held several large moss platforms in its arms. I wondered if any were the nests of marbled murrelets.

Deep in the darkness of trees, marbled murrelets nest. They are small seabirds, indistinguishable as they bob on the ocean. But they are amazing. They spend days out at sea, then fly back into the old-growth spruce and hemlock forests, reaching speeds of a hundred miles an hour, little bolts of brown feather bodies among thick stands of rainforest trees. Zip. Into the forest. Zip. Out to sea, to feed on the fish. Like needle and thread, sewing together land and sea, one inextricable from another.

I paused at the base of the tree, and, not able to find steady footing, grabbed hold of the trunk. I leaned into it, tried to encircle it with my arms, but could not. It was more than six arm-lengths in circumference. Old growth. This tree was protected now. No one will cut it down and sell its thick old wood. An earthquake might fell it, a tsunami, but not a chainsaw. Even if a marbled murrelet did not now nest in it, one could. Even if a river otter didn't make the trail I followed back down to the stream, one could.

It is the possibility of the wild that gives me hope. That this purchase, and others like it, leave open the possibility for the wild to live unhindered. That sounds like restoration. Atonement.

&

Of all that the Trustee Council has funded, habitat acquisition is the only thing that helps the place without inflicting more damage. It isn't perfect; to some Natives, selling their land sounds like a dangerous old story. It's only the best we imperfect humans can do. And, like double hulls and better-trained crews and more tugs, it is merely prevention. But as my friend David says, if we consider the Sound a patient, then we ought to remember the healer's Hippocratic oath: First, do no more harm.

With habitat acquisition, coastal forests slated for clearcutting by Native Corporations can be saved. Forests connected to oiled beaches and waterways; forests in whose streams spawning salmon lay eggs, the fry returning to the Sound; forests in whose trees nest birds who feed upon the fish in the Sound; forests along whose edges are fragile intertidal areas, nurseries where fresh and saltwater meet; forests entwined with the sea in mutually dependent relation: all can be saved.

Restoration funds have protected seven hundred thousand acres, completing millions of acres of intact ecosystems. Chenega lands were protected before they were cut, but not all of the Sound's forests were so lucky. Negotiations with two other Native corporations failed to prevent thirty thousand acres of clearcut since the spill. If the focus had been on this true restoration rather than science, these could have been saved.

Habitat acquisition allows for the only thing we are able to restore, what we most need to restore: our relationship with the place. Not through stewardship, where we humans have the arrogance to think we know what's best: that's what we use to justify science and technology. And not through abstinence, a total absence of human interaction with the place. Restoring our right relationship with Prince William Sound requires learning, or remembering, a way to be in the natural world that doesn't desecrate or overrun, but that maintains and respects.

This comes through attentive love: through action based on the love that comes from being aware, listening, noticing what the place and its inhabitants need and desire. Attentive love requires an ethic of humility, the opposite of arrogance. It sees excessive control as a liability;

it respects and reveres the process of life. Scientists like Barbara McClintock and Jane Goodall have shown this ethic: McClintock says she listened to the corn, Goodall let the gorillas show her what to do next.

Attentive love requires a "patient, loving regard" for an other who demands preservation and growth. This, says Sara Ruddick in *Maternal Thinking,* ". . . is governed by the priority of keeping over acquiring, of conserving the fragile, of maintaining whatever is at hand and necessary to the [other's] life." It is how we raise our children.

It requires faith in ourselves and in the other. And many people do it, in small and unrecognizable ways each day. Consider Roger who was constantly aware, constantly noticing every small thing about the place he has chosen to inhabit and be inhabited by. As he took us along Dangerous Passage into Eshamy, Granite, and Paddy Bays, he told us stories. Having lived in the Sound eighteen years, having served as caretaker for Chenega Corporation, Roger knew every inch. He stopped near a small island in Paddy Bay.

"There," he pointed to a tall Sitka spruce, "in the top. See the eagle's nest? This is the thirteenth summer they've nested here."

At the mouth of Eshamy, he pointed out a spit of land.

"A few falls ago," he told us, "I caught five bear hunters camped there. I chased them off, told them no hunting allowed on this land."

He told us stories about catching kayakers littering, a sailboater dumping used oil, hunters after bear and sheep. It was his job as caretaker to patrol these waterways, I knew, but I sensed he would continue no matter who owned it: in his eyes, the needs of the land don't change.

These are small acts, granted. But these ripples can grow into long deep ocean swells. Imagine the Trustee Council meeting to decide about research funding not in a conference room in Anchorage, but on the beach at Sleepy Bay, or on the hummock in the middle of Jackpot Bay. Never before have they gone to the Sound as the Council. Imagine, though, that they each had to spend time watching harlequin ducks in their habitat before they decided whether to fund another harlequin roundup.

Imagine a gathering each year like the gathering of earthquake survivors at old Chenega: remembering and honoring. Imagine such a gathering for the tenth anniversary of the oil spill, instead of what is happening: a two-day technology conference in Valdez or a three-day science conference in Anchorage.

In attentive love, the natural world remains wild. As Jack Turner says in *The Abstract Wild*, "A place is wild when its order is created according to its own principles of organization—when it is self-willed land." Attentive love enhances this self-willed nature by only doing what is asked. If we listen, the Sound will tell us that we don't need to capture harlequins, we don't need to band pigeon guillemots, we don't need to dart whales. The Sound will show us other ways of reaching restoration.

We are still groping in the darkness of the human-made veil for a way to connect, do good, match our desire to the will of the place. Attentive love can bring about true restoration, can reverse the rift between us and the natural world. I only hope it is not too late for Prince William Sound. Restoration: a reversal of the wrongs. Reversals are possible, if only I remember the waterfall. It is the Sound speaking of possibility.

❧

I hold an image, a scene that some friends who spent years observing sea otters in the Sound told me about when I asked, how will saving the forest help the sea otters recover? It reminds me not only that the habitat acquisition is the best use of restoration money. It also, and more importantly, reminds me that the Sound maintains much of its own self-will, that the possibility for restoration through attentive love remains.

In winter, when all the researchers have broken camp and gone home, when the cleanup equipment is stored in a warehouse, when the villagers are in their homes in Chenega Bay and Tatitlek, the reversing waterfall at Ewan is rife with life. Lined with a bed of mussels over a foot deep, the lagoon at low tide draws in sea otters. Just-weaned pups feast on mussels in shallow, still waters while their mothers haul out and rest on the boulders where water pours out and then in. River otters and other animals come down from the forest, too. It's an oasis for the sea otters from wild winter storms. It's a place of commingling, forest and sea entwined. It is the longest season, when the place is left to itself, there in the still lagoon, by the waterfall, which continues to flow back and forth with every tide.

—from *Orion*

The Grace of Geese

Kathryn Wilder

I've always wanted to be with a man I could call baby. A lifetime ago, in letters to my first love, a logger who wrote Hi Babe but spelled it Bab and lived a mountain range away, I said baby a lot. That is, until one day when spring had sprung and the snow and the earth had begun to thaw. Enough of the snowmelt had soaked down into the ground to nourish the shoots of what would become meadow hay; the rest lay atop the land, making it more marsh than meadow for a seasonal few weeks. Canadian honkers stopped in my valley every year on their way home, and my logger boyfriend, who had come to see me over the weekend, drove me out in his truck so we could park and watch the geese.

Five days is forever when you're young and in love, and that's how long we'd been apart. I could feel the heat of him through my worn-out workshirt and long patchwork skirt as I leaned into him, so close that we both watched the honkers over the steering wheel. He let the Ford's engine idle to keep the heater running, and the vibration helped to warm me, too. The geese at the marsh edge bobbed their heads up and down into the water. Others floated on currents made by spring wind. My hand journeyed up my lover's hill-climbing, tree-falling, rock-hard thigh—I was only eighteen but that didn't stop me from knowing what there was to love about a man.

He put his arm around my shoulder and rested his chin in my hair, and I felt his body stiffen and his breath draw in deep. "There's something I want to ask you," he said. A gray and black goose flapped along the water and rose into the air. Other goose necks craned at the action, and heads pivoted urgently. When they saw no danger they settled back to floating and feeding.

I didn't settle anywhere. What, I thought, the prom? Not *marriage?* Then it hit me and I felt like the sun—about to slip over the horizon forever. I remembered the finality of these special car rides, the ones where someone had something important to talk to me about. Words landed in my memory, without the grace of geese. My mother's when I was seven, on a long, tangled drive up a suburban hillside: "Your sister says that man hurt you. We're moving away so he can't hurt you anymore."

We did. My parents transported us to Hawaii, as far from the harmer's way as they could get us. And I left behind the friends I'd had my whole short life, never to see them again.

Later, at ten, my mother drove me down a highway lined with fields of blowing sugarcane. "I hate to tell you this," she said, "but I'm divorcing your father. The marriage is over."

My father's version of the same on the road curving along the empty coastline toward Lahaina, where he worked: "You're moving back to the Mainland. I'm staying here, but I'll see you every few months. And I'll call."

He didn't. I rarely saw him again.

The friends I'd made there joined the others, became names and faces I could no longer remember. A whole string of leavings followed. Relocations. Break-ups. Friends' parents heading for new towns. People'd come into my life, and then they'd go.

Back in my lover's truck, warmth beckoned me to stay while the memories pushed me toward the door. "In your letters. . ." my boyfriend began, but I was already scooting across the seat away from him.

He grabbed my hand. I could feel the calluses I loved against my skin. "Where are you going?" he said.

"Where are you going?" I reached for the door handle.

"Stop," he said. "Wait." I saw that he remembered my stories, too. He pulled me close, touched my face with callused fingers. I got shivers. I just want to ask you something about your letters, okay?"

I leaned toward him and bent my head to his chest like a goose seeking sleep. I could hear his breathing, feel his heart. I put my hand there, an anchor. "Okay," I said. "What about my letters?"

He took another deep breath. "I'm wondering why it is that in your letters you write 'baby,' " he said, "but you never say it to me."

I tucked my head deeper in hopes that he wouldn't see the heat spreading across my face. "I don't know," I whispered. I didn't. I couldn't.

He lifted my chin and kissed me. The word welled up inside. He slid over to the middle of the seat and I lifted my skirt and slipped onto his lap, my back to the honkers, my head bumping softly against the ceiling of the cab. He said, "I won't leave you, babe. I swear." As I hugged his body to mine I felt my version of the word pushing at the dam of my past, but release did not come in that form that day.

The marsh eventually dried up as it did every year and the honkers left, rising in clouds, circling the valley one last time before resuming their travels north, their voices calling back to me long after they were out of sight, the green meadow grasses waving after them in the wind. The word I wanted to call my love but couldn't lodged in my throat every time he'd cross that mountain range to see me when he wasn't falling timber. Sometimes, like in the cab of the truck, it came close to reaching air, but always in the end I swallowed it. And each time he left, it would choke me like a sob.

I never wrote it again, either, and the next fall, despite his promise, despite all that had flowed between us, my first love left me. He died flat under a pine tree on the side of a mountain, and went to his grave without ever hearing me say it: baby. I love you *baby. Baby* good-bye.

Twenty-five years later I sit in the same valley, on a rock near the river that wanders through. Summer-dried grasses sway in the wind and yellowing black oaks dot the surrounding coniferous mountainsides and line the river where it moves downcanyon. As the wind picks leaves off the oaks and rains them down onto the forest and canyon floors, I watch the geese come in. It's still early in the season so they fly in small skeins, not the larger flocks that will follow later in the fall. At a certain height above ground they spread themselves wide and air pillows under each great wing as they float down, silent in their descent, landing on the river with outstretched legs, webbed feet ready.

I feel time rising inside me. When it reaches air it evaporates, and even though my logger lover's been dead now longer than he was alive, I feel the heat of him right here beside me, sitting in these sunlit grasses near the riverbank, watching the return of the geese. I reach a hand out to rest on his thigh. Warm granite greets me.

What I know now is this: The word belongs to the love, not the man. And the love is here, by this river, in this valley, among these mountains, with the coming snows, the spring marshes, and Canadian honkers flying south and north, then south again.

Hours later I stand, straightening stiff knees with care, and a pair of geese rises in fright, honking loudly. A chill runs through me. I wrap my arms around myself and the rough touch of a callused hand brushes across my mind. The rest of the honkers start, some flapping their wings, all watching me and talking. In their voices I hear his.

"Bye baby," I say, and walk slowly away.

—first publication

Witness

John A. Murray

On no subject are our ideas more warped and pitiable than on death. Instead of the sympathy, the friendly union, of life and death so apparent in Nature, we are taught that death is . . . the arch-enemy of life . . . . Let children walk with Nature, let them see the beautiful blendings and communions of death and life, their joyous inseparable unity, as taught in the woods and meadows, plains and mountains and streams of our blessed star, and they will learn that death is stingless indeed, and as beautiful as life, and that the grave has no victory, for it never fights. All is divine harmony.

John Muir, *A Thousand-Mile Walk to the Gulf* (1867)

Having lived in Denver for about twenty-five years, I've learned most of the back streets, the little traveled avenues that run near and often parallel to the crowded main thoroughfares. These secondary routes—fugitive byways for long-term residents, a hopeless maze for out-of-towners—pass through quiet and often forgotten neighborhoods. These are urban areas with the sleepy atmosphere of a small town in western Kansas. Half a century ago, they were on the busy outer edge of the city. Now they are buried in its past. Most of the time the traffic is so slow that children can play entire games of kick-the-can without interruption. Squirrels actually live longer than a few months, even those that prefer to eat their fallen walnuts in the middle of the street. Sometimes, even at high noon, drivers will encounter a potbellied house cat walking across an intersection with the deliberate, measured gait of an African lion. Elsewhere, they only come out at night. Here they reign supreme. It is true that in such lost precincts there are stop signs every seven or eight blocks, but these only afford the opportunity to momentarily pause and enjoy the gardens, which are always lovely in the spring.

On the day I am thinking of it was late April—Earth Day, as a matter of fact. On NPR the commentator was reporting that the President had gone up the Potomac River to help rebuild a park trail, and that the next day, April 23rd, was the day that Shakespeare's birth is traditionally celebrated in his homeland. After that the real news came on and I turned the radio off and rolled down the windows so that I could smell the flowers, which filled the air with a heavy sweet fragrance. Along the streets the early period of the violet and crocus, hyacinth and daffodil, tulip and forsythia was over. In their place the fruit trees—apple, crabapple, cherry, apricot, plum, peach and pear— had begun to blossom. Some front yards were virtually white with blossoms, a cloudy mist that arrives only in those years when there is ample winter moisture but no late snow. Still to come were the peonies and poppies, lilies and iris, magnolias and gingko trees. After that it would be summer, a whole other season, in the city as in the country.

On this afternoon I was driving steadily—not quickly, but not slowly—down the empty side streets to the hospital, where someone I loved was at that hour being brought from surgery. I had been at the hospital earlier that day for two hours, trying to comfort her before the operation. I had told her jokes and done impersonations and related funny stories. I had finally gotten her to laugh during a spontaneous improvisation about how my old college roommate Roger and I had agreed with Blue Cross to do the operation for five hundred dollars and a case of beer, how we had studied the instructional videos over pizza all night and would try our best to use the correct instruments and perform the procedures according to the accepted sequences. I had even invented a bit of table-side dialogue: "Gee, Rog, did we complete step 84?" "Uhhh. . . I thought you were supposed to do step 84." "No, man, that was your responsibility." But, but, but. . . ." I had tried everything I could to make her laugh and I had finally succeeded. If these were her last conscious moments, I wanted them to be happy ones. And now I was on my way back. For several days I had had the persistent feeling that something bad was going to happen. After they had wheeled her away that morning—smiling bravely, blowing one last kiss—I had gone home to rest for awhile. I knew that if something unfortunate was going to occur, someone was going to have to be calm and clear-minded.

Once in the vicinity of the hospital I found an open stretch for parking along South Dexter. On either side of the street there were two and three-story red-bricked apartment buildings. They were shaped like inverted-U's, with grassy courtyards in the middle. Because it was Wednesday afternoon, everyone was at work. They were clean, practical buildings, the sort of comfortable but unadorned places where nurses and medical students, laboratory technicians and hospital security guards live. There was laundry hanging from some of the windows, for the day was very warm, and on a few of the window sills potted plants had been left out in the sun. I walked quickly, feeling a little light-headed from the lack of sleep and regular meals since the week-end, and looked far ahead, not at the pavement, as I had on the asphalt drill fields of Quantico a long time ago when I was learning how to drill a platoon. At one point I stepped off the sidewalk and onto the grass, so that a pregnant woman, walking unsteadily, could pass by without difficulty. She smiled at the kindness. She looked to be literally due at any moment, and had that slightly bewildered "What have I gotten myself into this time?" look of a woman who has not had a baby before. I remember thinking that if she could manage in that condition, then I could certainly make it around alright.

On the second floor of the hospital—that airless antiseptic smell—I got off the elevator and followed the signs to the Surgical Intensive Care Unit, a right, a left, another right, walking briskly, following the signs, hoping that everything would be fine now, that my concerns had been unfounded, that she would be home in a week and life would be as it had before all this started.

At the end of the last corridor there were a pair of swinging doors and I walked through them—slowly now, as in a strange dream—into the brightly lit intensive care area.

The first side room was dark and empty.

I looked ahead and saw that in the next room about a dozen people were crowded around a hospital bed. Between two of these people I saw her face turned toward me, ghostly white, her eyes closed, a breathing tube in her mouth. She was absolutely still, not moving, like a stone in the field. At first I thought the people were medical student's making rounds, and that I must be patient and wait for them to leave, but then I remembered that Rose was not a university hospital. As I looked more closely I saw that something about her expression was not quite right. There is the look of a person under deep anesthesia, and there is another look, the vacant look of someone who is there, but who is not really there.

I was trying to make sense of what I was seeing, and of what they were doing, when a tall young doctor in a green surgical gown, an intern or a resident, turned around, his face hard and tense, and asked who I was.

I pointed to the bed and said I was her middle son.

His face softened, the tone of his voice changed.

"We are having a problem with your mother."

"What's wrong?"

"She is very sick."

"Is it bad?"

I felt my mouth becoming dry, so that it was difficult to speak.

"It is very bad. Can you stand over there?"

He motioned to a desk and I walked over. I heard a sobbing and turned to see my father, hunched in a chair, crying into his hands, his back to my mother's room.

I put my hand on his shoulder.

On the desk was a book I had recently given him, a documentary history of baseball from 1900 to 1948, and next to the book were his Irish walking hat and bifocal glasses. Beside them I placed the gift I had brought for my mother, a collection of nature writings by women on the Grand Canyon. He was wearing his old blue jacket and I saw in a plastic bag on the floor of my mother's room the arm of her blue jacket. Like many elderly couples, they had since retirement become more and more like one person, spending every day in each other's company, sharing a complex private language and, increasingly, even dressing in the same style of clothing. To use another metaphor, they had become as two timberline trees growing together on an exposed point, that finally become so intertwined it is impossible to tell where one begins and the other ends.

My father was speaking but I was only half-hearing what he was saying—"I can't live without her. . . . I can't live without her. . . ."

Over and over.

I was not certain what was happening, and so I told my father that she would be alright and not to worry and after a while his sobbing diminished, if only because no one can endure that level of pain for long.

I was watching what they were doing and a white-haired doctor in a suit and tie had moved the defribrillator cart aside and was now pushing with both his hands on my mother's chest and looking up at the monitor over her head. A series of erratic green EKG lines flowed across the computer monitor, which was emitting a warning sound. Someone yelled for something and a nurse ran to a medicine chest. She moved smoothly, quickly, efficiently and grabbed a syringe and some medicine and ran back to the doctor. He bent over my mother's chest, did something, and looked again at the computer monitor.

No change.

Voices could be heard, the doctors now like hikers lost after nightfall on the forested side of a mountain, searching for the trail home, talking back and forth, exchanging ideas, developing theories, considering alternatives, some composed and others less so, all searching for the familiar path they had somehow lost.

My father was saying "Oh god no. . . . Oh god no. . . ."

I asked him if he wanted a tissue and I found a clean one folded in my shirt pocket and gave it to him.

He was saying that she had always been stronger than him and that he had prayed every night that he would go first, because he could not do this, he could not live without her.

I asked him if he had called my older brother at work and he said yes and I was hoping my brother would arrive soon, because he was closer to my father than I was, and could more easily provide comfort.

Inside I was empty. I was not crying. I could not have cried if I had wanted to. I was thinking very clearly, very sharply. There was a sink to my right and I was drinking cup after cup of water and watching them work on her. Perhaps I should not have, but I wanted to show myself that I could, as I had watched the birth of my son, and I also wanted to be there for her, if she was there, to have a family member looking on so that she, who had always been so fearful, so full of anxiety, would know that one of her boys was being strong for her, and that everything would be alright. I did not pray. It was beyond that. There was no use in praying. Prayers would not help. It would be like throwing a life preserver to someone who has just been swept over Niagara Falls, or opening an umbrella in a hurricane, or any other gesture of futility. There would be no miracles here today. What I was seeing was the laws of physics. The heart was a pump and for too long a fluid had been driven through that pump at too high a pressure.

A nurse came out of the room and bent beside my father. She had a plain round face and short brown hair and her cheeks were red. She cleared her throat and put her hand on his shoulder and told him that my mother had gone into cardiac arrest, and that the best doctors in the hospital were trying to save her life.

My father could not speak. He was bent over with his head between his shoulders and his hands covering his face, like a soldier in a foxhole during an artillery attack.

"Has she passed on?" I asked.

"Oh no," she said, not wishing to violate protocol on such an announcement, "but she is very sick and they are trying to stabilize her condition."

I understood that she had been sent out as a scout to survey the family and say as little as possible and then report back to the doctors. By asking her that question I was letting them know that I understood what the situation was. I was trying to make it easier for them. This was the hardest part of their job. In the days to come there would be official reviews and internal reports, after-hour meetings and all the necessary bureaucratic unpleasantness of a hospital fatality, but this— the telling of the family—this would be the most difficult task for them.

Another, older nurse came over to listen. She had thin lips and a narrow face and oversized glasses that made her face appear even smaller. She was not as warm or kind as the first nurse and I began to realize that not everyone responds to death, or to people's suffering, in the same way. I asked her, thinking aloud, if they could attach an electrical pacemaker to my mother's heart if all else had failed, and she looked at me as though I had just spoken Mandarin.

"It's not like that," she said, "To try to save her they had to do a lot of things they don't like to do. Her brain may have been involved, too."

That told me everything I needed to know.

A life that had begun with happiness and hope on October 20, 1926 in a hospital in Philadelphia, that had climbed all the peaks and crossed all the valleys of the twentieth century, that had created and nurtured three children along the way, was coming to an end on the second floor of a Denver hospital on April 22, 1998.

The nurses returned to the room where everyone was standing back now, their arms folded, staring blank-faced at the bed, the whole team stunned and defeated, as one lone doctor, the senior cardiologist judging from the whiteness of his hair, continued to search for a miracle.

Within moments a rabbi appeared, a short, heavy-set, balding man with a friendly, honest face. I pointed to my father, who was crying and saying "This can't be happening. This can't be happening."

The rabbi put his arm around my father and led him into a conference room at the other end of the intensive care unit. They sat down together and the rabbi began talking softly and asking gentle questions. It occurred to me that a rabbi was the best person of faith for my father, who had been raised Episcopalian but whose closest friends had always been Jewish. It was one of those odd coincidences—the rabbi just happened to be on duty that day—that seem in retrospect a blessing.

A minute later Dr. Parker, the surgeon, rushed by. We had met the previous afternoon, when the four of us had reviewed her angiograms—X-ray photographs of the inside of her coronary arteries—and again that morning, before surgery. Our eyes met for an instant, acknowledging the likely outcome, and he put his hand on my shoulder. He had muscular hands and his eyes were alert and steady, like the eyes of a surfer or a rock climber or anyone else who pursues a life of danger.

He left behind a pungent scent of Ralph Lauren cologne and, ironically, cigarette smoke.

When he got into the room with my mother he tore his jacket off, did not wait for a gown or gloves, and began repeating everything the team of doctors had just done. He had the pads in his hands and was telling everyone to stand clear and when that didn't work he began pushing and pounding on her heart with his hands, talking to my mother as if she was still alive and conscious ("Come on Pat. . . help me out here. . . ."), all the time looking up at the computer monitor. I could tell from the tight expression on his face and the tone of his voice that he was angry this had happened, that all his delicate work that morning intended to give this woman ten more good years had gone for naught—had been ruined, in fact, by what the intensive care people had just done—and he was trying to find out what happened, who did what. Doctors were speaking in low voices, so that I would not hear, but sometimes I did hear.

Suddenly she was nearby. I felt her presence in the corridor immediately beside me and even as I did something very cold and palpable passed through me. It was like an unexpected gust of wind on a mountain top, or a cold wave that breaks across you at the beach. My entire body was covered with goose bumps. Every hair on my body prickled. It was as though I had been physically touched by some sort of an electrical field. I sensed it was her spirit, trying to embrace me one last time. She had always believed in friendly spirits and now, perhaps, she was giving me some empirical evidence. I have no way of proving this theory, but neither does anyone have a means of disproving it, at least in this lifetime. I have never felt anything like that before, and I doubt I ever will again. After all, you only have one mother, only one person who carried you inside her for the better part of a year, only one person who nourished you with her own milk, only one person whose presence you would instantly recognize, even when she is no longer in her body.

After that I knew that she would not be returning to this world, on that day or on any other day.

Death in our time is not often seen as I was seeing it. Families are spread over the country and hospitals usually withold the last moments from loved ones, in the belief that it will be too much for them. In former times this was not the case, as the event often occurred at home and was shared by the family. I can only say that I was grateful for having been present at her passing. It gave me complete closure on her life, and my relationship with her, and in the oldest and the best way. When death is seen for what it truly is, and when it comes painlessly at the end of a fulfilled life, it is as the evening, or the autumn, or the concluding chapter of a long and interesting story. When families are deprived of this experience, and of this valuable knowledge, death becomes something that it is not, a weird jungle temple from which no one ever returns, a tortured false myth that everyone mistakenly believes to be true. Death is not, I saw, the enemy of life, but is its friend, not a punishment, but a release, not an end, but a beginning, not a division but rather a reunion, and is not always untimely in its occurrence, but sometimes comes as naturally as a river delta opening on the sea, an awakening from a dream, a butterfly emerging from a cocoon.

I looked at my watch and noted the time. Twenty-five minutes had elapsed since I first arrived. I continued to drink water and watch Dr. Parker, who now appeared to have abandoned the resuscitation efforts and to be lecturing the younger doctors as he undertook a post mortem. He was probing and pulling, examining and returning, and finally, with rhythmic arm movements, he began sewing up her chest.

My older brother arrived, I heard his voice at the other end of the unit, and I turned to see him walk into the conference room and put his arms around my father.

I walked down to the room and stood at the doorway.

My older brother Bill was dressed in a handsome suit and shoes, the sort of attire my father wore when he worked for the same government agency, the Environmental Protection Agency. He looked very distinguished and I was proud of him for being my older brother. He had the red hair and blue eyes of the Murray side of the family and, except for the goatee, closely ressembled my father at forty-eight. Like many eldest children, he had become a version of the parent for whom he had been named, with a similar career, personality, and even marriage. My younger brother Mike, who had been so wild in his youth, had also settled into a successful life, becoming, of all things, a clinical psychologist. He, too, had inherited most of his features from my father. Between them was me, the middle son, a mixture of the two brothers, and yet very much unlike either, very much an independent soul, very much like my mother, with her darker hair, green-brown eyes and artistic nature. Like most middle children, I had often found myself as the broker, the peace-maker, the diplomat, in conflicts between my brothers, my parents, and, most typically, my mother and paternal grandparents. As a result, I had grown into a person most comfortable when balanced between two extremes, the neutral emissary, the stabilizing electron, the arch between canyon walls, the outside observor with few entangling alliances.

Staring at me, his arms around my father, not told anything yet, my older brother said reassuringly, "Well, Dad, I'm sure Mom will be just fine."

My father's head was turned so that he could not see me and so rather than say anything that might upset him I looked straight into my brother's eyes and shook my head so that he would understand. His face dropped and became incredibly sad. All the light went from his eyes, as when the moon passes before the sun and the earth turns dark in the middle of the day. He buried his face against my father's shoulder, as he hadn't since he was six years old, and I was three, and the world was such a different place—our parents then like all-powerful, all-knowing, and seemingly immortal giants, Zeus and Hera, Ulysses and Penelope, the faithful keepers and guardians of the hearth.

There were phone calls to make, especially to our younger brother in North Carolina, and the rabbi dialed the numbers with a hospital phone card.

I stepped outside and saw Dr. Redstone, my mother's internist, walking toward the conference room. He was a slender man with curly grey hair and a neatly-clipped gray moustache. His shoulders were stooped and he had his hands in his pockets. He was the picture of sadness. My mother had been fond of him, and he of her.

He shrugged as our eyes met.

"We tried everything."

"I know," I said, "It wasn't your fault. You did everything you could with what you had."

He nodded, and as he nodded it occurred to me that for him this was a common, perhaps weekly conversation, while for people like me it was a once or twice a lifetime experience. To be a physician is to be continuously in view of the deep at the base of the cliffs, Land's End, the dizzying gulf where seagulls fly.

I paused for a moment.

"What do you think happened?'

"We couldn't figure it out. Maybe a clot in the grafts, or something with the potassium levels or the electrolytes. It's tough to say."

"My father is going to need some medication."

"Does he have a doctor?"

"I don't know who that might be. He's in bad shape. Sunday was their fifty-first wedding anniversary."

He winced and said, "Alright, I'll talk to Dr. Parker and get him a prescription for some Adavan. It's a mild relaxant."

As we stood there Dr. Parker walked out from my mother's room, his tie loose and flung over his shoulder, the top button of his shirt undone. His face was tired, drawn. There were only nurses in her room now, like dazed people cleaning up after a tornado.

Dr. Parker put his right arm around my shoulder.

"We couldn't bring her back, John. It just wasn't going to happen. Her heart was like a piece of jello. We call it ventricular fibrillation. No organized movement whatsoever."

As we walked along he raised his left hand to the ceiling in frustration, and said "It just went."

Although he was trying to conceal it, I could sense that he was quite upset. I also knew there would be some things he would not be telling me. The fact was, what had just occurred was rare. The bypass procedure has a ninety-five percent success rate, and those who die ordinarily have a risk factor such as diabetes, obesity, or some chronic disease.

We walked into the conference room together. My brother rose from his chair and Dr. Parker sat beside my father, put his arm around him, took my father's right hand in his.

My father was staring straight ahead, bracing himself for what he was about to hear, like a driver on a freeway who realizes he can't avoid a horrible collision.

"Bill, we lost her. Sometimes we have great victories and other times we have tremendous failures. Its hard to say why this happens. All that I can tell you is that right now I feel so inadequate. Being a cardiac surgeon is never easy. On days like this it seems like the hardest job in the world."

My father's head was in his hands again. I was alarmed by his state—in forty-four years I had never seen him like this—but I also realized that I would have been even more disturbed had he shown no emotion. In fact, he was at that moment being more of a human being than I was, and I privately wondered about myself—Was I capable of truly feeling anything? Had my heart after all these years finally turned to stone? Did a philosophy of endurance lead to a psychology of indifference? Was I being strong or was I being weak, afraid to face the feelings?

Or was it all just shock?

Dr. Parker continued: "We don't know what happened. It was very sudden. I just performed a quick autopsy and we weren't able to determine anything. I don't know if that would even change anything. The fact is that she's gone, and everyone in this room feels terrible."

There was a silence. All eyes were on my father. Dr. Parker pretended to wipe a tear from the corner of his right eye with the second knuckle of his right index finger. In fairness, I think he was a man, like me, who is incapable of showing emotion in public, and he was doing the best he could under the circumstances to share the family's pain.

Dr. Parker then assumed a slightly more formal tone and said that there were two official matters that needed to be attended to. The first was the question of whether the doctors could salvage organs for transplant purposes and the second was the question of whether the family wished to have an autopsy performed by the coroner, because the patient had died within twenty-four hours of surgery.

I told him that I had often talked to my mother about organ transplants and that I could state emphatically that it was her wish that her organs be put to good use to help others.

My brother looked at me sharply, and then asked my father what he thought.

There was a confused silence.

The rabbi volunteered that most people who wished to be cremated didn't mind if their organs were transplanted, and Dr. Parker nodded his head in agreement. Apparently my father had already told the rabbi that they both wished to be cremated. After some thought—three votes for, two undecided—my father said that he guessed it would be alright, and Dr. Parker produced a piece of paper, the 'Consent for Donation of Anatomical Gifts' form, for him to sign. The doctor also stated that because of the damage to my mother's internal organs, all that would be salvageable were her corneas.

"Thanks," he said, looking at me. "You just gave two people the gift of sight."

We then discussed the matter of an autopsy and all agreed it would not be necessary. We just wanted her back, her ashes in an urn in the house she loved so much.

There was a nurse standing at the door and I walked out and motioned for her to follow me up the hall.

"We'd like to see my mother one last time so that we can kiss her good bye."

"Of course. We've been getting her ready."

"Let's have a look and make certain everything is alright."

We walked into the room and there she was, yellow and waxen, looking so small, the spirit gone out of her, her blood on the pillow, the breathing tube still in her mouth. I wanted to hug her and tell her how much I loved her and somehow by sheer force of will squeeze my life into her, but I stood there motionless and shed not one tear.

I pointed to the endotracheal tube and asked the nurse if it could be removed and she explained what would happen if it were taken out and I agreed that we should not do anything. I asked her for a pair of scissors and a half dozen plastic bags, to gather locks of my mother's hair for her two sisters and for my younger brother and his daughters.

"She had such beautiful hair," the nurse said.

This was the same nurse who had earlier told my father and I that my mother was in cardiac arrest.

"Yes," I said, "She was very proud of it."

As I spoke those words I came very close to crying, but somehow held myself together. The afternoon had turned into a marathon run and I could see I had another four or five steep miles before the end, when I could finally allow myself to rest.

Just then my father and brother walked in. When my father saw my mother with the plastic tube in her mouth and the blood on her pillow, he physically recoiled, turned away, and then looked again, cursing in disbelief: "God———. . . ! God———!"

He stopped short of saying "damn," but the searing way he said "God ———!" without the profanity was actually more of a condemnation than if he had. It was an expression of deepest betrayal— he had lived a good life, worked hard, done all the right things, prayed every night, and now this—the ultimate worst thing—had happened. It was the howl of the wolf over his fallen mate, the roar of the mother grizzly over her dead cub, the cry of the eagle at the loss of her life-partner. It was the most ancient utterance on Earth, the sound of a creature asking the creator why there must be suffering and death on what is otherwise a pretty nice world.

The nurse brought in a chair and my father sank down, his face wet with tears, and exclaimed, loud enough for everyone in the unit to hear, "She didn't deserve this. She didn't deserve this."

There was a long awkward moment. Everyone was reluctant to speak. I was standing on the other side of the bed at my mother's head and I finally told my father I was going to cut some locks of her hair.

"I want one," he said.

"Alright," I said, relieved that he was raising no objections. `You can have the first one. Let's take them from the back."

The nurse picked up my mother's head and I cut six or seven locks from the back of her head and put them in plastic bags.

When I gave my father a lock of my mother's hair he took it in both hands and held it to his heart.

Dr. Parker, who had been waiting at the door for an appropriate moment to enter, walked in and gave my father the prescription.

"Don't be afraid to take these, Bill. You're going to need a full night's sleep in the days to come so that you can stay healthy and strong."

"I don't want to stay healthy and strong."

"But you need to. . . for your sons."

"They don't need me. They're grown men. I just need to get my papers in order and then I'll. . ."

"Don't talk like that, Dad," I said, disturbed by the implication.

"Don't you understand?" he said, "I just lost my wife."

"Yes," I said, "And I just lost my mother."

At that moment Rebecca, my older brother's wife, appeared at the door. She was nine months pregnant with their third child and had the happy life-filled glow of a woman about to give birth. She was wearing a flowing blue dress with tiny yellow flowers and her eyes were full of warmth and good cheer.

The last she had heard, two hours earlier, my mother was progressing well after surgery.

My brother whispered in her ear.

Her hand went to her face. "Oh Mom…. Oh, no… not like this…."

She was crying freely now and went over to embrace my father. Her extended embrace, her strong female presence, had a dramatic calming effect on him.

He blew his nose and wiped the tears from his face.

"Dr. Parker," my father asked, clearing his voice, "do you have a minute?"

"Bill, I have all the time you need."

"I'd like to tell the story of how Pat and I met. It was fifty-five years ago. November, 1943. I was a nineteen-year-old paratrooper stuck for the holidays in Philadelphia. My family was in Cincinnati and I had no one to spend Thanksgiving with. So I put an ad in the newspaper. It read: 'Lonely GI with no family in town would like a family to spend Thanksgiving with.' Patty, who was sixteen at the time, spotted the ad and asked her father if they could invite me. I'll tell you, it was love at first sight. She was the most beautiful young woman I'd ever seen. We wrote letters all through the war and as soon as I got back from Europe we were married. You know, she wanted to become a doctor, and she would have made a good one, but she gave up everything for me. After we were married she moved back with me to Cincinnati and worked to put me through college and then have my children. Cincinnati. God but she hated that town. It was so conservative. She always said that when she died she'd go to heaven because she'd spent twenty-four years in purgatory.

Everyone laughed.

"She was also fond of quoting Mark Twain, who said that "When the world ends I want to go to Cincinnati, because everything happens there ten years later."

Everyone laughed again.

"See, that's what you need to concentrate on Bill," said Dr. Parker, "on the positive memories that you and Pat shared."

My father nodded without conviction.

Dr. Parker glanced at his watch and asked, "Bill, is it alright if I leave? I have a—"

"Oh yes, I'm sorry, I'm just an old man bluthering on here. You've got other patients."

They hugged and Dr. Parker left.

Now came the time to make the final good-byes.

One by one, my brother, my father, and then Rebecca hugged and kissed my mother and said good-bye. All through this I remained at the head of the bed, with one hand on her head and the other on her arm.

When they had finished with their farewells my father kissed my mother's right hand and said, his voice breaking, "Oh, Patty, you were the spice of my life."

He had a look in his eyes like someone who has been struck.

Rebecca and Bill put their arms around him and helped him leave and his bad leg, first injured during the war, nearly gave way as they walked out the door.

After they were gone I stayed behind. A peacefulness slowly filled the room, a quiet that poured in steadily from some place far away. It was like the stillness in the forest after a pack-string of horses has passed by, or the snowmelt that gathers in a clear pool beneath a high glacier, or the desert sky after the sun has set and the colors have come and gone and there is still a light to the west, the magic time of deer moving and nightbirds calling. As an artist my mother would have recognized this moment for what it was—the afterglow of the day, the golden twilight, the tranquil evening canvas of Bierdstadt and Moran.

I had been the last family member to speak to my mother that morning when she was conscious ("See ya soon!" I had cheerfully said), the last family member to kiss her when she was conscious, and I wanted to be the last to be with her when she was dead. We had always been so similar, and shared such a special bond, a closeness that repelled us in the early years but ultimately brought us together at the end, so that we became as best friends.

I held her hand—the same hand that had made us so many meals, that had knitted baby outfits for our children when they were born, that had wrapped hundreds of Christmas presents for everyone over the years. I told her that she had been the best mother in the world and that I would always love her. I told her not to worry, that I would take good care of my father. I apologized to her for any wrongs that I had ever done, and asked for her forgiveness. I offered her the same and then I kissed her on the forehead, gave her one last wink, and whispered "I love you, Mom."

After that there was nothing more left to do.

I picked up the plastic bag that held her clothes, slippers, wedding ring, bifocal glasses, toothbrush, dental plate, comb, make-up kit and library book, and walked into the empty corridor toward the elevator.

Outside on the street it was a very bright spring day and the sky was very blue and people were busily coming and going from the hospital, some happy and some sad, no one pausing, everyone in a hurry as people always are around hospitals. The sun had moved toward the west and there were shadows forming among the trees and on the eastern side of the buildings. It would be evening soon. As I walked back to the car I reminded myself of my firm rule that even on a bad day— especially on a bad day—one must find something good to embrace and so when I spotted a fallen white apple blossom in the grass, I knelt down and picked it up and carried it in my hand. Once home I would place the white petals in the pages of my oldest book, along with a note. It would mark that time each year when the fruit trees blossom. I knew that is what she would have wanted me to remember.

—first publication

Notes on Contributors

&

Carol Ann Bassett is a journalism and creative writing professor at the University of Oregon, Eugene. For many years she worked as an independent writer, traveling and researching widely around the world. Her work has appeared in such venues as *The New York Times, Time* magazine and *Newsweek.* She is currently at work on a large format book that will feature her desert essays together with landscape photographs of the desert.

Kate Boyes teaches English at Southern Utah University in Cedar City, Utah. Her nature essays and poems have been widely published in journals and anthologies, and she has been a featured writer on several public radio programs. Each summer she moves from southern Utah to her permanent home, a remote cabin in northern Utah.

Emma Brown is a year 2000 graduate of Stanford University in Palo Alto, California. A native of Arlington, Virginia, she has worked the past several summers as a wilderness ranger in the Bridger Wilderness in northwestern Wyoming. Emma Brown has also traveled and explored widely in western North America, from coastal Alaska to the Mexican Baja.

Lisa Couturier writes from a small stone house along the Potomac River in Maryland where she recently moved after fifteen years of living in New York City. Her work has appeared in the anthologies *American Nature Writing 1998* (Sierra Club Books), *The River Reader* (Lyons) and in the national magazines *Wildlife Conservation, Women's Sport Traveler, and Iris: A Journal about Women,* among others.

Jan DeBlieu lives in Manteo, North Carolina with her husband and young son. She is the author of such popular works as *Hatteras Journal* and *Meant to be Wild.* In 1999 her pioneering work of natural history *Wind* (Houghton Mifflin) was awarded the John Burroughs Award for Distinguished Nature Writing.

Trudy Dittmar lives in a cabin in the mountains north of Dubois, Wyoming, just an hour's drive from the Tetons and Yellowstone. She has published widely in literary journals such as *The Georgia Review, Orion,* and *The North American Review.*

Penny Harter's recent books include five collections published since 1994: *Shadow Play: Night Haiku, Stages and Views, Grandmother's Milk, Turtle Blessing,* and *Lizard Light: Poems From the Earth.* She has published fifteen books of poetry. Her work appears in numerous anthologies and magazines worldwide, and she has won fellowships and awards from the New Jersey State Council on the Arts, The Geraldine R. Dodge Foundation, and the Poetry Society of America. She teaches in the English Department at Santa Fe Preparatory School.

Geneen Marie Haugen lives by the Gros Ventre River in Kelly, WY where she is a high-altitude gardener and potato farmer. She skis the backcountry, drifts rivers, watches birds and backpacks. Her essays about the human relationship to the wild have appeared in anthologies and journals. A book, *Tracking Artemis: A Hunt for a Way of Being,* is in progress.

Marybeth Holleman teaches creative writing and literature at the University of Alaska, Anchorage. Her work has appeared widely in literary journals and reviews and she is currently writing a book on Prince William Sound. She lives in the foothills of the Chugach Mountains with her young son.

Cynthia Huntington is a professor of literature and creative writing at Dartmouth College and Vermont College. She is the author of two books of poetry (*The Fish-Wife* and *We Have Gone to the Beach*). Her first book of prose, *A Salt House: A Summer on the Dunes of Cape Cod,* was published by the University of New England Press in 1999. She has received grants from the NEA, the New Hampshire State Council on the Arts and the Massachusetts Arts Council. In 1998 she received the John Kenyon Award for Poetry. She lives in Hanover, New Hampshire with her husband, an artist, and her fourteen-year-old son.

Susan Marsh has worked as a wilderness ranger in the Teton National Forest for over twenty years. She lives with her husband in Jackson. Her work appears regularly in *Orion* and other fine nature periodicals.

Ellen Meloy lives in Bluff, Utah with her husband, who is a BLM ranger on the San Juan River. She is the author of such noted works as *Raven's Exile: A Season on the Green River* (Henry Holt) and *The Last Cheater's Waltz* (Henry Holt). In 1997 she was a recipient of a Writer's Award from the Whiting Foundation.

Janisse Ray is an environmental activist who lives on a family farm in the coastal plains of southern Georgia. Her memoir, *Ecology of a Cracker Childhood* (Milkweed) is about growing up on a junkyard in the ruined longleaf pine area of the Southeast. She is a commentator for Georgia Public Radio and is currently at work on a manuscript about rural community.

Pattiann Rogers lives with her husband in Castle Rock, Colorado. She has published seven books of poetry, including *Firekeeper, New and Selected Poems* (Milkweed). In past years she has taught poetry in the writing programs at Washington University, the University of Montana, and the University of Texas, Austin, among others. She has been the recipient of a Guggenheim Fellowship, two NEA grants, and a Lannan Poetry Fellowship.

Adrienne Ross lives in Seattle, WA. A devoted environmentalist, she is active in community affairs. Her work has appeared in *Tikkun, Northern Lights, New Age Journal,* the anthology *An Intricate Weave: Women Write on Girls and Girlhood,* and numerous other publications.

Alianor True, a native of Douglasville, Georgia, is a 1997 graduate of Cornell University. Throughout her college summers she worked as a firefighter at national parks in the West, including Grand Canyon National Park and Sequoia National Park. In 1999 she received an MA in science education from the University of Michigan, Ann Arbor, and moved permanently to the west.

Kristen Vose Michaelides is pursuing an MS degree at the Yale School of Forestry and plans to work in the field of ecosystem conservation. She has explored the northern forest as a field assistant, a backcountry guide, and a naturalist in New Hampshire.

Kathryn Wilder has lived on the Colorado Plateau for much of the last ten years. She is the author of the children's book *Forbidden Talent* (Northland) and the editor of the anthologies *Walking the Twilight: Women Writers of the Southwest* and *Walking the Twilight II* (Northland). Her work has been nominated for the Pushcart Prize, the Western Heritage award, and won *Sierra* magazine's "Write on the Wild Side" competition.

Susan Zwinger lives on Whidbey Island near Seattle, Washington. Although formally trained as an art educator, a subject in which she holds a doctoral degree, Susan Zwinger has worked full-time as a professional writer for over a decade. Her nature books include *Stalking the Ice Dragon* and *The Last Wild Edge*.

Permissions